American Women Afield

NUMBER TWENTY

Louise Lindsey Merrick Natural Environment Series

American Women Afield

WRITINGS BY PIONEERING
WOMEN NATURALISTS

Edited by

Marcia Myers Bonta

TEXAS A&M UNIVERSITY PRESS
College Station

Excerpt from Althea Sherman's *Birds of an Iowa Dooryard*, reprinted courtesy of Christopher Publishing House, Hanover, Mass. Copyright © 1952. All rights reserved.

Cordelia Stanwood's "Tenants of Birdsacre," reprinted courtesy of *House Beautiful.* Copyright © October, 1920. The Hearst Corp. All rights reserved.

Excerpts from Ynes Mexia's "Camping on the Equator" and "Three Thousand Miles up the Amazon," reprinted courtesy of *Sierra Club Bulletin.* Copyright © 1937 and 1933, respectively, by Sierra Club, San Francisco, Calif. All rights reserved.

Excerpts from "Mary S. Young's Journal of Botanical Explorations in Trans-Pecos, Texas, August-September, 1914," reprinted courtesy of the Texas State Historical Association, Austin, Texas. Copyright © 1962. All rights reserved.

Excerpt from Ann Haven Morgan's *Field Book of Ponds and Streams*, reprinted courtesy of Putnam Publishing Group, New York. Copyright © 1930. All rights reserved.

Excerpt from Margaret Morse Nice's *Research Is a Passion with Me*, reprinted courtesy of Natural Heritage/Natural History, Inc., Toronto, Canada. Copyright © 1979. All rights reserved.

Excerpt from Margaret Morse Nice's *The Watcher at the Nest,* reprinted courtesy of Dover Publications, Inc., Mineola, N.Y. Copyright © 1939. All rights reserved.

Excerpts from pages 135-37 and 148-49 from Ruth Thomas's *Crip, Come Home.* Copyright © 1950, 1951, 1952 by Ruth Thomas. Copyright renewed. Reprinted courtesy of HarperCollins Publishers, Inc.

Excerpt from Rachel Carson's *The Edge of the Sea.* Copyright © 1955 by Rachel L. Carson, © renewed 1983 by Roger Christie. Reprinted courtesy of Houghton Mifflin Co. All rights reserved.

Excerpt from Rachel Carson's *Silent Spring.* Copyright © 1962 by Rachel L. Carson, renewed 1990 by Roger Christie. Reprinted courtesy of Houghton Mifflin Co. All rights reserved.

Library of Congress Cataloging-in-Publication Data

Bonta, Marcia, 1940–
    American women afield / by Marcia Myers Bonta. —1st ed.
        p. cm. — (Louise Lindsey Merrick natural environment series; no. 20)
    Includes bibliographical references.
    ISBN 0-89096-633-8 (cloth). —ISBN 0-89096-634-6 (paper)
        1. Natural history—United States. 2. Women naturalists—United States—
    Biography. 3. Naturalists—United States—Biography.
    I. Title. II. Series.
    QH45.2.B66 1995   94-3664
    508.73—dc20   CIP

To the late Chandler S. Richmond,
founder and former curator of the
Cordelia Stanwood Wildlife Sanctuary,
and the late Fred Pierce,
editor of Althea Sherman's posthumous book
Birds of an Iowa Dooryard.
Without their dedication, the work of Sherman and Stanwood
would have been forgotten.

Contents

Illustrations

Preface

DURING MY DECADE OF RESEARCH for *Women in the Field: America's Pioneering Women Naturalists,* I enjoyed reading a wealth of primary sources—both published and unpublished—by many women naturalists. Since the primary focus of *Women in the Field* was to feature the important contributions women field naturalists had made to society, I was able to feature some, but not all, of the women. Although I tried to illustrate how much their work meant to them by frequently quoting from their writings, my emphasis in that book remained on their professional accomplishments.

But I could not forget the memorable books and articles I had read by the women. Some of their books had been popular in their day, such as Susan Fenimore Cooper's *Rural Hours,* Mary Treat's *Home Studies in Nature,* Florence Merriam Bailey's *Birds of Village and Field,* Ann Haven Morgan's *Field Book of Ponds and Streams,* and, of course, Rachel Carson's best-selling books on the sea as well as her seminal *Silent Spring.*

Other books, such as Edith Clements's *Adventures in Ecology,* Margaret Morse Nice's *The Watcher at the Nest,* George and Elizabeth Peckham's *Wasps: Social and Solitary,* Anna Botsford Comstock's *Ways of the Six-Footed,* Ruth Harris Thomas's *Crip, Come Home,* and Phil and Nellie Rau's *Wasp Studies Afield,* were undeservedly less well known. All of these books, except for Carson's books and Comstock's recently reprinted *Ways of the Six-Footed,* are long out of print or difficult to find even in major libraries.

During the late nineteenth and early twentieth centuries, many of the women naturalists contributed to a wide variety of popular magazines and scholarly journals. Since there was little difference between scholarly and popular writing at that time, I found a variety of interesting and entertaining pieces by the women in such diverse periodicals as *Bird-Lore, Nature, Scientific Monthly, Wilson Bulletin, Sierra Club Bulletin, Harper's New Monthly Magazine, American Naturalist, Entomological News, Bulletin of the Brooklyn Entomological Society, Leaflets of Western Botany, Science, Annual Report of the Smithsonian Institution, National Geographic, Chicago Naturalist, Audubon,* and the *New Yorker.* Wonderful illustrations accompanied the older books and periodical pieces which added to the appeal of the material.

The women naturalists' books and articles, by and large, emphasized the how and why of their field work and their concerns about conservation issues long before most people were either aware of these problems or bothered to write about them. The women were sometimes self-deprecatory, often humorous, but usually focused on business at hand, whether it was watching birds, collecting plants and insects, or pleading for the conservation of forests. In addition, the women showed a special empathy for the natural world and were fearless in pursuit of natural history knowledge. They were oblivious to personal discomfort and, in some cases, even danger and privation, most notably Mary Sophie Young, Ynes Mexia, Agnes Chase, and Alice Eastwood. None of them exhibited the stereotypical female squeamishness towards nature. Instead they delighted in hand feeding spiders, taming wasps, camping under the stars, climbing unnamed mountaintops, tramping through swamps, and sitting patiently in the woods, all in pursuit of scientific knowledge. Obsessed by naming, knowing, and understanding what they saw, they specialized in straightforward narrative, although a few, such as Ruth Harris Thomas and Rachel Carson, were naturally gifted writers.

Many women field naturalists began in their dooryards by observing the near-at-hand, but some, depending on their circumstances, went farther afield. By the 1880s a handful were exploring their states, then several states or regions, and, finally, foreign countries. Those who were single, had the financial resources or professional support, or who were childless and married to supportive males were able to travel farther. Those who were married or had substantial family responsibilities continued to restrict most of their research to their immediate environs, for instance, Althea Sherman, Cordelia Stanwood, Margaret Morse Nice, Nellie Rau, Elizabeth Peckham, and Amelia Laskey.

All of the women had loved nature as children and had returned to it as adults to find meaning in their lives and to make a positive contribution to knowledge. Several expressed their disgust with society's expectations of proper womanly behavior and interests. They realized they were different from most women and were proud of it. A few of them, most notably Anna Comstock, saw the wisdom in appearing to be conventional, but probably only Susan Fenimore Cooper actually believed in the Victorian ideal of womanhood. "Scorn convention and you always can," Alice Eastwood said. Most of the other women naturalists seemed to agree with her.

Many of the twenty-five women whose works I have chosen to appear as excerpts in this book had a variety of male and female mentors throughout their lives, beginning with supportive fathers, mothers, or brothers and continuing with teachers, colleagues, friends, and spouses. Twelve of them were supported throughout their professional lives by a strong male mentor, either a husband or scientific colleague. At least six others had a network of supportive women. The rest seemed to need little or no help from anyone.

Although this book can be used as supplementary reading to *Women in the Field,* it can also stand by itself because I have included a short introductory biography of each woman naturalist. The cast of characters is slightly different too. Some of the most important professional women naturalists—Elizabeth Gertrude Knight Britton, Ellen Quillin, and Kate Brandegee—and some of the most interesting—Jane Colden, Maria Martin, Annie Montague Alexander, and Kate Furbish—did not write skillfully for the general public about their work. Others who did—for instance, Katharine Dooris Sharp and Ruth Harris Thomas—were known to their public primarily as writers, rather than naturalists.

I also included three examples of what Margaret Rossiter referred to in her book, *Women Scientists in America,* as "conjugal collaboration," in this case, husband and wife teams in which the husband was the primary scientist—Frederic and Edith Clements, Phil and Nellie Rau, and George and Elizabeth Peckham. The latter two couples, entomologists who specialized in wasps, coauthored books in which the woman's voice was as important as the man's. The Clementses' collaboration was of a different sort, with Edith's talents and interests supporting Frederic's work.

But with Edith Clements's book, as in all the other excerpts I chose, I wanted to show how the women did their work, what it meant to them, and how they were perceived. I also tried to choose material that was inherently interesting and entertaining and that best represented the personalities and aspirations of each woman.

Unlike many books about American natural history, this book does not concentrate on women in only one or two regions of the United States. The women are widely representative of the entire country, a probable indication of the universal appeal of nature to a select number of American women.

Because I am subordinating their professional attainments to their ability to write well about their work, I arranged the women's appearances in this book by birth order instead of discipline. This approach produces a splendid mix of women botanists, entomologists, ornithologists, and ecologists, all of whom characterized themselves first and foremost as "naturalists," whether their particular interest was birds, insects, plants, or mammals.

A love of nature characterized these women naturalists. But it is their desire to communicate that love to others that not only interests their readers in the natural world around them but also compels them to save it for posterity. Margaret Morse Nice in "The Awakening," from her posthumous autobiographical *Research Is a Passion With Me,* summed it up best when she wrote: "I thought of my friends who never take walks in Oklahoma, 'for there was nothing to see.' I was amazed and grieved at their blindness. I longed to open their eyes to the wonders around them; to persuade people to love and cherish nature."

Acknowledgments

ALTHOUGH MOST OF THIS BOOK is based on my previous research for *Women in the Field,* I did additional archival work for the new women I included. As usual, the librarians, professors, friends, and archivists I consulted, both for information and photographs, were eager to help.

Those people who took particular trouble for me include Penny Ahlstrand, Archivist, California Academy of Sciences, San Francisco; Patricia J. Albright and Elaine Trehub, Mount Holyoke College Library/Archives, South Hadley, Massachusetts; Dr. James Carpenter, Department of Entomology, American Museum of Natural History, New York; William A. Deiss, Deputy Archivist, Smithsonian Institution Archives; Dr. K. Elizabeth Gibbs, Department of Entomology, University of Maine, Orono; Claudia James, Director, Rachel Carson Homestead Association, Springdale, Pennsylvania; Richard and Jessie Johnson, Curators, Caroline Dormon Nature Preserve, Saline, Louisiana; Sandy Pesce, Librarian, Frederick and Amey Geier Collections and Research Center, Cincinnati Museum of Natural History; Stanley Richmond, President, Stanwood Wildlife Sanctuary; Martha Riley, Archivist, Missouri Botanical Garden, St. Louis; Muriel A. Sanford, Head, Special Collections Department, Raymond H. Fogler Library, University of Maine, Orono; Allison Smith, President, Vineland Historical and Antiquarian Society, Vineland, New Jersey; Dr. Ronald L. Stuckey, Professor of Botany Emeritus, Ohio State University, Columbus; Mary Linn Wernet, University Archivist, Eugene P. Watson Memorial Library, Northwestern State University of Louisiana, Natchitoches; Peter Whan, Preserves Manager, E. Lucy Braun Prairie, Lynx, Ohio; reference desk personnel, Kirkwood Public

Library, Kirkwood, Missouri; and the staff of the Pennsylvania State University Photo/Graphics.

In addition, I would like thank my husband Bruce, who used his academic reference librarian skills to help me locate the more obscure sources, and our son David, who read and critiqued the manuscript for me.

American Women Afield

Susan Fenimore Cooper

1813–94

THE DISCOVERY OF SUSAN FENIMORE COOPER'S BOOK *Rural Hours* started me on my quest in search of America's pioneering women natural-ists. First published in 1850, four years before *Walden* was written by Henry David Thoreau, *Rural Hours* was an unqualified success—"a great book, the greatest of the season," poet William Cullen Bryant wrote to his friend, the author's proud father, James Fenimore Coo-per.

Susan Fenimore Cooper was his oldest surviving child and his favorite. He managed to thwart one marriage proposal to her from a French nobleman during the Cooper family's Paris years abroad, and at least one historian claims that Samuel F. B. Morse of tele-graph fame was another unsuccessful suitor.

Feelings of affection were obviously mutual between father and daughter, since Sue, as he called her, dedicated *Rural Hours* to him. She wrote: "To the author of the *Deerslayer* these notes are very re-spectfully, gratefully and most affectionately inscribed by the writer." Cooper tried to follow in her father's footsteps as a writer. In addi-tion to *Rural Hours,* she had written an earlier novel. She also wrote several biographical sketches and a few articles, and she edited and annotated John Leonard Knapp's *Country Rambles in England,* an anthology of country poetry, which she dedicated to William Cullen Bryant, and *Pages and Pictures from the Writings of James Fenimore Cooper,* her best-known work after *Rural Hours.*

It was *Rural Hours,* though, which gave her a measure of fame. In this synoptic journal account of a typical year in rural Cooperstown, New York, most of the entries are concerned with plants or animals; the rest is devoted to sketches of rural life, all gained on foot in her neighborhood over a two-year period. *Rural Hours* remained in print for forty years, going through six American and two English editions, including a complete revision by Cooper herself in 1887.

In "Small Family Memories," Cooper credited her interest in nature to her maternal Grandfather DeLancey, with whom she and her family had lived in Mamaroneck, New York, when she was four years old. The Coopers then moved nearby to their own farm in Scarsdale and remained there until she was nine. During those formative early years, she often accompanied her grandfather on drives in the country. "In these drives, he taught me to distinguish the different trees by their growth, and bark, and foliage. . . . He would point out a tree and ask me to name it, going through a regular lesson in a very pleasant way. Such was the beginning of my *Rural Hours*."

After years of education in New York and Paris with her four younger siblings, Cooper and her family returned to her father's ancestral home in Cooperstown in 1833. There she remained for the rest of her life, known by her neighbors for her charitable works, her sweet nature, and only incidentally for her writing. Her obituary emphasized her founding of a town hospital and orphanage and her unselfish work on behalf of local underprivileged children.

Rural Hours remains the only evidence that Cooper had the soul of a naturalist, as well as a conservationist. In her book she does not hesitate to discuss society's willful destruction of nature through disinterest and greed. The book also reveals her wide interest in classical subjects and natural history, with anecdotes from the ornithological observations of John James Audubon and Alexander Wilson, frequent mention of the experiences of Dr. James Ellsworth DeKay, author of the 1842 *Zoology of New York,* and occasional references to English botanist Thomas Nuttall, Swiss botanist Augustin Pyramus de Candolle, and French zoologist Charles Bonaparte.

No doubt her knowledge was directly attributable to her fine education, which included skill in four languages, American and English literature, and history, zoology, and botany. As a result of her acute intelligence, she did not confuse conjecture with scientific facts, merely speculating, for instance, that "perhaps birds generally follow the same course, year after year, in their annual journeyings" because the "celebrated canvas-backs pass us every year possibly on their way to the Chesapeake."

When she did conduct her own scientific research, however, she was definitive in her conclusions. For instance, one mild October day she counted the flowers of a mullein stalk and discovered that it bore 570 flowers, "or rather seed vessels," she corrected herself, "for it was out of blossom, [and] each of these seed vessels were filled with tiny dark seed." Furthermore, she observed that the birds did not seem to like mullein seeds because "they are not seen feeding on the mullein stalks."

Her vivid descriptions provide a wistful glimpse for modern readers at passenger pigeons flying over the valley in "large unbroken flocks several miles in extent" and at Carolina parakeets "found in great numbers as far north as Virginia [which] fly in flocks, noisy and restless, like all their brethren; their coloring . . . green and orange, with a shade of red about the head." Cooper's words remind readers that *Rural Hours* was written long ago, for the birds species she mentions have disappeared, driven into extinction by humanity's greed.

Cooper was one of the first American nature writers to warn Americans about the dangers of their profligate use of natural resources, a warning that was not heeded, as the excerpt makes clear. With only a few deft changes, her description of humanity's disregard for conserving the natural world could have been written today. Although Cooper's lyrical description of an eastern American ancient forest before the arrival of Europeans is sheer nostalgia for modern readers, her suggestions for preserving forests are as valid today as they were in her time.

SUMMER

SATURDAY, [JULY] 28TH. —Passed the afternoon in the woods.

What a noble gift to man are the forests! What a debt of gratitude and admiration we owe for their utility and their beauty!

How pleasantly the shadows of the wood fall upon our heads, when we turn from the glitter and turmoil of the world of man! The winds of heaven seem to linger amid these balmy branches, and the sunshine falls like a blessing upon the green leaves; the wild breath of the forest, fragrant with bark and berry, fans the brow with grateful freshness; and the beautiful wood-light, neither garish nor gloomy, full of calm and peaceful influences, sheds repose over the spirit. The view is limited, and the objects about us are uniform in character; yet within the bosom of the woods the mind readily lays aside its daily littleness, and opens to higher thoughts, in silent consciousness that it stands alone with the works of God. The humble moss beneath our feet, the sweet flowers, the varied shrubs, the great trees, and the sky gleaming above in sacred blue, are each the handiwork of God. They were all called into being by the will of the Creator, as we now behold them, full of wisdom and goodness. Every object here has a deeper merit than our wonder can fathom; each has a beauty beyond our full perception; the dullest insect crawling about these roots lives by the power of the Almighty; and the discolored shreds of last year's leaves wither away upon the lowly herbs in a blessing of fertility. But it is the great trees, stretching their arms above us in a thousand forms of grace and strength, it is more especially the trees which fill the mind with wonder and praise.

Of the infinite variety of fruits which spring from the bosom of the earth, the trees of the wood are the greatest in dignity. Of all the works of the creation which know the changes of life and death, the trees of the forest have the longest existence. Of all the objects which crown the gray earth, the woods preserve unchanged, throughout the greatest reach of time, their native character: the works of man are ever varying their aspect; his towns and his fields alike reflect the unstable opinions, the fickle wills and fancies of each passing generation; but the forests on his borders remain to-day the same they were ages of years since. Old as the everlasting hills, during thousands of seasons they have put forth and laid down their verdure in calm obedience to the decree which first bade them cover the ruins of the Deluge.

But, although the forests are great and old, yet the ancient trees within their bounds must each bend individually beneath the doom of every earthly existence; they have their allotted period when the mosses of Time gather upon their branches; when, touched by decay, they break and crumble to dust. Like man, they are decked in living beauty; like man, they fall a prey to death; and while we admire their duration, so far beyond our own brief years, we also acknowledge that especial interest which can only belong to the graces of life and to the desolation of death. We raise our eyes, and we see collected in one company vigorous trunks, the oak, the ash, the pine, firm in the strength of maturity; by their side stand a young group, elm, and birch, and maple, their supple branches playing in the breezes, gay and fresh as youth itself; and yonder, rising in unheeded gloom, we behold a skeleton trunk, an old fir, every branch broken, every leaf fallen,—dull, still, sad, like the finger of Death.

It is the peculiar nature of the forest, that life and death may ever be found within its bounds, in immediate presence of each other; both with ceaseless, noiseless, advances, aiming at the mastery; and if the influences of the first be most general, those of the last are the most striking. Spring, with all her wealth of life and joy, finds within the forest many a tree unconscious of her approach; a thousand young plants springing up about the fallen trunk, the shaggy roots, seek to soften the gloomy wreck with a semblance of the verdure it bore of

4

old; but ere they have thrown their fresh and graceful wreaths over the mouldering wood, half their own tribe wither and die with the year. We owe to this perpetual presence of death an impression, calm, solemn, almost religious in character, a chastening influence, beyond what we find in the open fields. But this subdued spirit is far from gloomy or oppressive, since it never fails to be relieved by the cheerful animation of living beauty. Sweet flowers grow beside the fallen trees, among the shattered branches, the season through; and the freedom of the woods, the unchecked growth, the careless position of every tree, are favorable to a thousand wild beauties, and fantastic forms, opening to the mind a play of fancy which is in itself cheering and enlivening, like the bright sunbeams which checker with golden light the shadowy groves. That character of rich variety also, stamped on all the works of the creation, is developed in the forest in clear and noble forms; we are told that in the field we shall not find two blades of grass exactly alike, that in the garden we shall not gather two flowers precisely similar, but in those cases the lines are minute, and we do not seize the truth at once; in the woods, however, the same fact stands recorded in bolder lines; we cannot fail to mark this great variety of detail among the trees; we see it in their trunks, their branches, their foliage; in the rude knots, the gnarled roots; in the mosses and lichens which feed upon their bark; in their forms, their coloring, their shadows. And within all this luxuriance of varied beauty, there dwells a sweet quiet, a noble harmony, a calm repose, which we seek in vain elsewhere, in so full a measure.

These hills, and the valleys at their feet, lay for untold centuries one vast forest; unnumbered seasons, ages of unrecorded time passed away while they made part of the boundless wilderness of woods. The trees waved over the valleys, they rose upon the swelling knolls, they filled the hollows, they crowded the narrow glens, they shaded the brooks and springs, they washed their roots in the lakes and rivers, they stood upon the islands, they swept over the broad hills, they crowned the heads of all the mountains. The whole land lay slumbering in the twilight of the forest. Wild dreams made up its half-conscious existence. The hungry cry of the beast of prey, or the fierce deed of savage man, whoop and dance, triumph and torture, broke in fitful bursts upon the deep silence, and then died away, leaving the breath of life to rise and fall with the passing winds.

Every rocky cliff on the hillside, every marshy spot on the lowlands, was veiled in living, rustling folds of green. Here a dark wave of pine, hemlock, and balsam ran through a ravine, on yonder knoll shone the rich glossy verdure of oak, and maple, and chestnut; upon

5

the breast of the mountain stood the birch, the elm, and the aspen, in light and airy tufts. Leaves of every tint of green played in the summer sunshine, leaves fluttered in the moonlight, and the showers of heaven fell everywhere upon the green leaves of the unbroken forest.

Sixty years have worked a wonderful change; the forest has fallen upon the lowlands, and there is not a valley about us which has not been opened. Another half century may find the country bleak and bare; but as yet the woods have not all been felled, and within the circle which bounds our view, there is no mountain which has been wholly shorn, none presents a bald front to the sky; upon the lake shore, there are several hills still wrapped in wood from the summit to the base. He who takes pleasure in the forest, by picking his way, and following a winding course, may yet travel many a long mile over a shady path, such as the red man loved. . . .

It is to be feared that few among the younger generation now springing up will ever attain to the dignity of the old forest trees. Very large portions of these woods are already of a second growth, and trees of the greatest size are becoming every year more rare. It quite often happens that you come upon old stumps of much larger dimensions than any living trees about them; some of these are four, and a few five feet or more in diameter. Occasionally, we still find a pine erect of this size; one was felled the other day, which measured five feet in diameter. There is an elm about a mile from the village seventeen feet in girth, and not long since we heard of a bass-wood or linden twenty-eight feet in circumference. But among the trees now standing, even those which are sixty or eighty feet in height, many are not more than four, or five, or six feet in girth. The pines, especially, reach a surprising elevation for their bulk. . . .

It is often said, as an excuse for leaving none standing, that these old trees of forest growth will not live after their companions have been felled; they miss the protection which one gives to another, and, exposed to the winds, soon fall to the ground. As a general rule, this may be true; but one is inclined to believe that if the experiment of leaving a few were more frequently tried, it would often prove successful. There is an elm of great size now standing entirely alone in a pretty field of the valley, its girth, its age, and whole appearance declaring it a chieftain of the ancient race—the "Sagamore elm," as it is called—and in spite of complete exposure to the winds from all quarters of the heavens, it maintains its place firmly. The trunk measures seventeen feet in circumference, and it is thought to be a hundred feet in height; but this is only from the eye, never having been accurately ascertained. The shaft rises perhaps fifty feet without a branch, before it divides, according to the usual growth of old forest trees. Unfortunately, gray branches are beginning to show among its summer foliage, and it is to be feared that it will not outlast many winters more.

In these times, the hewers of wood are an unsparing race. The first colonists looked upon a tree as an enemy, and to judge from appearances, one would think that something of the same spirit prevails among their descendants at the present hour. It is not surprising, perhaps, that a man whose chief object in life is to make money should turn his timber into bank-notes with all possible speed; but it is remarkable that any one at all aware of the value of wood, should act so wastefully as most men do in this part of the world. Mature trees, young saplings, and last year's seedlings, are all destroyed at one blow by the axe or by fire; the spot where they have stood is left, perhaps, for a lifetime without any attempt at cultivation, or any endeavor to foster new wood. One would think that by this time, when the forest has fallen in all the valleys—when the hills are becoming more bare every day—when timber and fuel are rising in prices, and new uses are found for even indifferent woods—some forethought and care in this respect would be natural in people laying claim to common sense. The rapid consumption of the large pine timber among us should be enough to teach a lesson of prudence and economy on this subject. It has been calculated that 60,000 acres of pine woods are cut every year in our own State alone. But unaccountable as it may appear, few American farmers are aware of the full value and importance of wood. They seem to forget the relative value of the forests. It has been reported in the State of New York, that the produce of tilled lands carried to tide-water by the Erie Canal, in one year, amounted to $8,170,000 dollars worth of property; that of animals, or farm-stock, for the same year, is given at $3,230,000; that of the forests, lumber, staves, etc., at $4,770,000. Thus the forest yielded more than the stock, and more than half as much as the farm lands; and when the comparative expense of the two is considered, their value will be brought still nearer together. Peltries were not included in this account. Our people seldom remember that the forests, while they provide food and shelter for the wildest savage tribes, make up a large amount of the wealth of the most civilized nations. . . .

But independently of their market price in dollars and cents, the trees have other values: they are connected in many ways with the civilization of a country; they have their importance in an intellectual and in a moral sense. After the first rude stage of progress is past in a new country—when shelter and food have been provided—peo-

7

ple begin to collect the conveniences and pleasures of a permanent home about their dwellings, and then the farmer generally sets out a few trees before his door. This is very desirable, but it is only the first step in the track; something more is needed; the preservation of fine trees, already standing, marks a farther progress, and this point we have not yet reached. It frequently happens that the same man who yesterday planted some half dozen branchless saplings before his door, will to-day cut down a noble elm, or oak, only a few rods from his house, an object which was in itself a hundred-fold more beautiful than any other in his possession. In very truth, a fine tree near a house is a much greater embellishment than the thickest coat of paint that could be put on its walls, or a whole row of wooden columns to adorn its front; nay, a large shady tree in a door-yard is much more desirable than the most expensive mahogany and velvet sofa in the parlor. Unhappily, our people generally do not yet see things in this light. But time is a very essential element, absolutely indispensable, indeed, in true civilization; and in the course of years we shall, it is to be hoped, learn further lessons of this kind.

How easy it would be to improve most of the farms in the country by a little attention to the woods and trees, improving their appearance, and adding to their market value at the same time! Thinning woods and not blasting them; clearing only such ground as is marked for immediate tillage; preserving the wood on the hill-tops and rough side-hills; encouraging a coppice on this or that knoll; permitting bushes and young trees to grow at will along the brooks and watercourses; sowing, if need be, a grove on the bank of the pool, such as are found on many of our farms; sparing an elm or two about the spring, with a willow also to overhang the well; planting one or two chestnuts, or oaks, or beeches, near the gates or bars; leaving a few others scattered about every field to shade the cattle in summer, as is frequently done, and setting out others in groups, or singly, to shade the house—how little would be the labor or expense required to accomplish all this, and how desirable would be the result! Assuredly, the pleasing character thus given to a farm and a neighborhood is far from being beneath the consideration of a sensible man.

FURTHER READING

Cooper, Susan Fenimore. *Rural Hours.* Rev. ed. Syracuse, N.Y.: Syracuse University Press, 1968.

Cunningham, Anna K. "Susan Fenimore Cooper: Child of Genius." *New York History Magazine* 25 (July, 1944): 339–50.

2

Graceanna Lewis

1821–1912

GRACEANNA LEWIS WAS, ACCORDING TO HER BIOGRAPHER, Deborah Jean Warner, "the best informed woman naturalist of her generation." Combining her artistic and scientific talents, she spent more than fifty years of her life teaching, lecturing, and writing about many facets of natural history, frequently accompanying her verbal and written works with her accurate and beautifully executed charts, graphs, and watercolors.

Born and raised in Chester County, Pennsylvania, Lewis maintained that her interest in nature had been nurtured by her mother, encouraged by teachers and friends, and pursued in earnest after the Civil War, when she finally had time to sit quietly in her garden and observe the birds around her. But without the use of field glasses or access to the wealth of books that ornithologists have today, she found that learning the habits of even the most common dooryard birds was difficult.

A lifelong Quaker, Lewis was surrounded by an intelligent and supportive group of men and women. Two of them—amateur naturalists Ezra Michener and Vincent Bernard—taught her all they could, then introduced her to John Cassin, fellow Quaker and Curator of Birds at the Academy of Natural Sciences in Philadelphia. Cassin was one of three authors of *The Birds of America,* which Lewis had been using in her bird research. The other authors, George N. Lawrence and fellow Pennsylvanian and Assistant Secretary of the Smithsonian Spencer Fullerton Baird, also helped her with her ornithological studies.

But it was Cassin who actively encouraged her interest by opening the Academy and its wealth of natural history information to her, championing her abilities to his friend Baird, and allowing her to study the hundreds of bird skins that he had collected from around the world and used in his taxonomic work. When Lewis identified a new bird species from the skins, Cassin proudly acknowledged her find in the *Proceedings of the Academy.*

When Cassin died unexpectedly, Lewis was left bereft of the loss of her mentor and friend. In 1868, the year before his death, she had published, with his encouragement, the first part of her proposed ten-part *Natural History of Birds,* which was met with general acclaim. Now, however, without Cassin's support at the Academy, in what was essentially a male enclave, she felt unwelcome. Leaving her Philadelphia residence, she returned to nearby Chester County. Despite winning membership in the Academy with the help of anatomist Joseph Leidy, Curator of Birds George Tryon, and Academy librarian Edward J. Nolan, she was able to work only intermittently—teaching at private schools and doing research for periodical articles in such publications as the *American Naturalist* and *Friends' Intelligencer and Journal.*

When she tried to get an academic appointment teaching natural history at Vassar College in 1877, she received strong support from women scientists Rachel Bodley and Maria Mitchell. But of all the male scientists she asked, only Baird agreed to write a letter of recommendation for her. Although she was eminently qualified, Vassar wanted a male to fill the position. Bitterly disappointed, Lewis finally resigned herself to her role as a popularizer of natural history and took on as her literary mission the duty of reconciling for Christians the development of Darwinian natural processes with her perception of God's foreordained design of the universe. She outlined her final conclusions in an article she wrote in 1896 for *Friends' Intelligencer and Journal* called "Truth and the Teachers of Truth." In it she claimed that "life is not a mere struggle for existence with the blind forces of nature," as many Darwinians were claiming at the time. Instead, she considered the struggle (Darwin's "survival of the fittest" idea) to be part of God's plan to perfect humanity and nature.

With financial help from a stepdaughter she had raised and from occasional teaching, writing, and lecturing jobs, she managed to support herself. She continued to expand her natural history knowledge through her own observations and by voraciously studying everything from algae, reptiles, fish, wildflowers, and paramecia to paleontology, geology, and jellyfish. She reared her own butterflies so she could correctly illustrate amateur entomologist Henry Edwards's work on butterflies, and she painted for the Pennsylvania Forestry Commission fifty large watercolors of Pennsylvania tree leaves, a

Portrait of Graceanna Lewis. *Courtesy Smithsonian Institution Archives.*

project which won her a bronze medal and diploma at the Chicago Columbian Exposition in 1893. Those paintings, as well as the ones of wildflowers, Lewis made into a series of charts that she marketed and sold to schools for fifty cents each.

Her interest in and study of natural history never waned, even in old age. When she was eighty-seven years old, she wrote a series of scientific articles for the *Delaware County Institute of Science Proceedings,* including a detailed report of the jellyfish she had observed during her annual vacations to Longport, New Jersey. She

11

apparently accompanied that painstakingly written and researched piece with what was described in a footnote by the Institute as "beautiful watercolor sketches [whose] accuracy of outline and delicacy of color cannot be surpassed." Painting from nature, in fact, became one of her major outlets in later years.

"Birds and Their Friends," written when she was almost eighty years of age, is one of several interesting articles she wrote for *Friends' Intelligencer and Journal* about the natural history of her hometown of Media. In it she describes her early years as a budding naturalist, before her advent into the superior facilities of the Academy, and she details the difficulties she had in identifying the most common dooryard birds. She also includes her observations of unusual bird behavior by American robins, brown thrashers, song sparrows, and wood thrushes, and she encourages ordinary people to take up bird-watching.

She concludes that her interest in birds led to an interest in nature in general "until the broad outlook of Naturalist was attained." To Lewis, being a naturalist was the highest calling she could reach here on earth and a "fitting preparation for [her] advancement in eternity."

BIRDS AND THEIR FRIENDS

Many years ago, when I began the study of birds, I had no plates and no specimens,—nothing but a book of verbal descriptions, with the technical terms of which I was unfamiliar. It took me three weeks to know the common song-sparrow. I kept my book open at the description of this bird and when one came near I watched its markings. But a bird with a will of its own and wings to obey that will, cared little for my mental picture of it. Almost before my eye could seize a point, the animated little creature would be beyond sight. By perseverance I finally came to know these birds so as to be able to distinguish them from any one of the numerous other sparrows. They repaid me amply, meeting as they did in the vines and shrubs, and even on the ground about the house, some of them coming nightly to roost near our door where they had nested. One of them sang for us all winter long, until on a fatal day in February, it was carried off by a hungry sparrow-hawk [American kestrel] whose plumage and bearing I had been admiring, as he sat in full view perched on a grape-vine arbor. I thought it a great good fortune to see such a beautiful bird, but when the musical voice had been hushed for ever, I had no love for sparrow-hawks, with all their bravery of black and white and rust color.

In the same laborious manner as that applied to the song-sparrow, I learned all of the common song birds which visited my home or which were found in our woods. The best place for observation, I found, was seated quietly under a cherry tree when the fruit was ripe. There, in an hour, I could see a greater variety of birds than would be met with in a whole afternoon in the woods. Having exhausted my home resources, I afterward went to the Academy of Natural Sciences, in Philadelphia, where could be seen the birds of the world in such overwhelming numbers that at first I was completely confused by them. Gradually, by the aid of books and specimens, the birds of different countries took their place in their proper systematic order, forming a whole of vastly increased interest. I remember giving an entire winter to the birds of Australia alone. The birds of Europe, Asia, Africa, and South America, with those of Oceanic Islands, required similar studies. In time I could fairly call myself an ornithologist, but I was in no haste about it. The problems of a natural classification occupied my mind very deeply, and I felt I must have a wider knowledge to be able to build upon any sure foundation. The beginning I had made led to the study of animal life in general, and thus I became a zoölogist. Still later I took up the more systematic study of plant life, and all these studies led to far wider reaches until the broad outlook of Naturalist was attained, all beginning with the little brown song-sparrow of my country home, and the sights and sounds of country life,—the dearest I have ever known.

The beginner of the present day has many aids to the study of birds, not at first accessible to me. Many popular writers, such as Olive Thorne Miller [noted birdwatcher and prolific author], John Burroughs [popular nature essayist of late nineteenth and early twentieth centuries], and Bradford Torrey [American naturalist and writer who wrote nine popular nature essay books between 1885 and 1913 with a special emphasis on birds], have awakened public interest in the subject, and the study is now rendered comparatively easy by the numerous excellent works on Ornithology, chief of which remains to be the classic of Alexander Wilson [called the "father of American ornithology" and author of the nine-volume *American Ornithology* describing 262 bird species], with which I was early supplied.

Few who have not entered upon this study can imagine the pleasure to be found in it. Much can be learned from mere observation. To wander at will, in field and wood, with the ear open to catch any note or song of bird, and the eye trained to notice the least flutter in the branches, cannot fail to result in an interesting knowledge of bird-life. Every student should possess an opera-glass. It is an efficient aid to the eye, and will often enable one to recognize a bird, when otherwise there might be much difficulty in its identification. The habits of birds are also much more readily watched without alarming any shy inhabitant of the wood, or interfering with the maternal cares of the more domestic species.

I well remember at one time seeing a robin teaching its little one to *hop*. With a delectable morsel in its mouth, it would stand *almost* within reach of the birdling, on the ground, and would then move backward to entice the owner of the yellow throat to follow, reminding one of a human parent winning its child to its first steps. Probably the restless fledgeling [*sic*] had flown from the nest too early, a calamity which frequently befalls young robins. Should an uneducated cat appear upon the scene, the distressed cries of all bird-dom will arouse the most inattentive ear. Even the English sparrow will unite in the general outcry, and will sometimes, as I have seen, risk its own life by flying at the intruder. On occasions when the birds, seemed to ask and expect human help, I have relieved the anxiety by placing the unfortunate young adventurer in a crotch of a tree where it could be guarded by its parents, and have at the same time been taught a lesson by the birds whose sympathies are so spontaneous, and are so urgently manifested without regard to specific differences. Cat-bird, robin, and sparrow are equally affected when a nestling is in danger, and all unite in the clamor until safety is assured.

On very hot days I have seen robins standing on the edge of the nest watching the brood, but at the time affording the necessary air. In feeding her young, the mother is careful to give each one in succession, a cherry, or to divide a worm impartially, so that each may have a bit of the proper size to swallow.

When undisturbed, robins are especially confiding, often building in situations exposed to hourly observation. In one instance, the nest was placed in a fork of a tree standing on the pathway from the house to the barn; another selected a position not a yard from our door; still another built amongst the timbers of a tram-way where cars for the transportation of iron-ore were constantly passing to and fro above them, and I am happy to record that not one of eighteen workmen employed betrayed the trust reposed in them, but instead seemed to take a pride in the preservation of the nest, and in seeing that the brood was reared in safety.

In a utilitarian town, devoted to business interests, I once knew a man who waited to roof his house until the young robins were fledged because the parent birds had chosen to build amongst his bare rafters. He was an uneducated man whom no one would have suspected of either enthusiasm or sentiment. In contrast with this we may happen to know of song-birds which are illegally shot by wealthy owners of strawberry patches, and decide for ourselves where true gentleman-liness is to be found.

Individual robins, even in the wild state, are superior to others in melody. Morning after morning one may hear one sweet voice rising above the somewhat monotonous chorus, proving the capabilities of the vocal organs in this species.

I was once attracted by a bird-song which I knew to be that of a robin, but which reminded me of the mocking-bird and also of the wood-thrush. Inquiry revealed the fact that the rare singer was a common robin which had been reared from the nest as a pet bird, and had been fed on richer and more abundant food than it could have obtained in its native haunts, the result being that in captivity the vocal organs had been developed at the expense of liberty.

The robin, while not ordinarily a fine singer, belongs to the family of the thrushes which includes some of our very best musicians. One of these, our common brown thrush [brown thrasher] or "thrash-er," is associated in my mind with the month of May and an apple orchard with millions of fragrant blossoms. Seated in the midst of these, in the dewy morning, this delightful songster would greet the sun with such a joyous and thrilling strain that one would wish all the world might hear. In the evening the *quality* of the song was wholly different. The bird seemed to feel the influence of the evening hush and the quiet of the waiting stars. Sweet, tender, sacred, one asked not for the world, but only for the dearest of the home circle to listen. An embodiment of music and of the spirit of the hour, all the muscles of the little body were in accord. The very feathers, as well as the wings and tail, would rise with the high, or fall with the low, quiver with the tremulous, dying notes, before darkness fell, and the song melted into silence.

The wood-thrush, or wood-robin, was formerly considered a very shy bird, and is so described by Wilson, and Thomas Jefferson. It does love shaded streams, but, like its cousin, the robin, when undisturbed is extremely confidential toward those who protect it. It seems to have learned by generations of experience where its safety will not be endangered. Perhaps it would be more true to say that birds are fearless until they are taught by generations of experience to distrust. Like most other song-birds, shade, water, fruit, and insect food, and *human kindness,* are its requirements. Where these can be obtained, it will multiply in peace, and become almost, if not quite, as familiar as the common robin. Amongst other places known to me where it has found happy conditions are Germantown, Pa., parts

15

of West Philadelphia, and the woods adjoining Media. At my country home in northern Chester county, one of these birds alighted near our parlor door, picking up sticks, evidently for the purpose of building. The door being open it entered the parlor and hopped to the middle of the room. A friend and myself were sitting there at the time, but our presence seemed in no wise to alarm the small explorer. We kept perfectly still, and after satisfying herself that our parlor was not in good taste for a wood-thrush, she hopped out again and entered a woodshed which she examined critically for a good building site. She finally retired, unsatisfied, and in a wood belonging to an adjacent farm we heard the notes of a wood-thrush, probably her mate, during all the time of song.

In Media, this year, a pair built in a tree in the yard of one of my friends, and there hatched their eggs, much to the delight of the children of the family. Congratulations on the founding of a colony there were brought to an end by a homeless, prowling cat, but as wood-thrushes are abundant in a continuous copse leading down to a sheltered stream, we hope for better success another year.

FURTHER READING

Baird, Spencer Fullerton. Papers. Smithsonian Institution Archives, Washington, D.C.
Hanaford, Phebe A. *Daughters of America.* Augusta, Maine, 1876.
Lewis, Graceanna. "At Longport, New Jersey, in September." *Delaware County Institute of Science, Proceedings* 4 (1909): 103–10.
———. "Birds and Their Friends." *Friends' Intelligencer and Journal* 53 (1896): 762–63, 779–80.
———. "Lectures on Zoology." Academy of Natural Sciences Library, Philadelphia, Penn.
———. Letters to Friends and Relatives. Lewis Manuscripts. Friends' Historical Library of Swarthmore College. Swarthmore, Pa.
———. "Science for Women." Papers Read at the Third Congress of Women. Syracuse, N.Y. (October 13–15, 1875): 63–66.
Warner, Deborah Jean. *Graceanna Lewis: Scientist and Humanitarian.* Washington, D.C.: Smithsonian Institution Press, 1979.

3

Mary Treat

1830–1923

MARY TREAT WAS DISSUADED BY NO ONE from publishing her natural history discoveries, even if they were contrary to the opinions of prominent male scientists. "You know none of the botanists agree with you," Asa Gray, America's foremost botanist, wrote to Treat after she had told him that the sticky secretion inside pitcher plants intoxicated the insects.

"I cannot help it," she replied. "It must go in [to the article] for I have now seen it for myself, and know *it is* so." Twenty years later botanists corroborated her statement.

A modest, reserved, but determined woman, Treat specialized in closely watching the lives of insects, spiders, and birds in the backyard of her home in Vineland, New Jersey, but she often ventured farther from home. She drove a horse and buggy into the nearby Pine Barrens to collect wildflowers and ferns, botanized from a rowboat on Florida's Saint Johns River, and dug up anthills near Green Cove Spring, Florida. Such forays led to the discovery of the rare local fern *Schizaea pusilla* in the Pine Barrens, a new amaryllis lily, the Zephyr-lily (*Zephranthes treatae*) along the banks of the Saint Johns River, and both a new harvesting ant species (*Aphaenogaster treatae*) and a cynipid oak fig root gall (*Belonocnema treatae*) growing on a Virginia oak tree in Florida.

Unhappily married then widowed in early middle age, Treat had to make her own way in the world, and she did this by writing about her nature observations. Highly respected not only by Gray but also by other prominent scientists in both the United States and Europe, she shared her findings and specimens with many leading scientists— ant expert Auguste Forel of Switzerland, entomologist Gustav Mayr

Portrait of Mary Treat, circa 1904. *Courtesy of Vineland Historical and Antiquarian Society, Vineland, New Jersey.*

of Vienna, director of the Kew Gardens Sir Joseph Hooker, and American entomologists Henry C. McCook, C. Valentine Riley, and Samuel Scudder. Scudder, one of the founders of the Cambridge Entomological Club of Massachusetts, made certain Treat was elected a member.

Her most famous champion and correspondent was Charles Darwin. Like her friend Asa Gray, Treat supported Darwin's theory of evolution, but that opinion did not stop her from setting him straight about how bladderworts (*Utricularia clandestina*) captured insects. Darwin thought the insects used their heads as wedges to enter the plants. To disprove him, Treat put the tiny bladders into water along with minute insects, then, watching carefully through her microscope, discovered "a depression at the entrance of the utricle [bladder], a pretty vestibule that seems to attract the little animals into the inviting retreat, where just beyond is a fatal trap or valve which if touched springs back and engulfs the unwary adventurers."

"It is pretty clear I am quite wrong about the head acting like a wedge," Darwin wrote to her, and in his book, *Insectivorous Plants,* he acknowledged that "Mrs. Treat of New Jersey has been more successful than any other observer" in understanding how bladderworts capture insects. Carnivorous plants, in fact, were her specialty. She spent a great deal of time studying not only bladderworts and pitcher plants but also sundews, butterworts, and Venus flytraps and their mechanisms for trapping insects.

Her articles appeared in many popular magazines of the day, most notably *Harper's New Monthly Magazine, American Naturalist,* and *Lippincott's Magazine.* Out of those pieces she constructed several of her books, including *Chapters on Ants* and her best-selling *Home Studies in Nature.*

The first selection that follows, "Plants That Eat Animals" from *American Naturalist,* illustrates her insatiable curiosity about nature, which she subsequently confirmed with carefully planned experiments. She was not averse to name-dropping, mentioning that she had written about her discoveries to Dr. Asa Gray and Mr. Darwin but that "at that date he [Darwin] had not worked the matter up as far as I had." She conceded, though, that "with his superior facilities he may have far outstripped me."

"Home Studies in Nature," from *Harper's New Monthly Magazine,* is only a small portion of her book by the same title. This excerpt is based wholly on her studies of insects and spiders carried out in what she alternatively called her "Insect Garden" or "Insect Menagerie." There, on a one-acre backyard plot, she discovered two new species of burrowing spiders—*Tarantula tigrina* and *Tarantula turricula*—and observed their habits, as well as those of both the digger and social wasps. Ahead of her time in her nonjudgmental observations of predators, whether insects or birds, she exhibited little patience for the prejudices most people had against spiders. Still, when she dug up spider nests and put them into glass candy jars for closer observation, she was careful to "cover the surface with moss, and introduce some pretty little growing plants, so that my nervous lady friends may admire the plants without being shocked with the knowledge that each of these jars is the home of a large spider."

Those experiments and observations led her to conclude that "the more I limit myself to a small area, the more novelties and discoveries I make in natural history," a principle as true today as it was in the last half of the nineteenth century.

Plants That Eat Animals

The Bladderwort is a common plant, growing in shallow ponds and swamps; Dr. [Asa] Gray [Professor of Botany at Harvard University, considered the "father of American botany"] in his "Manual of the Botany of the United States," describes twelve species found within this range, and almost every muddy pond contains one or more of them. Some grow wholly or nearly out of water; but the species which I am about to describe are immersed, with finely dissected leaves on long stems floating in the water. Scattered among the leaves, or along the stems which are destitute of leaves, are numerous little bladders, the use of which we had supposed was to float the plant at the time of flowering. The flowering stems of most of the species are smooth and free from leaves or bladders, and shoot up straight from the water to a hight [*sic*] of from three to twelve inches, bearing at the top from one to ten curiously-fashioned flowers of a yellow or purple color. It has always been taken for granted that these little bladders were made to float the plant, although I had noticed that the stems most heavily laden with bladders sank the lowest in the water.

About a year ago (in Dec. 1873), a young man, now at Cornell University, and myself, on placing some of the bladders under the microscope, noticed animalcules—dead entomostraca, etc., apparently imprisoned therein. But our attention was not sufficiently aroused to follow up the subject very closely; we laughingly called it "our new carnivorous plant." But as the bladders always seemed to be open, the significance of the fact of the imprisoned animal was not very apparent. We thought it could hardly be for the purpose of feeding the plant, but a kind of wanton cruelty. Still, my curiosity was aroused. I soon found larger animals in the bladders—dead larvae of some aquatic insect—large enough to be seen distinctly with the naked eye. But I was not aroused to earnest work until I watched the movements of an imprisoned living larva, and saw its struggles and final death. This was in October, 1874. I now visited the ponds and procured abundant material.

The plant that I experimented with mostly was the one known to botanists as *Utricularia clandestina.*

My next work was to see what prevented the escape of the animal from the bladder, and to this end I directed all my attention for several days. The animal that I found most commonly entrapped was a Chironomus larva, about the length of the mosquito larva, but more slender and of lighter color. I have frequently trapped these snake-like larvae and seen them enter the bladders. They seem to be wholly vegetable feeders, and specially to have a liking for the long hairs at the entrance of the bladders. When a larva is feeding near the entrance it is pretty certain to run its head into the net, whence there is no retreat. A large larva is sometimes three or four hours in being swallowed, the process bringing to mind what I have witnessed when a small snake makes a large frog its victim.

I worked with this larva for several days, determined, if possible, to see him walk into the trap.

I put growing stems of the plant in a small dish of water with several larvae, and set it aside. In a few hours thereafter I would find the living larvae imprisoned. This served for another purpose, but not for the object I was aiming at. Forced to give up this plan of seeing the larvae enter the bladder, I now directed my attention to the smaller ones—animalcules proper,—I placed the bladders in water inhabited by numerous tiny creatures, and soon had the satisfaction of seeing the *modus operandi* by which the victim was caught.

The entrance into the bladder has the appearance of a tunnel-net, always open at the large end, but closed at the other extremity. I find that the net is simply a valve turned in from the mouth of the bladder, with the outer edge surrounded with a dense mass of hairs, which impels the larva forward and prevents the possibility of retreat. The little animals seemed to be attracted into this inviting retreat. They would sometimes dally about the open entrance for a short time, but would sooner or later venture in, and easily open or push apart the closed entrance at the other extremity. As soon as the animal was fairly in, the forced entrance closed, making it a secure prisoner.

Entomostraca too were often captured—*Daphnia, Cyclops* and *Cypris.* These little animals are just visible to the naked eye, but under the microscope are beautiful and interesting objects. The lively little Cypris is encased in a bivalve shell, which it opens at pleasure, and thrusts out its feet and two pairs of antennae, with tufts of feathery-like filaments. This little animal was quite wary, but nevertheless was often caught. Coming to the entrance of a bladder it would sometimes pause a moment and then dash away; at other times it would come close up, and even venture part way into the entrance and back out as if afraid. Another, more heedless, would open the door and walk in; but it was no sooner in than it manifested alarm, drew in its feet and antennae and closed its shell. But after its death the shell unclosed again, displaying its feet and antennae. I never saw even the smallest animalcule escape after it was once fairly inside the bladder.

So these points were settled to my satisfaction—that the animals were entrapped, and killed, and slowly macerated. But how was I to know that these animals were made subservient to the plant? If I could only prove that the contents of the bladders were carried directly into the circulation, my point was gained. This now was my sole work for several days, to examine closely the contents of the bladders. I found the fluid contents to vary considerably, from a dark, muddy, to a very light, transparent color. Hundreds of these bladders, one after another, were put to the test under the microscope, and I found that to a greater or less extent, I could trace the same color that I found in the bladder, in the stem on which the bladder grew, though the observation was not so clear and satisfactory as I could wish. After more critical examination I arrived at the conclusion that the cells themselves and not their contents, change to a red color; the stems also take on this color, so as to make it appear as if a red fluid was carried from the bladders into the main stem, which is not specifically the fact so far as the observations yet made determine; though the main point, that the contents of the bladders are carried into the circulation, does not seem open to question.

The next step was to see how many of the bladders contained animals, and I found almost every one that was well developed contained one or more, or their remains, in various stages of digestion. The larva of Chironomus was the largest and most constant animal found. On some of the stems that I examined, fully nine out of every ten of the bladders contained this larva or its remains. When first caught it was fierce, thrusting out its horns and feet and drawing them back, but otherwise it seemed partly paralyzed, moving its body but very little; even small larvae of this species that had plenty of room to swim about were soon very quiet, although they showed signs of life from twenty-four to thirty-six hours after they were imprisoned. In about twelve hours, as nearly as I could make out, they lost the power of drawing their feet back, and could only move the brush-like appendages. There was some variation with different bladders as to the time when maceration or digestion began to take place, but usually, on a growing spray in less than two days after a large larva was captured, the fluid contents of the bladders began to assume a cloudy or muddy appearance, and often became so dense that the outline of the animal was lost to view.

Nothing yet in the history of carnivorous plants comes so near to the animal as this. I was forced to the conclusion that these little bladders are in truth like so many stomachs, digesting and assimilating animal food. What it is that attracts this particular larva into the bladders is left for further investigation. But here is the fact that animals are found there, and in large numbers, and who can deny that the plant feeds directly upon them? The why and wherefore is no more inexplicable than many another fact in nature. And it only goes to show that the two great kingdoms of nature are more intimately blended than we had heretofore supposed, and, with Dr. [Joseph] Hooker [Director of Kew Gardens in London and one of the world's premier botanists], we may be compelled to say, "our brother organisms—plants."

About the 1st of December, after I had made most of my observations, I wrote to Dr. Asa Gray and to Mr. Darwin, both on the same day, telling them of my discovery. Dr. Gray then informed me that Mr. Darwin had been engaged in the same work on *Utricularia,* and also sent me a note from him, bearing date Aug. 5. From this note it would appear that at that date he had not worked the matter up as far as I had—at least had not found so many imprisoned animals; but with his superior facilities he may have far outstripped me.

FROM HOME STUDIES IN NATURE

I sometimes think the more I limit myself to a small area, the more novelties and discoveries I make in natural history. My observations for the past four summers have been almost wholly confined to an acre of ground in the heart of a noisy town. A bit of natural woodland occupies about a quarter of the acre, and here I have made several discoveries new to science.

The most interesting creatures that have rewarded me in my search are two species of large burrowing spiders that had heretofore escaped the attention of naturalists. These spiders build beautiful, complicated structures above their burrows, with which they take as much pains as most birds do in building their nests.

The Rev. Dr. [Henry C.] McCook [entomologist, author of scientific and popular works on ants, spiders, and related animals, including *The Natural History of the Agricultural Ant of Texas*] has named one of these spiders *Tarantula tigrina,* or tiger-spider, from the fact that the legs have annular stripes of gray and black like a tiger's.

This species digs a tube in the earth six or seven inches in depth, and uniformly straight. But its skill and wisdom are displayed in erecting the upper part of its domicile, which is evidently for concealment. It first builds a broad, silk-lined funnel at the mouth of its burrow; the background is composed of whatever material it can reach with its long hind-legs while its fore-legs rest in the edge of its tube. This funnel is the foundation of a concealed room, which sometimes takes it several nights to complete. It does not work during the day.

I had repeatedly tried to see one go on with its building, but the light of the lamp or my near proximity seemed to disturb it; but at last I had the satisfaction to see a fine large female go on with her work undisturbed by the light or my presence. She first spins a canopy of web over the funnel, leaving a place of exit on one side. She next comes out and steps carefully over the canopy, as if to see whether it is strong and secure. Seemingly satisfied that it is all right, she steps down, just letting her fore-feet touch the edge of the web, while with her hind-legs she feels, examines, and handles various things, which she rejects. Finally she selects a dry oak leaf about two inches broad and three in length, and lays it over the canopy, and proceeds to fasten it down all around except at the entrance. After the leaf is made secure, she reaches up and pulls down blades of grass, and lays them over the leaf, and fastens them down with web so dexterously that it can not be seen except with the closest scrutiny. This makes a strong roof over her domicile. Now she goes within, and seems to be putting some finishing touches on the inside. This done, she stands in the door of her neat apartment waiting for any chance insect that may come within her range. I see a beetle slowly crawling along, evidently in search for its supper. I carefully direct its course toward the spider. Quick as a flash she seizes it, and goes within her home to make her meal. Former experience has taught me that she will be a long time making this meal, so I leave my post of observation for that night.

In a few days thereafter I find that she has completely closed the entrance to her domicile, and if I did not know the precise spot in which it is located, I should not be able to find it.

I have twenty-eight of these spiders under observation. I visit them all, and find that more than half of the number, both males and females, have closed their doors very firmly. Some of these burrows are situated in beds of moss, and the moss is so cunningly arranged over them that the most expert naturalist would find it difficult to tell where they are. I have often tried my friends, to see if they could

24

find one of these concealed burrows, and have limited the space to a few square inches, within which it was located, but they scarcely ever hit upon the right spot.

It is August, and a digger-wasp is making sad havoc among these spiders. She wants them to feed her young, and nothing but this particular species will do; and woe now to all the spiders with unclosed doors, for she is sure to find them. The wasp is large and strong, and has steel-blue wings, and two bright orange spots on either side of the abdomen. She runs over the ground swiftly, peering here and there, until she alights upon an open burrow, down which she speedily goes, and soon comes out, dragging her victim, which she has paralyzed with her powerful sting.

Sometimes two wasps are hunting in the same vicinity, and when one finds a spider, the other tries to wrest it from her. And now a fearful battle ensues. They drop the prey, and clinch in deadly conflict, seemingly trying to stab each other with their stings. The victorious party returns to the spider, which is heavier than herself, and proceeds to drag it to her nest. She runs backward for a time, dragging it over the ground; then tries flying a short distance, but the burden is so heavy that she soon comes to the ground again. She is so active and quick in her movements that I am obliged to walk quite fast to keep even with her. She carries the spider several rods from where she obtained it, lays it down on a gravelled walk, and hunts over the ground. She soon finds the burrow which she has previously dug, returns to the spider, seizes it, and disappears within. She comes out empty-handed, and proceeds to fill up the hole with the earth which she has thrown out. She works so rapidly that I can scarcely tell which feet she uses the most. She seems to dig with her fore-feet, and to rake the earth in backward with her hind-feet. Soon the hole is full; and now she makes a battering-ram of herself by repeatedly striking her body on the ground, as it to pound the earth down. This done, she rakes the ground all over and around the place, to make it level, and then seizes a small pebble in her mandibles, and lays it over the spot; and scatters other pebbles all around it, so that it looks noways different from the surrounding ground.

The wasp is gone, and now like a thief I venture to dig up the treasure. I find the spider about four inches below the surface, with an egg sticking in the body which the wasp has placed there. The egg hatches into a legless white grub, which at once begins to feed upon the spider.

Some strange knowledge more than we possess enables the mother wasp to so prepare the spider that the meat will keep fresh and sweet from four to six weeks, or until the helpless baby wasp is full grown, and passes into the chrysalis stage. It remains a chrysalis until the following summer, when a full-fledged, bright-colored wasp emerges. In this state it does not feed upon spiders, but upon nectar and honey.

The wasps continue their raids for two or three weeks, only the spiders with closed doors escaping. Sometimes one has kept herself shut up for two weeks, and then timidly opens her door and looks out; but the raid is not yet over, and, sooner or later, she is sure to become the wasp's prey.

Toward the end of August I see no more of the wasps, but out of twenty-eight spiders, only five are left. These now soon open their doors, and occasionally one cuts the threads of web in such a manner as to make a sort of trap-door, leaving a hinge on one side. But more usually there is a hole in one end of the oven-shaped cover, which the spider can soon close by drawing the material together and fastening it with web.

In November they all hermetically close their doors, and keep them shut until the following April, when the spiders again come forth, the females each with a cocoon of eggs attached to the spinneret. The eggs hatch in May, and the young spiders crawl on to the mother's back—in fact, literally covering her body. After a few days they leave her, and all at once come rushing out of the burrow. For two or three months these young spiders flit about here and there, over bushes and on the lower branches of trees, seemingly ambitious to get in high places. Toward the end of July their roving life ceases, and they settle down and dig little burrows in the earth, which the first season they do not conceal. The wasps do not molest these young ones.

The following spring—when a year old—they are a little more than half grown, but during the summer they grow rapidly, and moult several times, each time changing their appearance. By August they seem to be nearly full grown, when their enemy the wasp makes such havoc among them.

By thus tracing the life history of this spider, we find it to be two years old before the first brood of young are hatched; and if no accident befalls it, it probably lives several years.

These spiders make very interesting pets. I capture them by cutting out the nests with a sharp trowel or large knife, and have ready some glass candy jars from twelve to fourteen inches in height, in which I carefully place them. I then fill in with earth all around, making the jar about half full, and cover the surface with moss, and introduce some pretty little growing plants, so that my nervous lady friends may admire the plants without being shocked with the knowledge that each of these jars is the home of a large spider.

Some of these spiders take kindly to their new surroundings, and at once begin to repair their domiciles. Others utterly refuse to take advantage of my kindness, and try to climb up the side of the jar—which is impossible for them to accomplish—to make their escape. It is of no use to keep a discontented individual, for it will not build, however tame it becomes. Such a one I always let go to shift for itself, which it very soon does by digging a burrow, sometimes within a few feet from where I sent it adrift.

The male tiger-spider is a handsome fellow, and fully as large as the female. In color the body is a light snuff-brown, with dashes of dark purple, while the legs are striped like a tiger's. The female is nearly black. The male takes as much pains in building his domicile as the female. In fact, one of the males in a jar entirely outdid the female in making a tasteful retreat. He utilized a little twining plant by winding it around, and making a living green bower over his burrow.

He has a voracious appetite, scarcely refusing anything I give him, even taking large hairy caterpillars. He has moulted three times during the summer, and now in September must be full grown.

But another species—of which this is the first public mention, so far as is known—excels the tiger-spider in its curious architectural attainments. It belongs to the genus *Tarantula,* and is as large as the tiger, but quite different in color. The male is a soft velvety black, while the female is grayish-brown, or like faded velvet. She has a light gray spot on top of the thorax, and on the abdomen are three dark brown longitudinal stripes alternating with light gray. In young specimens these markings are quite distinct, but in old ones the colors blend somewhat. The two sexes do not differ in size, the male being fully as large as the female. The body is a little more than an inch in length, and the legs are large and long, which gives it quite a formidable appearance, but it is perfectly harmless.

I have provisionally named it *Tarantula turricula,* reserving a further description. The name was suggested from its manner of building.

It digs a burrow in the earth six or seven inches in depth, but the upper part of its domicile is entirely unlike that of the tiger-spider. This species builds a little round tower above its burrow. It procures sticks from one to two inches in length, and arranges them very symmetrically one above the other, laying them so as to make a five-sided wall.

It is usually a most contented species in confinement. Early in July I took a fine female, surrounded and almost covered with baby spiders about ready to leave the mother—the young can readily run up the side of the jar and escape. As soon as they left her, I removed the jar to my study; I did not take the nest with this spider, as I wished to see what she would do with entirely new surroundings. The earth in the jar was about six inches in depth, and well pressed down. I gave her sticks and moss to put around the top of her tube.

She soon began to dig a burrow, and when it was about two inches in depth, she commenced to build a tower above it. She takes a stick from my fingers and places it at the edge of her tube. She works while inside of her burrow, holding the stick with her fore-legs until it is arranged to suit her; she then turns around and fastens it with a strong web. She takes another stick and proceeds in the same way, and continues this until she has laid the foundation of a five-sided wall. She now goes down to the bottom of her tube and brings up a pellet of earth, which she places on top of the sticks; she goes all around, making a circle of these pellets, which she flattens by pressing her body against them, and arranges them in such a manner as to cover the sticks on the inside, making the walls perfectly round and silk-lined. Now she is ready for more sticks, which she continues to alternate with the pellets until the tower has reached the height of two and a half inches above her burrow. I sometimes gave her bits of green moss an inch or two in length, which she would use by fastening them to a stick with web. This makes the wall on the outside fringed with moss.

If she is not in a mood for building, and I offer her a stick, she takes it in her mandibles, and with her fore-feet gives it a quick blow, often sending it with force enough to hit the jar; and when she is digging and bringing up pellets of earth which she does not wish to use in her tower, she throws them from the top of the walls with sufficient force to make them land a foot or more from the burrow, if it were not for the intervention of the glass. This accounted for the fact that I could never find any fresh earth near the burrows of these spiders.

She is also a very neat housekeeper; she leaves no débris in the cellar under her tower; the remains of all insects are thrown from the top in the same manner she throws the pellets. The tiger-spider always leaves the skeletons of insects in the bottom of its tube, and in time this makes a rich black mould around the bottom of it, and as a result of this the spider is often driven from its home by a great mushroom starting from the bottom of the burrow, which pushes its way upward, and completely demolishes it, forcing the spider to seek new quarters. Such a catastrophe never happens to our neater tower-builder.

28

In confinement the female tiger-spider will kill and eat the male, but the tower-builder has no such wicked tendency; the two live in perfect harmony. I soon introduced a male into the jar with the female, which I captured in July, but he would not build for himself, neither would he assist her, but he often seemed to be watching her movements, and would go up on her tower and look down, but I never saw him venture within her burrow.

Toward the last of July the female appeared with a cocoon of eggs, about as large as a hazel-nut, attached to the spinneret. I now set the male free, and he dug a burrow not more than two rods distant from where I liberated him. His tower is not so fine as the female's, and as yet it is only about an inch above the burrow, and he has been at work on it for two months or more, but meanwhile two disasters have happened to it—probably some bird, catching a glimpse of the builder, demolished the structure in the vain hope of capturing him.

The female in the jar exercises the greatest care over her cocoon. On cool days she keeps out of sight down in her tube, which is now about eight inches in depth, including the tower. But when I set the jar in the sun, she soon comes up and puts the cocoon in the sunshine. When cool enough for a fire, if I set the jar near the stove, she places the eggs on the side next to the stove. If I turn the jar around, she soon moves the cocoon around to the warm side, letting it hang outside of the walls of her tower.

On the 6th of October the young spiders are hatched, and very comical they look, perched on the mother's back, and even on her head and legs. When I captured her three months ago in this same condition, she was wild and frightened; now she is tame and quiet. She carried the cocoon two months before the eggs hatched.

She never leaves her home, her favorite position is sitting on the top of her tower, with her legs folded beneath her. But any unusual noise, like the sudden closing of a door, always alarms her and sends her quickly within; but she has become so accustomed to my presence that she allows me to move the jar without leaving her position, and she takes food from my fingers, yet if a stranger comes into the room she always seems to know it.

She takes strong insects, like grasshoppers or large moths, into her cellar to kill them; and when their struggles have ceased, she brings them up, and deliberately proceeds to divest them of their wings and legs, which she throws away, and then sucks the juices from the body and throws away the dry carcass.

Another individual of this species I kept several weeks in a similar jar; but she refused to build, and would not even repair her old home. However, she became quite tame, and I had the satisfaction to see how she killed her prey. The moth was not allowed to flutter its wings; the spider would get astride of it, and hold its wings down with her legs, and pierce it with her sharp mandibles until it was dead.

Among country people there is much superstitious dread of spiders; and the more ignorant, the greater the superstition. . . . [People] in Florida believe the bite of a spider causes sickness and death. [Someone] informed me that the bite of an ant—a species of *Campanotus* that makes its home in fallen timber—would give them "the fever."

Fallen trees on the barrens, that would make several cords of excellent wood, would at once be abandoned by the chopper if these ants were found in them. But we need not go to Florida to find the existence of senseless superstition.

The handsome large black and yellow spider *Argiope* is perhaps the most dreaded, on account of its large size and bright colors. A fine specimen of this species had hung her pretty geometric web in a blackberry bush in a large field devoted to this fruit. On walking through the field I noticed the pickers had day after day left the fruit on this bush, and I supposed they did not wish to disturb the spider. At last she was gone, and upon making inquiries I learned that a woman more courageous than the rest had armed herself with a large stick and killed the monster!

This beautiful creature, with her exquisite web, is one of the most charming studies in nature.

"The spider's touch, how exquisitely fine!
Feels at each thread, and lives along the line."

She is readily tamed, and her solicitude over her great pear-shaped cocoon of eggs is often quite pathetic.

Some species of wasps are very interesting studies, especially the social wasps. A tree was being trimmed in the grove, when I noticed three or four wasps apparently much excited, and not willing to leave a particular spot. I soon found the cause of their grievance. A small branch had been cut off and thrown down, upon which was fastened their curious paper nest. I took the branch and stuck it in the ground under the tree. The wasps at once found it, and manifested so much intelligence that I resolved to watch them, and see if they could be tamed.

They belonged to the genus *Polistes*. The nest is firmly fastened to the branch by a slender, strong pedicel, which is on one side of the mass of cells. The cells are so arranged as to form a concave curve. . . . One side is lower than the other, which makes a slanting roof.

To bring these wasps under subjection I supposed would require much and long continued patience, but, to my surprise, I found them very tractable and easily won.

My first experiment is to handle the branch, which they resent by acting quite waspish; but I am very gentle with them, and they never sting me, and they soon allow me to hold it in such a manner that I can see them feed their young, and go on with their work, building their paper cells. They manufacture their paper out of wood. I place a weather-beaten board near them. Two of the wasps use it; some of the others try it, but seem to conclude that they have a better manufacturing establishment of their own finding.

I hold a small dish of moistened sugar and fruit syrup in my hand, which they find and relish highly. I never leave this for them to help themselves, as I wish to teach them that I am their benefactor, and they soon learn this, and come to meet me. If I neglect to bring the syrup, they flit all around me, sometimes alighting on my hand, but they no longer make any demonstrations that look like stinging.

I one day witnessed a most singular proceeding among this family. A large fat baby wasp died in its cell. The mother wasp pulled it partly out, and stroked it with her antennae, and seemed to be licking it. At this time there were a dozen or more mature wasps—the queen and workers. Nine of these were hanging about the cells, an unusually large number to be at home, all at the same time, during working-hours. As soon as the mother stepped aside, another took her place, and went through the same motions, stroking and licking it; and this in turn was repeated by all of the sister wasps that were present. Then one of the number pulled the dead baby out of the cell, and flew away with it, followed by three or four of the family, and I soon lost sight of them.

All of the social wasps, so far as is known, commence the colony with one individual queen. The old queen, workers, and males die in the fall, while the young queens hibernate through the winter, under moss and leaves or beneath the bark of trees, and in the spring they select a spot to build, and lay the foundation for the future colony. As the queen has the entire work to do in building the first cells and feeding the larvae, the work progresses slowly; only two or three cells are completed when the first worker emerges. And now the work goes on more rapidly. The foundations of other cells are at once made, in each of which the queen places an egg, which develops rapidly, and soon the mature wasps appear, which join their mother and sisters in the work, until the colony—in the genus *Polistes*—often numbers a hundred or more individuals.

A small earthen wren-house had been fastened under the eaves of a building to accommodate the birds. I had often noticed a pair of wrens chattering and scolding and peering in at the door, but never venturing within. Wishing to learn the cause of their behavior, I mounted a step-ladder and looked in. I found that the rust-red social wasp (*Polistes rubiginosus*) had selected this novel place to build in, much to the chagrin of the birds, which were evidently afraid to venture within.

In the autumn, after the wasps are gone, I investigate their work, and find this had been their home for five years. Four large clusters of cells were suspended from above. This species attaches its nest from a central point, unlike the first-mentioned species. These four nests just about filled the space; the one last made was some-what crowded and irregularly built—no space left for future progeny.

In the spring a queen returned to the ancestral hall, took in the situation, and resolved not to forsake the home of her forefathers. She selected a stick about an inch in length, and firmly welded it across near the lower edge of some of the old cells. This made a strong brace, capable of sustaining the future colony. She suspended her nest from the brace, where the colony was successfully reared.

Further Reading

Gershenowitz, Harry. "The Mrs. Treat of Darwin's Scientific World." *Vineland Historical Magazine* 55 (1979): 3–7.

Harshberger, John W. *The Botanists of Philadelphia and Their Work.* Philadelphia: T. C. Davis & Sons, 1899.

Scudder, Samuel. Papers. Museum of Science, Boston, Mass.

Smith, Nancy. "Mary Treat." *New Jersey Audubon* 9 (Winter, 1983): 18–20.

Treat, Mary. *Home Studies in Nature.* New York: Harper & Brothers, 1885.

———. Papers. Vineland Historical and Antiquarian Society, Vineland, N.J.

———. "Plants That Eat Animals." *American Naturalist* 9 (1875): 658–60.

Weiss, Harry B. "Mrs. Mary Treat, 1830-1923, Early New Jersey Naturalist." *Proceedings of the New Jersey Historical Society* 73 (1955): 258–73.

4

Martha Maxwell

1831–81

"I BEST LOVE THE HANDYWORKS OF NATURE in there [*sic*] wildest forms," Martha Maxwell once told her mother and stepfather, long before her days as a Colorado naturalist observing and collecting wild animals for her innovative museum displays. When she wrote those words, she was still a student at Oberlin College in Ohio, struggling to stay in school by scrimping on food, heat, and warm clothing. After two years she had exhausted her funds and was forced to return to Baraboo, Wisconsin, to live with her family and teach school.

A native of Dartt's Settlement in Pennsylvania's remote and rugged Tioga County, Maxwell had first gained a love of nature through walks in the woods with her maternal grandmother. Later, when Maxwell's widowed mother remarried, she acquired another crucial influence through her stepfather, Josiah Dartt, a young first cousin of Maxwell's deceased father. Dartt was an intellectual, religious man who appreciated nature and encouraged Maxwell's lifelong pursuit of knowledge and natural history.

When Maxwell returned to Baraboo, where her parents had moved when she was a youngster, she met a wealthy widower with six children. He offered to pay her way to Lawrence College in Wisconsin if she would both chaperon his oldest son and daughter there and help them with their studies. Eager to resume her education, she agreed. She did not accept his marriage proposal as readily, however, until Dartt urged her to reconsider. In 1854 Martha Dartt became Martha Maxwell, the wife of James Alexander Maxwell, owner of a store, gristmill, and large home. Three years later, he was financially ruined by the Panic of 1857.

Undaunted, they decided to make a new start, and in 1860 they

Illustration of Martha Maxwell from Mary Dartt's *On the Plains.*

left their two-year-old daughter in Baraboo with the Dartts and headed for the newly discovered gold fields of Pikes Peak, Colorado. But that venture, too, was a failure. After three difficult years, in which Maxwell ran a boarding house and her husband drove cattle from Omaha to Colorado, Maxwell returned to Wisconsin to visit her family. While she was there, she learned a skill that would serve her well for the rest of her life—the art of taxidermy.

She took quickly to what she saw as a way to combine her "deep love of all animal life, a passion for beauty, and . . . need for self-expression," as her daughter Mabel later explained in her book *Thanks to Abigail.* Returning to Colorado in 1868 with her daughter Mabel and her half-sister and lifetime best friend Mary Dartt, Max-

34

well was distressed by the reduction of wildlife that had taken place during the five years she had been away. This feeling inspired her to use her newfound talent in taxidermy to create a full collection of Colorado's fauna.

During her absence, her husband and stepson had developed a sawmill business. They often made trips into the wilderness, so Maxwell was able to go along to collect specimens. She also occasionally went by herself, shooting and trapping her quarry and camping under primitive conditions. In addition, she spent many hours observing the habits of live birds and other animals in their natural setting. Some of those animals she kept as pets in her home and used them as models so that her specimens would look as lifelike as possible. She developed her own way of preserving the animals by molding them in plaster, then covering them with their skins, which she had carefully preserved. When she opened her Rocky Mountain Museum in Boulder in 1873, the settings for the animals were as natural-looking as the specimens.

Altogether she collected 224 birds and 47 mammal species, including 3 black-footed ferrets which had been described by John James Audubon but never seen by scientists, and a subspecies of screech owl—the Rocky Mountain screech owl—named *Scops asio* var. *maxwellae,* or Mrs. Maxwell's owl, by ornithologist Robert Ridgway of the Smithsonian Institution.

By then she was also a regular correspondent of Spencer Fullerton Baird at the Smithsonian. She had sent him two bird specimens in 1874, and he, in turn, had supplied her with catalogs of birds and mammals.

Fascinated by her uniqueness as a woman naturalist and by her outstanding expertise in taxidermy, the Colorado legislature invited her to take her collection to the 1876 Centennial in Philadelphia as part of the Colorado pavilion. Dressed in her hunting outfit, she easily drew the attention of the press and was declared the "living heroine of this Centennial exhibition" by one enthusiastic journalist. More important to Maxwell, though, were the reactions of Ridgway and his fellow ornithologist Elliott Coues when they visited her collection. Ridgway commented, "It [the collection] illustrates very fully the avian fauna of Colorado." Coues later wrote in his introduction to a mammal list he prepared from her collection: "I was glad to see a collection of our native animals mounted in a manner far superior to ordinary museum work. . . . I regarded it as one of the most valuable single collections I had ever seen."

The following excerpts are taken from *On the Plains and among the Peaks; or, How Mrs. Maxwell Made Her Natural History Collection,* a book written by Mary Dartt with considerable assistance from Maxwell, according to her biographer Maxine Benson. Benson considers the book "in the main accurate and capable of independent verification . . . it also indicates to some degree how Martha Maxwell viewed herself, and how she wished to be perceived by others."

Dedicated "to Spencer F. Baird, the Sympathetic Friend of Nature's Friends," the book begins with Dartt's account of the Colorado centennial celebration and then recounts Maxwell's exploits in procuring her specimens. It also includes numerous asides about women's abilities, which reflected both Maxwell's and Dartt's beliefs "that capacity and ability, rather than birth, color, sex, or anything else, should determine where individuals belong, and what they shall do."

FROM ON THE PLAINS AND AMONG THE PEAKS

"'Woman's work!' What does that mean? Can it be possible any one wishes us to believe a *woman* did all this?"

"Couldn't say—I'm pretty sure I shan't stretch my credulity so much—it would ruin the article!"

"I should think so! Why one might think the ark had just landed here!—buffaloes, bears, birds, wild-cats, mice, and who but Noah or Agassiz could name what else! There must be hundreds of these creatures!" and the last speaker turned to me with the question:

"Does that placard really mean to tell us a woman mounted all these animals?" with an inclusive wave of a handsomely gloved hand.

"Yes," I replied.

Instantly a dozen lips were parted and questions fell, "like leaves in Vallambrosa," upon my innocent ears.

"How could a woman do it?"

"What did she do it for?"

"Did she *kill* any of the animals?"

"Well, I never! Can a body see her?"

"What sort of a woman is she?"

"Are you the one?"

It was my first day at the [1876] Centennial [in Philadelphia], and I had volunteered to relieve Mrs. Maxwell by standing for an hour, and answering questions, behind the iron paling that separated her "Natural History Collection" from the rest of the Kansas and Colorado Building, one side of a wing of which it occupied.

Within the enclosure was a miniature landscape, representing a plain, and a mountain side, apparently formed of rocks and crowned with evergreens. Down the rugged descent leaped a little stream of sparkling water, which expanded at its base into a tiny lake, edged with pebbles and fringed, as was the brook-side, with growing grass and ferns. The water and the banks which confined it were peopled by aquatic creatures: fishes swimming in the lake—turtles sunning themselves on its half submerged rocks, while beavers, muskrats and water-fowl seemed at home upon its margin. Between the cascade and lakelet appeared the irregular vine-fringed mouth of a cave, its dark moss-grown recesses soon lost from sight in shadowy gloom. Above it and upon the upper heights of the mountain side—suggesting the altitudes at which they are found—were grouped those animals that frequent the Rocky Mountains; fierce bears, shy mountain sheep, savage mountain lions or pumas, and a multitude of smaller creatures, each in an attitude of life-like action. On the limited space allowed to represent the Plains that stretch eastward from that elevated chain were huge buffaloes, elk, antelope and their native neighbors. The attitudes and surroundings of all were so artistic and unique as to form an attraction even among the many fascinations of the century's gathered productions.

As the landscape was designed and made, the animals procured, stuffed and arranged upon it, by a woman, Mrs. M. A. Maxwell, the words "*Woman's Work*" were printed on a card suspended near the cave. It was this which called forth the exclamation we first mentioned.

From the opening of the Exhibition gates in the morning until darkness made sight-seeing impossible, thousands of people pushed and crowded and jammed and jostled each other against the railing of that mimic landscape.

The idea of facing so many was at first not a little terrifying, but I fortified my courage with the thought of relieving Mrs. Maxwell, and that the American people are usually so polite, the task could not be a very unpleasant one. Alas! I had never measured their capacity for asking questions!

I had not finished assuring the large fat man in the white hat that I was by no means the person who had performed the work he saw before him, when the tall woman in the linen duster, and the short one in the white finger-puffs, and the young one in the idiot fringe, and the old gentleman with the gold-headed cane, and the man with the blue cotton umbrella, and the rough with the battered felt, and—I couldn't possibly begin to tell who else—all began at once to ask:

"Is she a young woman?"

"Is she married?"

"Where is she at?"

"Did she kill all these animals?"

"Did she kill them all?"

"How did she do it?"

"What did she do it with?"

"Where did she get them?"

"How did she stuff 'em?"

"Did she kill 'em *all*?"

"Did she kill them buf'lo" (I positively believe this question, with variations to suit the linguistic attainments of different speakers, to have been asked, on an average, every ten minutes through all the Exhibition!)?

"I don't believe them critters was shot; I've looked 'em all over and I can't see any holes. Did she pisen 'em?"

"Does she live in that cave?"

"Is all this (with a gesture) made to represent the place and the cave she lived in in Colorado?"

"Is game as thick as this all over the Rocky Mountains?"

"If she's married, why ain't it called Mr. Maxwall's collection?"

"How old is she?"

"Is she good-looking?"

"Has she any children?"

"Is she a half-breed?"

"Is she an Indian?" and as that crowd surged by, another wave continued the inundation of like questions!

I kept hold of my departing senses with an effort, and leaned forward to catch the words of some dear old Quaker ladies. They were asking in soft, confiding voices:

"Will thee be so kind as to tell us something of the history of this collection?"

Blessings on their sweet, motherly faces! I would have attempted anything for them!

Gentlemen of scientific proclivities echoed the request—people of all kinds repeated it with an emphatic, "Do tell us who she is, and how she did it!"

The promise was made, and, though it is rather late, here is its fulfillment!

Mrs. Maxwell is the woman who made a collection of the animals of Colorado, procuring herself, either by shooting, poisoning, trapping, buying, or soliciting from her acquaintances, specimens of almost every kind of living creature found in that region, skinning, stuffing, or in other ways preserving them.

Colorado commissioned her to represent with this collection the fauna of its mountains and plains. She complied by arranging, singly, or in artistic groups, upon or near the miniature landscape we have described, over a hundred mammals and nearly four hundred birds. Before leaving Colorado she had these and many other objects of interest gathered in a museum, an idea of which can be obtained from the graceful pen of H. H., in "Bits of Travel at Home," in the *N. Y. Independent:*

"On a corner of one of the streets in Boulder is a building with a narrow and somewhat rickety staircase leading up on the outside. At the top of the staircase is the sign, 'Museum.'

"'What a place to find a museum, to be sure!' and 'Museum of what?' are the instinctive comments of the traveller at sight of this sign. The chances are a hundred to one that he will not go up the stairs, and will never give the sign a second thought. Yet whoever visits Boulder and goes away without seeing this museum loses one of the most interesting and characteristic things in Colorado. I smile to recollect how it was only an idle and not altogether good-natured curiosity which led me to visit it. Somebody had said in my hearing that all the animals in the museum were shot and stuffed by Mrs. Maxwell herself, and the collection was nearly a complete one of the native animals of Colorado. That a pioneer woman should shoot wild cats and grizzlies seemed not unnatural or improbable; but that the same woman who could fire a rifle so well could also stuff an animal with any sort of skill or artistic effect seemed very unlikely. I went to the museum expecting to be much amused by a grotesque exhibition of stiff and ungainly corpses of beasts, only interesting as tokens of the prowess of a woman in a wilderness life.

"I stopped short on the threshold in utter amazement. The door opened into a little vestibule room, with a centre-table piled with books on natural history; shelves containing minerals ranged on the walls, and a great deer standing by the table, in as easy and natural a position as if he had just walked in. This was Mrs. Maxwell's reading-room and study. On the right hand a door stood open into the museum. The first thing upon which my eyes fell was a black-and-tan terrier, lying on a mat. Not until after a second or two did the strange stillness of the creature suggest to me that it was not alive. Even after I had stood close by its side I could hardly believe it. As I moved about the room, I found myself looking back at it, from point after point, and wherever we went its eyes followed us, as the motionless eyes of a good portrait will always seem to follow one about. There was not a single view in which he did not look as alive as a live dog can when he does not stir. This dog alone is enough to prove Mrs. Maxwell's claim to be called an artist.

"In the opposite corner was a huge bison, head down, forefeet planted wide apart and at a slant, eyes viciously glaring at the door—

39

as distinct a charge as ever bison made. Next to him, on a high perch, was a huge eagle, flying with outstretched wings, carrying in his claws the limp body of a lamb. High above them a row of unblinking owls, labelled

"'The Night Watch.'

In a cage on the floor were two tiny young owls, so gray and fluffy they looked like little more than owls' heads fastened on feather pincushions. Mrs. Maxwell opened the cage and let them out. One of them flew instantly up to its companions on the shelf, perched itself solemnly in the row, and sat there motionless, except for now and then lolling its head to right or left. The effect of this on the expression of the whole row of stuffed owls was something indescribable. It would have surprised nobody at any minute if one and all they had begun to loll their heads.

"The walls of the room were filled with the usual glass-doored cases of shelves, and, to our great surprise, there were curiosities from all parts of the world. Japanese, Chinese, Alaskan, Indian—the collection was wonderfully varied. Mrs. Maxwell has the insatiable passion of a born collector, and, having visited San Francisco, has had opportunities of gratifying it to a degree one would not have believed possible. The collection of minerals and ores of the territory is a very full and interesting one. There are also fine collections of shells from various countries. These and the other foreign curiosities she has obtained by exchange and by purchase.

"The distinctive feature of the museum, however, is a dramatic group of animals placed at the further end of the room. Here are arranged mounds of earth, rocks, and pine trees, in a by no means bad imitation of a wild, rocky landscape. And among these rocks and trees are grouped the stuffed animals, in their families, in pairs, or singly, and every one in a most lifelike and significant attitude. A doe is licking two exquisite little fawns, while the stag looks on with a proud expression. A bear is crawling out of the mouth of a cave. A fox is slyly prowling along, ready to spring on a rabbit. A mountain lion is springing literally through the branches of a tree on a deer, who is running for life, with eyes bloodshot, tongue out, and every muscle tense and strained. Three mountain sheep—father, mother, and little one—are climbing a rocky precipice. A group of ptarmigans shows the three colors—winter, spring, and summer. A mother grouse is clucking about with a brood of chickens in the most inimitably natural way. And last, not least, in an out-of-way corner is a touch of drollery for the children—a little wooden house, like a dog-kennel, and coming out of the door a very tiny squirrel, on his hind legs, with a very tiny, yellow duckling hanging on his arm. The

40

conscious strut, the grotesque love-making of the pair is as positive and as ludicrous as anything ever seen in a German picture-book. Only the most artistic arrangement of every fibre, every feather, every hair could have produced such a result. We laughed till we were glad to sit down on the railing, close to the grizzly bear, and rest.

"But a funnier thing still was on the left hand—a group of monkeys sitting round a small table playing poker. One scratching his head and scowling in perplexity and dismay at his bad cards, and another leaning back smirking with satisfaction over his certain triumph with his aces; one smoking with a nonchalant air; and all so absorbed in the game that they do not see the monkey on the floor, who is reaching up a cautious paw and drawing the stakes—a ten dollar bill—off the edge of the table. Beard himself never painted a droller group of monkeys, nor one half so life-like. It will always be a mystery to me how to these dead, stiff faces Mrs. Maxwell succeeds in giving so live and keen and individual a look.

"The collection of birds is a beautiful one, nearly exhaustive of the Colorado birds and containing many fine specimens from other countries."

Of course only the Colorado department of this museum was represented at the Centennial, yet its groups of animals and birds were so numerous and so instinct with something fresh and life-like, that, weary as I became of ceaseless questions, I could but sympathize with the desire to know what circumstances could have enabled a woman to develop artistic power in such a direction, and what motive could have inspired her, even with any amount of skill, to undertake such a herculean enterprise. . . .

In 1868 it [Boulder] was a village of only about three hundred inhabitants—the centre for supplies of a gold, silver and coal mining region, since found to be very rich, but then only worked at a few points, and of an agricultural section but just beginning to be developed.

Cheyenne was then the terminus of the Union Pacific Railroad, and it and the towns beyond it along the unfinished road afforded a fine market for lumber, and the like products of the timber-growing region, in which Mr. Maxwell had an interest.

He often made journeys to these points, travelling distances of from eighty-five to one hundred and fifty miles, over the then almost unbroken plains.

As the road was inhabited at only a few points, he took his food with him, camped at night, built a fire and cooked it, and then retired to the privacy of his own blanket spread under his wagon, to enjoy the luxury of sleep!

That new specimens might be added to her collection, Mrs. Maxwell resolved to accompany him and share these novelties of travel.

All superfluous graces and ornaments of costume were dispensed with, and their place was supplied by a gymnastic suit of neutral tint and firm texture. Substantial shoes and stockings, a simple shade hat, a game bag, ammunition and gun completed her personal "out-fit."

When she had prepared as much food as they could eat while it would remain fresh and sweet, she was ready to take a seat on the top of the loaded lumber wagon beside her husband, or occasionally to occupy the saddle of a restless little "broncho" that was taken along to do duty whenever occasion demanded.

Many were the exciting adventures through which they passed; and many more the hardships. The latter were soon forgotten when the specimens were obtained for which they were endured.

Such success, however, was not always attained.

At one time they camped upon the banks of a lonely little lake in the Laramie valley. A ranch which had once served as a stage station on the overland route to California, occupied at this time by a single man, bore the only trace of humanity for miles around.

The borders of the lake were deeply edged with tall reeds and rushes, which had grown up year after year, and fallen undisturbed each winter about their submerged roots. On and around the water were large numbers of beautiful water fowl; how to obtain some of them was soon Mrs. Maxwell's absorbing thought.

They had no dog. The moment the water was rippled by the rude little skiff belonging to the ranch, the birds would retreat to the rushes and remain hidden while it was in sight.

It was soon apparent that there was no way to secure them but for either herself or husband to play dog, and by wading around among the reeds, frighten them out on to the lake where the other could shoot them.

Mr. Maxwell had hardly recovered from an attack of rheumatic fever, and such exposure was not to be thought of for him. He could, however, lend his boots and an extra pair of his lower garments.

Equipped in these, surmounted by her loose dress, Mrs. Maxwell waded boldly out into the half-submerged, tangled mass of decayed and growing vegetation. At every step, she sank, with a shiver, sometimes a few inches, sometimes to her waist in the cold water. She was soon compelled to make a disorderly retreat.

The boots were at the bottom of it! They tangled themselves in the rushes. They filled with water. They seemed determined to remain fixtures in the mud! It was only by an exertion that greatly endangered her equilibrium that they could be drawn up for the steps necessary to reach the shore. Once there, they were left in disgrace, while she returned in her stocking-feet.

This made the experiment a matter of far more ease, and secured her the tantalizing success of seeing numbers of the birds start up before her only to dodge into the covert in another place!

For nearly two hours she waded about among the slimy vegetation, curbing her fancy when it pictured snakes and leeches about her limbs, resolutely beating about to drive some fowl within range of her husband's gun, which he, in the skiff upon the lake, held ready to discharge.

Then darkness interfered, and compelled her to go into camp with nothing but her "clinging drapery" and benumbed limbs to reward her for her exertion!

The next day, approaching another pond, she met with better success.

Leaving the wagon as soon as they came within its neighborhood, she stole carefully between two knolls until within a couple of hundred yards of the water.

The pond was a naked one; that is, a little sheet of water held in a depression of a treeless, rockless plain, with no vegetation upon its border except short grass.

Plover, avocet and other waders frequented it; but the difficulty was to get within range of them unobserved. They are very shy, having learned that man is the most dreadful of all their enemies. Their long, stilt-like legs and swift wings—such good security against four-footed foes—are of little avail where man is concerned; so, if he would approach them, he must lay aside his superior dignity and put himself at least on a level with the beasts of the field.

There was not an object—not even a clump of grass—to shield her from view; so, gun in hand, she cautiously crept toward the water upon her hands and knees.

Tall avocets were standing in the shallows, occasionally thrusting their long, recurved bills into the mud for worms and tiny muscles [*sic*], or flying up to try their success in other spots. A few plover and an occasional snipe were running or flying about on the slimy soil left by the gradual evaporation of the water. Whenever they showed any signs of disturbance from her presence, she would lie perfectly still, close to the ground, for a time, and then creep forward.

When within good range, she waited until one shot would cover two or more of the birds; then, still reclining, fired one barrel of her gun, and, as the birds rose, discharged the other.

Two plover and an avocet were killed. The plover, victims of her last shot, had fallen not far apart, a few feet from the water; but the avocet had not been so accommodating. It had fluttered forward, and lay floating several feet beyond the reach of her ramrod.

It was too desirable a specimen to be lost. Her experience of the night before had not invested wading with any new charm; still, that avocet must be obtained. He was!

FURTHER READING

Benson, Maxine. *Martha Maxwell: Rocky Mountain Naturalist.* Lincoln: University of Nebraska Press, 1986.

Brace, Mabel Maxwell. *Thanks to Abigail: A Family Chronicle.* N.p., 1948.

Dartt, Mary. *On the Plains and among the Peaks; or, How Mrs. Maxwell Made Her Natural History Collection.* Philadelphia: Claxton, Remsen, and Haffelfinger, 1879.

DeLapp, Mary. "Pioneer Woman Naturalist." *Colorado Quarterly* 13 (Summer, 1964): 91–96.

Henderson, Junius. "A Pioneer Venture in Habitat Grouping." *Proceedings of the American Association of Museums* 9 (1915): 91.

Maxwell, Martha Dartt. Papers. Colorado Historical Society, Denver.

5

Annie Trumbull Slosson

1838–1926

NOT MANY WOMEN WOULD APPRECIATE having a slug named for them, but entomological collector Annie Trumbull Slosson not only enjoyed having insects named after her by others, she relished the naming of insects herself. As she wrote in *Entomological News* about her collecting in Lake Worth, Florida: "I have great hopes concerning my unnamed specimens. One large, oddly-marked Sphinx [moth] fills me with visions of a new genus as well as species, and I have already selected its name." In fact, over her forty-year career, which she began when she was already forty-eight, more than one hundred insect species were named for her by the many male entomologists whom she supplied with her specimens.

This ninth child of prominent Connecticut citizens—Gurdon and Sarah Trumbull—was born and raised in Stonington. She married Edward Slosson in 1855 but was widowed sometime during the following decade. They had no children. After his death she began writing popular literature, mostly tales of New England life, and continued to write the rest of her life.

A childhood interest in nature was probably nurtured in part by her older brother, James Hammond Trumbull. Before becoming a philologist, Trumbull had been interested in entomology. He had catalogued the reptiles, fishes, and shells of Connecticut, and his influence may have led to Slosson's first serious scientific pursuit, that of botany. She even corresponded with botanist Asa Gray about some of her discoveries. Her botanical interest, in turn, led her to wonder about the insects she saw when afield, particularly the butterflies.

Slosson was encouraged by a succession of supportive males. This

Portrait of Annie Trumbull Slosson, circa 1913. *Courtesy New York Entomological Society.*

group included her brother-in-law and amateur entomologist W. C. Prime, English actor-entomologist Henry Edwards, and other professional entomologists with whom she corresponded about her discoveries.

Although most of her time and energy went into collecting insects, she still managed to devote some time to supporting the fledgling New York Entomological Society. She was one of the Society's first elected members when it was founded in 1892, and she hosted many of its meetings at her own New York City home. She eventually persuaded Morris K. Jessup of the American Museum of Natural History to allow them to meet in the museum. Slosson also helped raise money for the Society and its publications by selling her beautifully mounted prize butterflies.

Numerous accounts of her collecting trips appear in the *Journal of the New York Entomological Society*, but she also wrote for *Entomological News*, the journal of the Entomological Society of America (now the American Entomological Society), as well as *Canadian Entomologist* and *Entomologica Americana*. Except for the usual obligatory lists (ten in all) of her discoveries that she published, including *Insects Taken in the Alpine Regions of Mt. Washington* (1894), Slosson's writing is lively and interesting, recording both her joy in collecting and the methods she used in such diverse areas as the summit of Mount Washington, the Pennsylvania side of the Delaware Water Gap, the mountains of North Carolina, and the waterways of Florida.

As one of the first collectors to explore the environs of Miami in the 1890s, Slosson made many of her original discoveries in that area, such as Slosson's slug—*Alarodia slossoniae*—a denizen of the mangroves along Florida's southern coast, and *Zethus slossonae*, a wasp species from Lake Worth.

Her correspondence in her later years with entomologist W. T. Davis, the so-called "Cicada Man" of Staten Island, portrays a woman determined never to give up despite the aging infirmities of body she suffered. No matter how badly she felt, she could always devise a way to keep collecting, if only by leaving the screens off her windows and the lights burning to entice moths inside on a warm summer night. When she was eighty-three years old, Davis described her as "cheery and vivacious as any woman of half her years." She was still "keenly interested in most things," and she fervently wanted to show people how easily they could fill their lives with "beauty, interest and keen enjoyment" by appreciating "what a museum of wonders is the piece of woods a stone's throw from your door."

Certainly Slosson never lost her appreciation for nature. She faithfully spent fourteen summers in her old age collecting at the Delaware Water Gap on the Pennsylvania side. In a letter to entomologist Philip Calvert, she described herself "as enthusiastic as ever and able to do more tramping and scrambling and net work than many a younger person."

As a result of her prolific work, she amassed a personal collection of thirty-five thousand specimens in addition to the thousands she sold or gave away to any scientist who wanted them. Shortly before her death, she donated her collection to the American Museum of Natural History.

"Experiences of a Collector" appeared in the *Bulletin of the Brooklyn Entomological Society* in April, 1917. It is an excellent account, told in Slosson's usual good-natured, humorous fashion, of her collecting techniques and of the unusual reactions she often encountered along the way.

"Collecting on Biscayne Bay, Part II" was published in *Entomological News* in May, 1899. In it she describes in great detail the various collecting methods she used according to the habitats she encountered. She also includes the scientific names and descriptions of some of the species she collected. This combination of interesting reading and scientific detail is a hallmark of most of her journal contributions.

EXPERIENCES OF A COLLECTOR

Some time ago I wrote, for a religious weekly, an article entitled Human Nature Study. In it I told of various experiences of my own in botanical and entomological collecting. I received many letters after its publication asking if it was truth or fiction and expressing surprise that any one in our enlightened age could show such ignorance as I spoke of encountering. But I am confident that the audience I address now will believe all that I may say on this subject. They have "been there":

I am, as most of you know, an old woman, though still an enthusiastic and strenuous collector. So as I tramp over hill and plain in rough, appropriate costume, butterfly net in hand, poison bottles hanging at my leather belt, with big bag, holding knife, forceps and other essentials, I suppose I am an odd looking character to the average passerby. So I make allowances and am rarely stirred to anger even by rude or discourteous questions or remarks. For many years I was more interested in botany than in any other branch of natural history and met with many amusing experiences in that kind of collecting. But this is not the place for them, and I will confine myself to the bug adventures.

Every one of you insect collectors has been asked again and again as to what one might call the lucrativeness of your pursuit. "How much are you paid for your work?" "What firm do you work for?" "What will you pay me to help you?" These are questions familiar to every collector. That one can walk miles over rough roads, climb rugged heights, stand for hours in mud or water, blister one's hands stripping bark from trees or turning big stones and this *without pay,* does seem hard to believe, I admit it. For these questioners know nothing of our real earnings, our full reward for all pains and exer.tions. The question most often asked, in one form or another, is *why* we do these things. And it is so hard to explain that *why* in a way they can comprehend. Often I find, after I have made what I think is a plain, lucid explanation of an entomologist's aim, that I have utterly failed to give the listener the faintest idea of it all.

"How many insects have you at home yourself?" asked a sweet faced old lady who joined me one day on a wooded road in Vermont. And when I told her there were thousands in my collection she exclaimed—"How do you ever feed them all?" And I found she thought they were all kept alive as pets or companions. Yet she herself was of more than ordinary intelligence and knew so many, many things I had no knowledge of. For she told me in what year the first missionary was sent to Africa and added many details as to his own and later missionaries' work and success. She talked of the different religious denominations in Vermont and had statistics concerning the comparative numbers of Baptists, Methodists and Congregationalists at her tongue's end. And she was fully as ardent and enthusiastic in this field as I in my small sphere of interest. Surely, as St. Paul says, "There are diversities of gifts, but the same spirit." I am often asked, in my wanderings, if I am employed by government to do this thing. At a summer resort, where I have been year after year of late, I find it is generally thought by the waiters and other employees of the hotel that I am in the employ of the state government, with a large salary. In vain I deny this—they only think I am guarding a state secret. A very intelligent woman in the south, after watching me night after night capturing moths at the electric lights, said to me very courteously, "I think now I understand your purpose in this. You are trying to see if you can find two of these night-flyers exactly alike. It is like trying, as I used when a child, to match two leaves of ribbon-grass." I afterwards learned that the woman was a teacher. I hope she does not conduct a nature course. In my frequent visits to Mt. Washington and my long sojourns on the summit I heard more strange and uncomplimentary comments upon myself and my doings than I ever heard at a lower level. You who have been to that delightful spot know how bleak and rugged is its external appearance and how little suggestion of animal life is there. A butterfly on that peak would seem to the casual observer or summer tourist an incongruous thing, a miracle. So each day when the train crept up the mountain, laden with travellers, looking, very often for the first time, upon the strange peak covered with pile upon pile of huge rocks I, happily and harmlessly following my beloved pursuit below the platform, would hear such remarks as these:

"What in the world is that old woman about? What's she got in her hand?" "Oh it's a butterfly-net! Did you *ever?*" "She must be crazy. Just think of a butterfly up here. Why do her folks let her do it?" "Let's ask in the house about her, they'll know." They did know and much of our good Miss Clarke's valuable time was spent in satisfying the curiosity of the "exertionists," as we call them up there, as to the manners and customs of the queer character they had seen. The "man with the hoe" was not half as well known up there as the "woman with the net." I tell you I know from experience how it feels to be considered "a rare alpine aberration."

"Come on, Ma," I once heard a sunburned youth say to a plain, homey old woman as I stood on the platform watching the tourists filling up the waiting train soon to start for the base. "Come, the cars is going d'rectly, we must get seats."

"Le'mme alone, John. Seems's if I hadn't seen all the sights yet. Let's see. I've got 'em writ down here," and she read from a crumpled scrap of paper: "Printin' office, Lizzie Bourne's grave stun, the Tip-over House and—there I ain't seen the old bug woman!" I did not introduce myself and nobody pointed me out. So the disappointed sight seer was dragged reluctantly to the train, her golden opportunity lost. "Excuse me, madam," said a tall Southerner of the Colonel Carter type, as he swung his hat from his head with an elaborate bow, when he met me at the edge of an orange grove in Florida one April day. "I venture to address you without an introduction as I see you are taxidermist." Then, almost before I could recover my breath, quite lost from the shock of this unjust accusation, he added in a trembling voice with a suggestion of nearby tears, "my mother-in-law was one also." Later I found that the said connection by marriage was a studier of ants and their habits. So that her pursuits and my own were really more alike than if she had followed taxidermy as her mourning son-in-law had intimated. The term entomologist does not seem generally understood throughout good collecting regions. Several times, in New Hampshire, when I have owned to being one I have found it understood to mean a member of some religious denomination. As one very old man in Jackson said when I owned the soft impeachment, "Well, I dare say, it's a good enough belief, but, as for me, I'm an old fashioned Hardshell Baptist like my folks before me and I ain't no use for your new sects." I did not set the old man right—what was the use?—but left him standing in the road gazing sadly after me and doubtless wondering how an intelligent being could accept other creed than that of the Hardshell Baptists'! I was once "held up" in a sandy Florida road by a solemn little girl of nine or ten, and denounced to my face as a "cruel, wicked woman" for putting to death harmless insects. I can see her now, as I look back, with her old fashioned, pale, pinched little face looking into mine, her thin little hand with uplifted finger being shaken at me, as she called down judgment upon my head. Did any of you ever try to defend your taking so many lives when talking with one who thinks it a sort of cruelty-to-animals pursuit? I never tried harder than I did that day. I told the child how painlessly the insects died by my hand; how short their natural lives were at the best, and how apt they were to die violent deaths, from storm, attacks of birds, etc. But oh, the look of scorn on that small face as she listened, and when I paused she said calmly, "Just talk, talk!" and I felt smaller than one of the flea-beetles I had just been capturing. I learned later that the child's mother was a vegetarian, thought it wicked to kill or eat any animal or wear its skin, carrying her ideas into everything and going to violent extremes. Small wonder that her child should try to do missionary work in the same field.

But I have had many, many pleasant encounters while collecting; acquaintances, yes, even warm friendships have been formed through chance meetings on the road, by stream, or in the woods. A courteous question as to my pursuit, an inquiry about a flower or tree, a sympathetic phrase about nature in one of its varied forms, such things as these have been the small beginnings of great things making life broader, happier.

COLLECTING ON BISCAYNE BAY, PART II

I spend many hours along the shore of the bay. There are several accessible stretches of sandy beach where at low tide I find some interesting things. Under wet seaweed or beneath bits of coral rock or pieces of wood are many beetles, some very rare ones. But it is not easy to discover or to capture them, for there are so many other living creatures to distract the eye and mind. As one turns over a heap of seaweed, hundreds of small shrimplike crustaceans, "sand flees" [*sic*] as they are called—jump and wriggle about in a bewildering way. As they strike the sand there is a pattering sound as of rain drops. Then large brown shining ear wigs glide rapidly out from under the seaweed, looking much like big *Staphylinidae* [rove beetles], or slender Carabs [ground beetles]. Pinkish earthworms crawl sluggishly along, tiny ants run on the sand, and occasionally an immature cricket, soft and pallid, hops up. All this movement and life is at first distracting, but the trained eye soon learns how to distinguish readily what it seeks. . . . When tired and stiff with sitting on the damp sand I change my position, take my net and going to the sandy stretch a little farther from the water I chase tiger-beetles, flies, and aquatic bugs. There are two or three species of *Salda* [shore bugs] which fly over the sand, one of them very pale in color, almost white and very difficult to detect on the white sand. In diptera [flies] there are some very pretty Dolichopodidae [long-legged flies], most of them of whitish green, to harmonize with the tints of the shore, an occasional robber fly and *Borborus venalicus* [dung flies] by thousands. I find also on the damp sand a species of the little three-toed cricket, Tridactylus, looking like a miniature mole-cricket. It is very agile and hard to capture. Still farther back from the water and on higher ground grow many flowers, and there I hunt bees, wasps, butterflies and bugs till time to wend my way homeward over the glaring white, hot coral road.

Sometimes I spend a morning on the Miami River in a rowboat. We row along the shore under the mangrove and search the leaves for larvae on coccoons [*sic*]. Here can be watched the whole life history of the dark blue butterfly, *Erycides batabano,* which was fully recorded a year or two ago by Dr. [Harrison Gray] Dyar [expert on butterfly larvae and the classification of mosquitoes]. It is a beautiful life in every phase, from egg to imago. It is still fascinating to me, after seeing it so many times, to peep into the carefully folded mangrove leaf fastened with finest, strongest silk, and see the lonely larva of rich purple red, the color he wears until his last moult. Then he becomes quite a different creature, of soft bluish white with head still of crimson. Then comes the graceful white chrysalis and last the butterfly of rich dark blue. On the mangrove too the little white moth, *Eupoeya slossoniae* lives its life. The genus is no longer Eupoeya, but I have forgotten its latest name and have nothing here to tell me of it. The larvae are lovely, soft, silvery green things, hard to distinguish when flattened and motionless on the green leaves, and the small white coccoon [*sic*] of parchment-like texture is a dainty cell in which to await its snow white wings. Among the mangroves fly several species of small dragonflies, easily caught from the boat with a net. And over and across the blue water are always flying scores of little gray and white Pyralid moths, a species of *Nymphaella,* I think; perhaps the same one we have by our northern waters, *N. maculalis.* They often fly within reach of our nets, sometimes even coming into the boat and resting there. Our mornings among the mangroves are pleasant ones. It is an indolent, luxurious way of collecting, not such hard work as grubbing in wet sand or hunting under dank seaweed, and I like it for a change. Sometimes we take a little naptha launch and go far up the river almost to the everglades. There, the other day, I landed and hunted about for half an hour. I took, for the first time on the east coast, *Burtia belae,* a pretty day flying moth, with scarlet body and transparent wings. I have taken many at Punta Gorda on the west coast, but these are much larger than any I have seen there. I took also the other day, on some flowers near the river, a moth I suppose to be *Harrisina australis,* Stretch. The type came, I think, from Florida. It is greenish black, with orange collar, and about the size of *H. americana,* perhaps a trifle larger. I caught too a ragged specimen of the butterfly *Apatura flora,* the first I have taken. Butterflies and moths are not nearly so abundant as in former years. The freezing weather of February 13th and one or two later cool waves destroyed much insect life. The flowering plants, too, were killed or temporarily injured, leaving few blossoms to attract insects. Our evenings have been very cool, as a general thing, and I have had little success in collecting at light. Last week a warm, still evening, following light showers, brought hundreds of beetles to the lighted piazzas. But the number of species was small.

Further Reading

Davis, William T. "Annie Trumbull Slosson." *Journal of the New York Entomological Society* 34 (December, 1926): 361–64.
Dougherty, Veronica. "Annie Trumbull Slosson." *American Entomologist* 2 (Summer, 1990): 126–27.
Edwards, Henry. "New Genera and Species of North American Moths." *Entomologica Americana* 3 (January, 1888): 181–85.
Leng, Charles W. "History of the New York Entomological Society." *Journal of the New York Entomological Society* 26 (September–December, 1918): 129–33.
Osborn, Herbert. *Fragments of Entomological History.* Columbus: Herbert Osborn, 1937.
[Skinner, Henry]. "A Loved and Respected Entomologist." *Entomological News* 30 (December, 1919): 300.
Slosson, Annie Trumbull. "Coleoptera of Lake Worth, Florida." *Canadian Entomologist* 27 (1895): 9–10.
———. "Collecting on Biscayne Bay." *Entomological News* 10 (April, 1899): 94–96.
———. "Collecting on Biscayne Bay, Part II." *Entomological News* 10 (May, 1899): 124–26.
———. "Collecting at Lake Worth, Florida." *Entomological News* 6 (May,

1895): 133–36.

———. "Collecting on Mt. Washington, Part I." *Entomological News* 4 (October, 1893): 249–52.

———. "Collecting on Mt. Washington, Part II." *Entomological News* 4 (November, 1893): 287–92.

———. "Experiences of a Collector." *Bulletin of the Brooklyn Entomological Society* 12 (April, 1917): 25–29.

———. "A Few Memories." *Journal of the New York Entomological Society* 23 (June, 1915): 85–91.

———. Letters to Philip Powell Calvert and Henry Skinner. Library of the Academy of Natural Sciences, Philadelphia, Penn.

———. Letters to William T. Davis. Staten Island Institute of Arts and Sciences, Staten Island, N.Y.

———. "May Moths in Northern New Hampshire." *Entomological News* 1 (February, 1890): 2–19.

———. "Winter Collecting in Florida, Part I." *Entomological News* 1 (June, 1890): 81–83.

———. "Winter Collecting in Florida, Part II." *Entomological News* 1 (September, 1890): 101–02.

6

Katharine Dooris Sharp

1846-1935

KATHARINE DOORIS SHARP WAS PART OF an army of female amateur botanists who made substantial, but largely unrecognized, contributions to botany during the nineteenth and early twentieth centuries. A native of Ireland, she was raised in Ohio and married a medical doctor—Henry James Sharp—at the age of twenty-six.

When she first began botanizing around her home in London, Ohio, both her husband and her sons indulged her in what they thought was a passing whim. She claimed she started botanizing in order to share the outdoors with her sons, but they were quickly embarrassed by their unorthodox mother and often refused to stop the carriage for her when she spotted an unusual specimen.

She frequently hitched rides with her husband when he visited his patients, and although she dedicated her charming book *Summer in a Bog* "To my Husband, in whose companionship, in his professional drives through the country, my first acquaintance was made with the Flora of Madison County, Ohio," she confessed that "he has very little sympathy for these excursions into woods and swamps. He has visions of snakes and other possible terrors which, I am glad to say, rarely enter my mind. His care and forethought are appreciated, but sometimes disregarded."

In contrasting his opinion of a weedy strip along the road with hers, she wrote:

> "If I owned that cornfield, I'd drain it better," said the Doctor critically, as we drove past it one afternoon.
> "It's just like a strip of lovely flowered ribbon," said I. "Here, stop and

Portrait of Katharine Dooris Sharp as a young woman. *Courtesy RLS Creations and Ronald L. Stuckey, Columbus, Ohio.*

let me off. I've been intending to visit that bog for more than a year, and I'll do it now."

Sharp was apparently no conformist. She cared little what people thought of her and poked gentle fun at a friend who begged to go botanizing with her and then spent her time worrying about snakes.

"I shall be so interested in seeking the specimens for which I have come that I shall not think of the poor creatures at all," Sharp told her friend.

To Sharp there were "no labors so purely delightful as those which we assume with Nature." Yet she showed considerable interest and delight in the people she met while botanizing—a ginseng collector, a geology professor, and a housekeeper attacked by her employer's bull. She also extolled the botanically inclined wives of male botanists, listing both married and unmarried female botanists, eleven altogether, including herself, who had contributed to the state flora collection.

Sharp maintained that "the qualities of mind are similar in the sexes," which is why she was also an active suffragist. Like many bright women in her day, she was a charter member of the local Women's Club and was involved in the usual club and civic activities of such prominent women. She had the financial resources to travel widely in the United States and Europe and was chiefly remembered as a writer of numerous magazine and newspaper articles, poems, and novels.

Yet from 1899 to 1906 she contributed at least 447 specimens to the State Herbarium of Ohio, including an aquatic species rare for the state—*Armoracia aquatica*. She showed her enthusiasm for collecting and her love of Ohio when she said that "it would be difficult to find a region of the globe which furnishes a richer and more varied field for the naturalist than our own beautiful Ohio."

She concludes *Summer in a Bog* with a conservation piece she wrote in 1900, called "Passing of the Wildwood," in which she asked: "Do we not owe a duty to posterity in making an attempt to save a tract like this for future students, in the neighborhood of each city, town or college? If the Government purchases and preserves the birthplace of a great man, the field of a celebrated battle, why not a strip of Mother earth, rich with indigenous vegetation?"

The following chapter, "The Woman Botanist" from *Summer in a Bog*, beautifully sums up the joys and dilemmas of being a woman botanist as well as a wife and mother. In the chapter Sharp hoped to show "that women may be imbued with a love of science for its own sake, and pursue it in spite of obstacles." This chapter describes not only Katharine Dooris Sharp—wife, mother, botanist, and writer—but thousands of other women botanists, married and unmarried, who struggled to make their contributions to the only science deemed suitable for women in their lifetimes.

THE WOMAN BOTANIST

> Always a voice is calling
> In the city's roar and clangor,
> Or the silence of the room;
> Now with tender message pleading,
> Or, again, with loud insistence
> When the world is all abloom.
>
> 'T is the voice of the lone wild-wood,
> Of the forests man-forsaken,
> Of the meadows flower-gemmed;
> Of the streams that murmur softly
> O'er the white and shining pebbles,
> 'Tween the banks with sedges hemmed.
>
> 'T is the voice of Mother Nature,
> From her cool and dim recesses,
> In the places undefiled.
> O, I hunger for the woodland,
> And I hear her, and I answer,
> And I seek her, I her child!

There is this advantage in being an amateur: one may break into verse if so inclined. A technologist or professor is not supposed to have any such inclinations.

The true botanist is born, not made—as you may have heard in regard to specialists in other fields. When, as a child, she sought the woods on holidays, bringing back the precious spoil of flower, fern, and sedge, the woman who would desire to name and classify was foreshadowed.

What is it for a woman to be a botanist? With maternal, domestic, or social duties, to say nothing of literary, if she incline that way, and each an occupation in itself, how shall she find opportunity to cultivate acquaintance with Nature and reduce her observations to a science?

She will do it because she was born to do it; because within her is the heaven-imparted kinship with Nature which is the open sesame to that kingdom of delight. But she will do it under difficulties.

"Who is it goes 'round the woods and 'round the roads and leaves a rag on every bush?" asks the facetious riddler. The answer is not "The snow," but, "The woman botanist." Let them have their fun; there is no truth in this, I assure you.

Yet she is no respecter of good clothes. One day she will go "calling" on her country friends, dressed in "best bib and tucker," quite determined to conduct herself like an ordinary Christian, to that end abstemiously leaving her vasculum at home; yet she will come back with her hat awry, her hair flying in strands and tangled up with bits of branch and leaf, her best lace handkerchief lost—she went back and found it in a roadside ditch—her fine mull gown with zig-zag tears in the front breadth, her sleeve torn up half its length—but radiantly happy and totally impervious to reproof. And why? Because in that sheaf of spoil she carries there are specimens of the wild flowers never before seen by her.

She will take impromptu Turkish baths in an attic, heated under its slate roof by the summer sun to the temperature of an enameling oven, or thereabout, while placing her specimens in press or changing the papers during the drying process. She will litter her vacant rooms with all manner of plant débris, though otherwise an immaculate housekeeper. Under the atlas and dictionary you will find her treasures, and she will contrive to invest them with a romantic and sensational personality almost astounding to her family, who, nevertheless, in their moments of disillusion and impatience, sometimes rail and scoff.

She may be said to lead a double life, if doing twice as much as an ordinary woman is a scale of measure of her achievements.

"Ah!" you say, "this is not the lady we know, who is an M.Sc. or Ph.D., and who calmly works in a laboratory, unharassed by household cares or maternal duty."

It is an extreme case, of course, but I am glad to quote it, since it shows conclusively that women may be imbued with a love of science for its own sake, and pursue it in spite of obstacles. The qualities of mind are similar in the sexes. We reap what we sow; twaddle and tittle-tattle in the one, aggressive war and crime in the other, under suitable culture, or a high standard of personal responsibility in both, if we so demand.

But while the road to scientific attainment is for the man broad and well-paved through centuries of use, there is generally for woman, when she dares to walk therein, a look askance and a cold reception. But she will not mind that greatly—the woman who truly loves Nature. She will be instant in season and out of season, and it need not discourage her if her devoted friends arrive at the conclusion that it is the latter.

Disappointments, discouragements, adversities constitute food for hardy natures, and no other need attempt the road of science.

When taking her rides abroad in company with unsympathetic companions, collecting, what had at first been conceded to her as a hobby of possibly brief duration, like any other fad, by reason of prolonged and persistent continuance, became burdensome; and finally, objection was not unfrequently made to stopping for botanical acquisition. In this emergency, and after being summarily whisked by coveted treasures, a new expedient suggested itself.

Gloves and hand-bags had mysterious ways of falling over the wheel into the road in near proximity to new and attractive weeds: in getting out to recover the one, she audaciously insisted on securing the other. Her soul is still harrowed by recollections of a much-desired specimen, dimly identified at a moment when nothing was at hand to drop—her hat being the only article possible to so use, and it tightly, alas! pinned to her hair. What a pity that heads could not be conveniently tipped off on such interesting occasions! And that specimen has never been seen since, and is still absent from her collection.

Too soon, however, the boys caught on to these tricks, and openly accused her of them, on the last occasion of the perpetration of the deception, riding defiantly away and telling her she could walk into town by herself. This she serenely proceeded to do, but was shortly met by the repentant though sulky driver, who, however much he might desire to bring her up in the way in which he thought she ought to go, doubtless had compunctions of shame about having strangers see his only mother walking along the dusty road like a common tramp, she not in the least appearing to care.

The social doings of her own sex lose something of their attractiveness to the woman who botanizes. An afternoon reception is on her tablet for the day, and if she has a new gown she dons it, feeling its strangeness, perhaps conscious that she is an object of observation. Or, having nothing new in her wardrobe, she spends valuable time in looking discontentedly over the old apparel, finally selecting something that "came out of the ark."

She attends the social function: is probably invited to partake of food for which she has no need; talks on topics in which she has not the slightest interest (but so "safe!") to persons who in no way attract her, and comes away, hoping to goodness that she has not said anything which will hurt any one's feelings.

Perhaps her companions indulge in post-prandial ridicule of the hostess or guests—it is horrible, the liberty some persons give themselves: they could ridicule the angels in heaven!

How different is an afternoon in the woods and fields! Let us hasten thither, for the time passes so quickly.

It is spring, and the fresh grass is sprinkled with buttercups and spring-beauties. How divine are the violets! Or the phlox fills the spaces with a misty flush.

June! O love and roses and the fullness of life!—can we ask any more? Kind Heaven, how good to all created! Let us lie full-length, with faces in the grass, and hear the stream ripple and sing over its rocky bed.

If it is autumn, a thousand hands reach out to grasp and hold us.

And the refreshments? A twig of sassafras takes us back into childhood; or the golden-brown, wrinkled berry of a May-apple. A rosehaw touched by the frost, or an amber ground-cherry, in its withered, bladdery calyx-cup, cheers and inebriates with the exhilaration of new-found old delights. "Mary, did you ever taste a leaf of the lady's-thumb?" and you trick her into it. O, don't mention pepper after that!

The sun sinks low, and we must hasten home. No one has had a thought of the clothes she wore; only of those she has seen, surpassing the glory of Solomon. If the plant-people have criticised, there has been no consciousness of it.

But the blood courses through the veins more healthfully. How bright and good and sweet a thing the world is after all! Ah! we have been in the Presence. Heaven seems so near. We will live worthy of it. We will love and help each other and be kind and true, keeping high faith with all the hearts that trust us!

Further Reading

Sharp, Katharine Dooris. *Summer in a Bog.* Cincinnati: Stewart & Kidd Co., 1913.

Stuckey, Ronald L. *Women Botanists of Ohio Born before 1900.* Columbus: RLS Creations, 1992.

7

Althea Sherman

1853–1943

"THE BIRDS UPON ONE ACRE FURNISHED more study than it is possible to master," self-taught ornithologist Althea Sherman once wrote. But she did her best to reach full mastery during the second half of her life, beginning her voluminous bird notebooks in 1903 and her studies of individual bird species, such as northern flickers, brown thrashers, American robins, and gray catbirds.

Trained as an artist and teacher at Oberlin College, where she received both her bachelor's and master's degrees, she was called home from her teaching in 1895 to tend her ailing parents on their eastern Iowa farmstead. She quickly discovered that the hamlet of National was "unsuitable for progress" in studying and teaching art, so she began studying birds instead, putting her artistic training to work by painting many of the birds she watched.

She first used a tent as a blind, but in 1907 she erected a wooden blind in a marshy ravine on the western edge of her property. The forty-six-inch-square blind had a door on one side, a window on each of the other sides, and was elevated on posts. Sherman had hoped to observe migrating birds from it, and over a twenty-year period she did watch 110 species, including sora, king, and Virginia rails. But after observing a pair of nesting sora rails in the marsh in 1909, the blind was preempted the following year by nesting screech owls and two years later by sparrow hawks, now called American kestrels. The new residents presented Sherman with the opportunity to study their nest lives and to publish the first in-depth studies of those birds. Her "Nest Life of the Screech Owl" appeared in the *Auk* in 1911 and was followed by "The Nest Life of the Sparrow Hawk," also in the *Auk*, in 1913.

Althea Sherman at her dooryard gate in National, Iowa. *Courtesy of Oberlin College Archives, Oberlin, Ohio.*

Although she made many new observations of both species, which were later used by Arthur Cleveland Bent in his multivolume *Life Histories of North American Birds,* her judgmental attitude toward those predators led her to declare war on them in later years. Citing her findings that 20 percent of the screech owl's diet and 18 percent of the American kestrel's consisted of songbirds, she made her dooryard safe for the "good" birds by eliminating the "bad" ones.

More to her liking was the northern flicker, a species that had been living in her barn since 1897. In 1908, hoping to obtain an intimate view of their nest lives, she took wooden soap boxes and attached them inside the barn wall beside three flicker holes. On the floor of each nest box she spread a covering of excelsior. She drilled an observation hole in the top of each box as well as a hole near the bottom, so she could easily remove nestlings to weigh, paint, and photograph them. Her many hours of observation led to her first published bird study, "At the Sign of the Northern Flicker," in the *Wilson Bulletin* in 1910. To Sherman, the northern flicker was the species that gave her more pleasure than any other she studied during her thirty-eight years of bird observations.

Her inventive, restless mind also led her to spend more than a dozen years experimenting with different concoctions before settling on the perfect winter bird food—"a cupful of cornmeal, a cupful of chopped walnut meats, three or four table-spoonfuls of corn syrup, and enough water to wet the mass. This is cooked for a few minutes and may then be filled into the holes of a feeding-stick or spread upon cards of corrugated pasteboard with thread or twine bound about to hold the food in place." She called her invention "food cards" and fastened them to old shingles or pieces of galvanized iron or hung them from the picket fence, branches of trees, or snowball bushes. These "cards" attracted many woodland species, such as red-bellied, downy, and hairy woodpeckers, white-breasted nuthatches, and black-capped chickadees, to what she called the "exposed, wind-swept location" of her home grounds.

Another bird feeding effort was directed towards attracting ruby-throated hummingbirds. Fashioning artificial flowers from white oilcloth and wire, she painted them to resemble tiger lilies and nasturtiums. Each "flower" had a tiny bottle of sweetened water attached to it and was then fastened to a bush in her yard. For seven years she manipulated the "flowers" by changing their positions, shapes, and colors. In a paper she read before the American Ornithologists' Union in 1913 (she was the fourth woman member ever elected to the A.O.U.), she concluded that hummingbirds remembered both the feeders and her from year to year but did not particularly care about either the shape or color of the "flowers" she used.

Of all Sherman's inventive ideas for attracting and observing birds, her most famous was her chimney swift tower. In the following excerpt from "The Home Life of the Chimney Swift," which appeared in her posthumously published *Birds of an Iowa Dooryard*, edited by Fred J. Pierce, she describes the tower itself and some of her original

64

observations. Altogether she studied the swifts for eighteen years, starting at the age of sixty-five and continuing until she was eighty-three, despite being badly crippled with arthritis, burdened by housekeeping for herself and her doctor sister Amelia, and living in a house with no running water or other modern amenities.

In 1928 she made four hundred visits to the chimney, which, she later calculated, involved climbing 12,000 steps. She also had 133 visitors and wrote 32 pages of notes during the 130 days the swifts were in residence. Altogether, she amassed 400 pages of notes, amounting to 91,000 words on chimney swifts, none of which she was ever able to assemble into publishable form as she had for her earlier studies. Instead, she spent many of her later years writing articles opposing the building of nesting boxes for house wrens.

The other excerpt is from her most notorious piece, "Down with the House Wren Boxes," which appeared in the *Wilson Bulletin* in 1925. Her biting wit and sarcasm toward ignorant lovers of "Jennie Wrens" made her many enemies.

But although Sherman was often unreasonable and sometimes even vindictive, she did remarkable work. "Tireless in her search for truth; neither tedium nor suffering deterred her," her fellow ornithologist and friend Margaret Morse Nice wrote in her review of *Birds of an Iowa Dooryard* nine years after Sherman's death. Of course, Sherman was right about her observations of house wrens. A house wren study conducted in 1989 not only amply documents the destruction of the eggs and nestlings of their own and other species that Sherman decried, but ornithologists who have studied them still have no answer to what elicits this destructive impulse.

The Home Life of the Chimney Swift

Many years ago I planned a building which was not built until 1915. For lack of a better name, it is called the Chimney Swifts' tower. Its dimensions are 9 feet square and 28 feet to the top of the chimney. The artificial chimney is 2 feet square, and runs down the center of the tower to a depth of 14 feet; the chimney was built of pine flooring with the rough sides of the boards turned within. A door opens into the chimney and a stationary ladder may be climbed for closing and opening the top of the chimney in fall and spring, respectively. Auger-holes serve as peep-holes on two sides, while on the other two sides are windows. The frames of these windows are not vertical but are in two planes which meet in an obtuse angle. Into this space which juts into the chimney one's head can be introduced, and through the glass a view to the bottom or to the top of the chimney may be obtained without unduly frightening the birds. A paper screen often is placed over one window and back of it a lighted lamp or lantern gives sufficient illumination for one easily to watch the swifts' home life at night. The illumination is even a little better than it is by day. Although my chimney was planned without a very full knowledge of Chimney Swift life, after many years of use and observation made within it, I have failed to see how any improvements could have been made in the planning of it. . . .

The first year of Chimney Swift nesting in my tower, four eggs were laid; the second and third years there were five; and the fourth and fifth years there were six eggs laid.

During the period of ten or twelve days occupied by the egg-laying, a swift is seldom found in the day time in the chimney, and very rarely is one seen on the nest for a few minutes. Real incubation appears to begin a little while before the last egg is laid, since usually the hatching of one is a little later than that of the others. Both swifts share in the incubation and the brooding of the young. Occasionally the eggs are left uncovered for a short time. When the nest was new and the sticks on both sides curved upward to the same height, there were but three positions possible for the sitting bird's head. It could be held upright or bent to the right or to the left. The returning bird grasped the front edge of the nest and instantly dropped to the eggs with its breast against the chimney's wall. This was true of the first season. After the sticks near the top of the left side of the nest were broken off the swifts could sit crosswise of the nest, which they seemed to prefer to do. Certainly they looked comfortable that way, while they did not look comfortable the other way.

The nest duration from the laying of the first egg to nest-leaving has been 42, 45, 47, 45, and 50 days for a five-year period, giving an average of 46 days. Of this period incubation has taken 18 days for the first and second years and 19 days for the other three years; 19 days was the time in the nest watched by Miss [Mary F.] Day [who wrote in *Bird-Lore* in 1899 about her observations of nesting chimney swifts].

As the eggs hatch the shells are not carried out, but are tossed to the floor of the chimney. These shells suggest that the head of the embryo swift must lie in the egg in somewhat different position from that of all other species known to me, since other birds' shells are divided in the middle, while the division in the swift's egg is scarcely more than a third of the way down, the large end portion suggesting a lid for the remainder of the shell.

Structural similarities in the Chimney Swift and Flicker led orni-

66

thologists to place the two species near each other in classification. Although there are striking differences to be noted while studying the home life of both species, still there are equally striking similarities. In both species the young when hatched are perfectly naked, there being no vestige of natal down. In both species there is a continuous infant crying or moaning by the young when they are unbrooded. Both are fed by regurgitation; both make a great clamor when the parents come to feed them; both sleep hanging to the wall, although the swift has never been seen to sleep with head turned backward and bill hidden in the feathers of the back. Both species are free from lice or vermin of any kind. Unlike the Flicker's, the swift's feeding is done with gentle movements and is finished quickly, though at times two or three nestlings may receive a part of the meal brought in. Unlike young Flickers, the swifts are never quarrelsome. During the many summers of intimate living with the Chimney Swift, I have never found it a subject for criticism in any respect—no evil has been detected in its relations with its own or with other species. In short, it appears to be a paragon of perfection—the bird that properly might be chosen as the emblem of peace.

During my early study of the Chimney Swift I made the very broad assertion that the bird does not feed its young at night. My subsequent years of study of this species have in no way caused me to alter my opinion. During numerous summers, with lighted lamp before their window, I have frequently sat up in night-watching of the swifts. I have chosen the nights most favorable for their going out—when there was bright moonlight, many insects abroad, and the young were large and needing their greatest supply of food. Not once has a swift left the chimney. I know that others have told us that [they] have seen swifts go out at night. I do not dispute such statements, but what I do contend is that the parents do not feed the young at night. From twenty minutes to a half hour after sunset is the latest in the evening that I have seen the parents bringing food. It is dusk then within my chimney, the hole of which is twice as large as that of an ordinary chimney.

In the first place, the young are sufficiently fed during the day time. My notes show that there is plenty of time for more feedings by day if it were necessary. Moreover, the hard-worked swifts have another way of meeting exacting requirements. None of us has forgotten that the summer of 1921 was extremely hot and dry. That was the season our swifts raised six young ones, the feeding of which may have overtaxed their parents' energies. One day while I was watching them, an old bird came in, fed, and remained to rest. Very soon another bird did the same, and a few minutes later a *third* swift came in, fed, and rested also. I looked and counted again. There was no mistake—three adult swifts were hanging on the wall, while the nest held six blind nestlings. This was the first time I had seen this phase of Chimney Swift life, which Miss Day also witnessed in her New Jersey nest. The third swift continued in the role of nurse-maid. The lamp before the window showed that she stayed with the family at night. When the young had left the nest all nine swifts could be counted on the wall. The third bird continued to act as nurse-maid for at least several days. So beautifully ordered was the family life that no one could tell which was the willing servitor, but I guessed that the two hanging under the young were the parents, and the nurse was the one at the side of the young. One cannot help speculating as to the manner of the introduction of the nurse-maid into the family. Was she invited or did she come as a volunteer missionary? I have always thought that it was a female swift—quite likely an old maid. That there are old maids among the birds is as probable as that there are old bachelors, widows, widowers and grass widows and widowers, of all of which we have had ocular proof.

Many people have the Chimney Swift nesting inside their chimneys. If you ask them their opinion regarding the night feeding of the young, they are pretty confident that it is done, for very often from their bedrooms they have heard a noisy chatter exactly like that heard in the day time when food is brought. By my night watchings I have learned that a very slight movement made by one swift starts all the young ones to chattering. Not until some one has witnessed an actual feeding at night by good artificial light, shall I believe that such a thing takes place.

Down with the House Wren Boxes

If, when a felon is on trial for high crimes and misdemeanors he is confronted by numerous eye-witnesses, who are trustworthy and fully competent to testify, if by their evidence it is proved that for upward of twenty-five years he has been seen committing the most flagrant crimes against his neighbors; if the depositions of these expert witnesses have been spread upon the public records and printed in volumes accessible to every one, it would appear that the public ought to demand for the good of our country that the felon be sentenced, and that the sentence be executed without dangerous delay.

In the case of the people of North America versus the House Wren together with his subspecies the Western House Wren, the eye-witnesses of his crimes are numerous, trustworthy, and exceedingly competent; among them are men, who rank with our most eminent ornithologists: men whose professional business during many years has been the careful study of birds. Besides these there are many other men and women less famous, but equally trustworthy as witnesses, who from the Atlantic seaboard to the Pacific coast and from the Gulf states to the farthest north range of the House Wren in Canada have made numerous statements regarding this species. Their observations cover a period of more than a quarter of a century and have been published in various ornithological books and magazines, which are open to the examination of all.

In this prosecution the public must be jury, judge and executioner and, most unfortunately, a large part of the public is unfitted to act in any of these capacities: as jurymen, because they have already formed an opinion; this opinion is not based on any real knowledge on the subject, either first-hand or otherwise, but having a wren-box on their narrow village lot they refuse to listen to the warnings of those who have seen the House Wren at his nefarious work. They are fond of *their* bird and are angry when the truth is spoken about it; they act precisely like the parents of vicious children, refusing to believe the evil things their darlings do. They did not see the rattlesnake strike its fangs into the tender flesh of the little child that died last summer, yet the dying child was found and the rattlesnake near it: good enough circumstantial evidence for them was this, but the testimony of most trustworthy and competent witnesses of the evil done by the House Wren they flout and vilify. Neither are they fitted to act as judges. A judge in law must have knowledge of the literature of law, but with little or no knowledge of ornithological literature many people feel themselves supreme judges of this Wren; they will not take the bird magazines wherein they could find much convincing testimony. . . .

Any policeman will tell you that in a time of peril a gentle admonition will turn some people into a path of safety, but that on others he must use his club. It must be confessed that in connection with the danger here discussed, there is scarcely one of us who has not deserved the club. It is now a full score of years since Mr. Otto Widmann [Missouri ornithologist, author of numerous journal articles and *A Preliminary Catalogue of the Birds of Missouri*] wrote the following gentle warning: "I would also say to those who put up bird houses of any kind to keep a watchful eye on the House Wren. He is as great a nuisance as the English Sparrow. He enters homes in the absence of the owners, ruins their nests, pierces and throws out eggs and can do enough mischief in one season to threaten the existence of a whole colony of martins. Nor are his attentions confined to bird houses either; open nests also suffer from his sneaking visits, and much of the damage laid at the English Sparrow's door may be traced to the innocent-looking Jennie Wren."

In the same number of *Bird-Lore* Mr. Robert Ridgway [eminent ornithologist, Curator of Birds at the U.S. National Museum, author of the eight-volume *The Birds of North and Middle America,* and co-author of *A History of North American Birds* with Spencer Fullerton Baird and Thomas Brewer] gave similar testimony. In speaking of his bird houses he said: "These nesting-places are occupied solely by House Wrens, for they will not allow any other bird to use them. Each spring a pair of Carolina Chickadees build their nest in one of them and have begun incubation by the time the House Wrens arrive, but that is as far as the poor Chickadees get, for the wrens immediately oust them and destroy their eggs." Again in the same magazine ten years later he writes: "The House Wren is equally ty-rannical, and no small bird can nest in its vicinity. Several pairs of Carolina Chickadees and Tufted Titmice, and a pair of Bewick's Wrens, that had been with us all winter, and would have nested in boxes near the house but for the rascally House Wrens, who, though possessing boxes of their own, drove the other birds away." Farther on he speaks of this destructive little demon, saying: "The first House Wren ever seen or heard by me in southeastern Illinois was noted in the vicinity of Olney some time near the year 1870. . . . Bewick's Wren was THE 'House Wren' of the entire region. . . . In the vicinity of Olney, the House Wren is now by far the more numerous of the two, especially in the town itself; and, wherever it has chosen a home, Bewick's Wren is forced out, for Troglodytes [*T. aedon,* or house wren] will not brook the presence of any species, Wren, Chickadee, Tit-mouse, or Nuthatch, which requires similar nesting-sites. Thryomanes [*T. bewickii,* or Bewick's wren] on the other hand is exceedingly tol-erant of other species, and therefore is far the more desirable, espe-cially since it is equally tame and a far better songster. . . ."

That the gentle admonitions of Mr. Ridgway have influenced the editor of one Audubon publication is attested by his magazine, which has ceased to advocate the placing of wren-boxes; but most of us seem to have needed the club. Speaking for myself, it must be con-fessed that I may have sinned against my small bird neighbors, when for purposes of study, there has been tolerance, years ago, of two nestings each of Screech Owls and Sparrow Hawks. But there is only one sin that causes constant mourning in sackcloth and ashes, that causes me to lie awake nights visioning the future condition of our country with its bird population consisting mainly of those undesir-able aliens, the Starling and the English Sparrow, together with

Screech Owls, Bronzed Grackles, and House Wrens: that sin was the putting up of bird houses and allowing them to be occupied by House Wrens. It may comfort some people to learn that for this sin full punishment is being meted out in this world: except the Traill's Flycatcher, whose vigilance and pugnacity protects his nest, and the Goldfinch, whose nesting comes after the wren's frenzy has abated, can any other little birds hatch their eggs, since the House Wrens became numerous; the successful breeding here of small species is ended, they are becoming scarce as has been reported from Olney, Illinois.

The cheerful twitterings of the Wren are pleasing, but no more so than the songs of the Warbling Vireo, the Yellow Warbler, the Maryland Yellowthroat, and other small birds that he has robbed and routed. Some of these by second trials in more remote spots are still perpetuating their species, but in greatly diminishing numbers, wherever the House Wren has largely increased. For corroboration of this statement the regional lists of birds given in the ornithological magazines are cited. Some of the reports give the Chipping Sparrow as now rare where formerly it was abundant. To be sure the species has other enemies; in some places the Blue Jay as well as the Bronzed Grackle, the latter a bird that, most unfortunately, is increasing in many places. Bad as it is it does not sneak through all the small bushes and into bird houses. As for injury done by the English Sparrow one would do better to choose twenty of these rather than one House Wren. . . .

The reason for this great increase must be clear to every one. It is the result of the campaign for erecting boxes for wrens; boxes with small openings that protected the wrens from their natural enemies and enabled them to breed in undue numbers. That the species needs no such protection, but survives in plentiful numbers in the remote portions of its breeding range is another fact proved by the regional lists printed in the bird magazines. How many persons have searched for such records? Those who have done so, have read of the House Wren having been found breeding "abundantly" in the wild portions of Pennsylvania and of West Virginia, in the mountains of Virginia, in the northern woods of Michigan and Wisconsin, in South Dakota, Saskatchewan, Alberta, British Columbia, Washington, Montana, Colorado, and in the higher altitudes of New Mexico and Arizona. Certainly enough instances to prove that this bird needs no special protection.

This protection has been given by some unwittingly, by others obstinately, those who refused to believe the emphatic warnings of Robert Ridgway and Otto Widmann spoken twenty years ago. An example of one open-minded searcher for truth was afforded by a conscientious and learned ornithologist, who could not quite accept the words of Mr. Widmann, hence set the men of his state to seeking proof. How long they sought was not stated, but it was considerably less than seven years. It calls up the picture of a woman bent on vindicating her wren, who takes her tatting, sits in the shade of her apple tree in sight of her wren-box, and while she tats an entire afternoon she sees no eggs destroyed, consequently declares that there is nothing but malicious lies in the whole story. Such zeal on the part of one investigator might provoke a smile if the subject were not so serious; but those of us who for twenty to fifty years have studied thoroughly and carefully the life of the House Wren know the difficulty of catching him red-handed. More often than otherwise the detection comes accidentally. Fingerprints are deemed trustworthy evidence against the human criminal. One "fingerprint" of this wren is the dropping of the egg, its contents uneaten, outside the nest; but this evidence is lacking at times. It may be said, in brief, that the collecting of evidence is not rapid work; it takes years, yes, *years*. A man who begins this work today, possibly, may know as much a score of years hence as does the man who began twenty years ago, but no more. However, it is very doubtful if he will know as much, since he begins in a world crowded with House Wrens, whereas the other man had a nearly wrenless background. And will the word of the beginner of today be any more reliable than the words of the eminent men who have spoken erstwhile?

The word of a truthful, competent, observant man can be trusted *seemingly* about most things, but not about the destruction done by the House Wren. He may tell of a dozen or more things seen in this wren's life that very few besides himself have ever witnessed, and all his statement will be accepted if he does not mention the menace of the wren to other bird life; on this subject he can not be trusted. It is not because the menace is a new idea to them nor because its workings have not been seen by them that they are obstinate, for they readily accept new truths about things that they have not seen, such as statements about vitamins, endocrine imbalance, sex-linked inheritance, chromosomes, the atomic world, and relativity.

Were a criminal belonging to the human race on trial, had his trial dragged along for many years during which he had time and again been confronted by the testimony of witnesses who were expert, competent, and veracious, it is certain that public sentiment would demand that a verdict be given and a sentence be passed. In the case of the felonious House Wren have not numerous jurymen pronounced him guilty? Capital punishment has not been demanded, though if no steps are taken to stop his unrestricted breeding it is safe to predict that the time will come when all true bird lovers will wring his neck as cheerfully as they now wring the neck of the pestiferous English Sparrow. By no means is it asked that the death penalty be exacted; instead of that drastic measure a mild sentence is urged—merely that the wren-boxes be taken down, thereby returning this wren to the place in nature that he occupied before man's interference destroyed the natural balance. In order that this restoration be not short-lived it is hoped there may come a true appreciation of his disposition, so that no one will suffer a breeding House Wren on his premises any sooner than he would tolerate vermin on his person.

Bird-Lore has a splendid motto: "A bird in the bush is worth two in the hand." But if we are to have that bird in the bush in future years, and if it is to be any other than a House Wren, then we need the slogan, "Down with the House Wren Boxes." The stand we take on this question will affect more than present interests, and each one should so act that a kind Providence need not protect his memory from the just execrations of future generations.

FURTHER READING

Bonta, Marcia. "The Chimney Swift Lady: Althea Sherman." *Bird Watcher's Digest* 7 (March–April, 1985): 36–40.

Boyle, Barbara. "The Great Wren Debate Revisited." Wings: *Newsletter of the Johnson County Songbird Project* (Summer, 1993): 1, 10–14.

Brown, Joseph K. "Althea Sherman." *Iowan* 21 (Spring, 1973): 5–9.

Kaufman, Dianne. "Althea Sherman and Her Chimney Swifts' Tower." *Wings* (Fall, 1992): 2–4.

Nice, Margaret Morse. Papers. Department of Manuscripts and University Archives, Cornell University Library, Ithaca, N.Y.

_____. "Some Letters of Althea Sherman." *Iowa Bird Life* 22 (1952): 51–55.

Palmer, T.S. "Althea Sherman." *Auk* 64 (April, 1947): 348–49.

Sherman, Althea R. "Birds by the Wayside in Egypt and Nubia." *Wilson Bulletin* 27 (September, 1915): 369–93.

_____. "Birds by the Wayside in Europe, Asia, and Africa." *Wilson Bulletin* 27 (March, 1915): 243–71.

_____. *Birds of an Iowa Dooryard*. Boston: Christopher Publishing House, 1952.

_____. Manuscripts. State Historical Society of Iowa, Des Moines, Iowa.

_____. "Nest Life of the Screech Owl." *Auk* 28 (April, 1911): 155–68.

_____. Papers and Paintings. Garnavillo Historical Society, Garnavillo, Iowa.

_____. "Summer Outings of Bats during Fourteen Seasons." *Journal of Mammalogy* 10 (November, 1929): 319–26.

Taylor, Mrs. H. J. "Iowa's Woman Ornithologist Althea Rosina Sherman 1853–1943." *Iowa Bird Life* 13 (June, 1943): 18–36.

Wood, Sharon E. "Althea Sherman and the Birds of Prairie and Dooryard: A Scientists's Witness to Change." *Palimpsest* 70 (Winter, 1989): 164–85.

Youngworth, William. "T.C. Stephens: The Complete Birdwatcher, Ancedotes from Other Days." *Iowa Bird Life* 24 (June, 1954): 31–33.

8

Elizabeth Gifford Peckham

1854–1940

IN AN OBITUARY PUBLISHED IN 1914 for *Entomological News,* R.A. Muttkowski wrote: "In dealing with the work of Dr. [George] Peckham, we cannot separate therefrom the work of his wife and collaborator. From the time of their marriage these two are inseparably linked in all phases of their work, in their researches, in their travels, in their very thoughts."

Although natural history husband-and-wife teams were not uncommon at this time, the tone of this obituary was, because scientific husbands, who collaborated with their wives, usually received most, if not all, of the credit for their work. So readers of George Peckham's obituary found Muttkowski uncharacteristically generous, yet truthful, in his praise of Elizabeth Peckham's contributions.

Muttkowski also claimed that she told him that she had no interest in carrying on her work after her husband's death. But apparently she quickly changed her mind because she continued to be an active and productive scientist for several more decades. She had already been cited as a "special student of entomology and joint author with husband of works and papers on *Arachnidae;* Habits and Instincts of Hymenoptera, etc." in Volume 8 of *Who's Who in America, 1914–1915.* Furthermore, unlike many women scientists, married or unmarried, she had been listed not only in the 1906 and 1910 editions of *American Men of Science* but also in the 1921 edition, a full seven years after the death of her husband. In fact, as soon as two years after his death, Elizabeth Gifford Peckham was the recipient of a Ph.D. from Cornell University in 1916 when she was already sixty-two years old.

Elizabeth Gifford Peckham was born and raised in Milwaukee and received her bachelor's degree from Vassar College in 1876. She married Dr. George Peckham four years later. Although he was trained in both medicine and law, he chose to work in a Milwaukee high school as a biology teacher. He later became principal, then superintendent, and finally ended his public career as Director of the Milwaukee Public Library. But he and his wife were first and foremost "nature students," and all their spare time was devoted to studying the psychology of spiders and wasps and the taxonomy of spiders.

During the 1880s the Peckhams had three children. Elizabeth Peckham also managed to earn her master's degree from Vassar in 1888, the year before their third child was born. Joint papers on spiders started appearing early in the same decade, primarily in publications of the Wisconsin Natural History Society and in the *Transactions of the Wisconsin Academy of Sciences, Arts and Letters*. Both Peckhams were leaders in the Wisconsin Natural History Society, but it was George who became president of the Society as well as of the Wisconsin Academy of Sciences, Arts, and Letters. He received an honorary Doctor of Laws from the University of Wisconsin in 1896.

Two years later their magnum opus "On the Instincts and Habits of Solitary Wasps" appeared as Bulletin No. 2 of the Wisconsin Geological Survey. In 1905 an enlarged and revised version—*Wasps: Social and Solitary*—was published by Houghton Mifflin and Company and illustrated by natural history illustrator-sculptor and arachnologist James H. Emerton. According to entomologist Howard Ensign Evans in his own classic book *Wasp Farm*, the Peckhams' book caused "quite a splash in the biological world" because of their account of tool-using by one species of solitary wasp—*Ammophilia urnaria*. That part of the book, Evans claimed, was "one of the most widely quoted paragraphs in the literature on solitary wasps."

But there was much more to their book than just that discovery. Naturalist-writer John Burroughs in his introduction to *Wasps: Social and Solitary* called it "a wonderful record of patient, exact, and loving observation," which indeed it is. Inspired by French entomologist Henri Fabre's *Souvenirs Entomologiques*, the Peckhams, nevertheless, often corrected Fabre's observations based on their own experiences. They especially questioned his assertion that all insects "are inspired by automatically perfect instincts, which can never have varied to any appreciable extent from the beginning of time," because such a "deviation from the regular rule would mean extinction." The Peckhams, on the other hand, were constantly discovering through close observation that "the one preeminent, unmistakable and ever present fact is variability. Variability in every particular," including behavior.

They did most of their wasp watching at their summer home in Pine Lake, Wisconsin, sometimes assisted by their children, "who made themselves useful by reporting finds in the shape of nests." In addition to watching, the Peckhams devised experiments for testing the intelligence and homing ability of wasps. They frequently dug up their nests, then took them home to observe, keeping records of larval food, hatching periods, parasites, and other details of their habits.

Their patience was extraordinary. Once they sat observing the great golden digger wasps in 98-degree temperatures from ten in the morning until 6:45 at night. But their longest stint was forty-two straight hours, including two nights, when they watched *Crabro stirpicola* build her nest in a berry stem. At night they put a bottle over the stem to catch the chips of pith as they fell, so they could measure how much was removed. A check by lantern light revealed that the wasp was still working at a greater rate even than during the day. "We have studied wasps for a number of years, and feel that we are on terms of more or less intimacy with many of the species, but never before have we known one to work after day was done," they wrote.

The following excerpts from *Wasps: Social and Solitary* include the story of how they began watching wasps, their special fascination for the genus *Ammophiles,* and their famous account of tool-using, an account, incidentally, which has since been observed by many entomologists in several *Ammophiles* species.

COMMUNAL LIFE

As the tendency of mankind to crowd into towns grows stronger the joys of country life and the workings of Nature are more and more excluded from the daily experience of humanity. In a few the primal love of the wild is too strong for suppression, and turning from the hot and noisy streets they find it a refreshment of spirit to meet our little brothers of earth and air in the wider spaces of their own territory.

We were walking through the woods one hot day in the middle of August when our attention was attracted by a stream of yellow-jackets issuing from the ground. They came in such surprising numbers and looked so full of energy that we stopped to watch them, and this was our introduction to the study of these "bold sons of air and heat," although a perusal of Fabre's [a French schoolteacher who specialized in writing about insect observations for a popular audience] fascinating "Souvenirs Entomologiques" [which set the stage for more accurate and erudite nature writing by later entomologists] had prepared us to feel a lively interest in them. We were at our summer home near Milwaukee, where meadow and garden, with the wooded island in the lake close by, offered themselves as hunting grounds, while wasps of every kind, the socialistic tribes as well as the extreme individualists of the solitary species, were waiting to be studied.

The Vespas [yellow jackets] that had aroused our interest received our first attention, and a nest in the ground proved to be a most convenient arrangement. Experiments that would have been dangerous to life and limb had we tried them with a paper nest hanging in the open, were easy here so long as we kept calm and unflurried. Intent upon their own affairs, and unsuspicious of evil, perhaps because they knew themselves to be armed against aggression, they accepted our presence, at first with indifference; but as we sat there day after day we must have become landmarks to them, and perhaps before the summer was over they considered us really a part of home.

While poor humanity takes comfort in a mid-day siesta, wasps love the heat of noontide, and with every rise in temperature they fly faster, hum louder, and rejoice more and more in the fullness of life. The entrance to the Vespa nest was but an inch across; and once when they were going in and out in a hurrying throng, jostling each other in their eagerness, we counted the number that passed, one taking the entrances and one the exits. In ten minutes five hundred and ninety-two left the nest and two hundred and forty-seven went in, so that we saw eight hundred and thirty-nine or about eighty to the minute. This must be a strong swarm, wonderful indeed when we thought that it had all come from a single queen mother. We imagined how she had made an early start, digging a hole in the ground, building within it a paper comb with five or six cells around a central column, and laying therein some neuter eggs; how she had then spent a month in attending carefully to the beginnings of things, feeding the young larvae as they hatched, and watching over them through their childhood and youth; and then how her solicitude was rewarded by the filial devotion with which this first set of workers took upon themselves the labor of excavating, building, and feeding the young, everything indeed except the egg-laying. These queens, surrounded though they are by respectful and attentive subjects, have much the worst of it in our estimation, never going out, and passing their lives in a dull routine. Through the early summer only neuters are produced, but when fall approaches the future generation is provided for by the development of males and females. The activity of the little colony is limited by the season, for as the days grow colder the males and females leave the nest and mate, and a little later both males and workers lose ambition, become inactive and finally die, while the queens hide away in protected corners to reappear in the spring. The eggs and larvae, left unfed and uncared for, become a prey to moulds and to hordes of insects, and thus the swarm comes to an end.

AMMOPHILA AND HER CATERPILLARS

Before we had worked long on our Vespa family we were beguiled by tempting opportunities into running after the solitary wasps. The solitaries, so far as species are concerned, are immensely more numerous than the socials; but they have only two sexes, and the males and females usually see but little of each other after the mating is over, although we occasionally find them living happily together until the end of the season. In the early summer they begin to emerge from the nest in which the eggs were laid the year before. Solitary indeed they come into the world, the generation that gave them birth having perished in the fall. For a time their career is one of unmixed pleasure, and yet, free and unguided though they are, basking in the sunshine, feeding on the flowers, or sleeping at night under some sheltering leaf, they are hourly acquiring experience, so that when the cares of life descend upon them they are no longer creatures of mere instinct. With these sobering cares an almost absurdly heavy sense of responsibility for future generations transforms the hitherto happy-go-lucky females into grown-up wasps with serious views on marketing and infant foods. Each one makes a separate nest and provisions it by her own labor; and in many cases a new nest is made for each egg. There is no co–operation among them; although in certain genera, as Aphilanthops [hunting wasps] and Bembex [wasps that burrow in sand and stock their nests with captured and paralyzed horseflies], a number of individuals build close together, forming a colony. The nests may be made of mud, and attached for shelter under leaves, rocks, or eaves of buildings, or may be burrows hollowed out in the ground, in trees or in the stems of plants. The adult wasp lives upon fruit or nectar, but the young grub or larva must have animal food; and here the parent wasp shows a rigid conservatism, each species providing the sort of food that has been approved by its family for generations, one taking flies, another bugs, and another beetles, caterpillars, grasshoppers, crickets, locusts, spiders, cockroaches, aphides [*sic*], or other creatures, as the case may be.

When the egg-laying time arrives the female secures her prey, which she either kills or paralyzes, places it in the nest, lays the egg upon it, and then, in most cases, closes the hole and takes no further interest in it, going on to make new nests from day to day. In some genera the female maintains a longer connection with her offspring, not bringing all the provision at once, but returning to feed the larva as it grows, and leaving the nest permanently only when the grub has spun its cocoon. The males never acquire this interest, so admirable for the development of character, and aid little, if at all, in the care of the family. The egg develops in from one to three days into a footless, maggot-like creature which feeds upon the store provided for it, increasing rapidly in size, and entering the pupal stage in from three days to two weeks. In the cocoon it passes through its final metamorphosis, emerging as a perfect insect, perhaps in two or three weeks, or, in many cases, after the winter months have passed and summer has come again.

Most graceful and attractive of all the wasps—"*taille effilée, tournure svelte,*" as Fabre describes them, the Ammophiles [digger wasps, which stock their nests with caterpillars], of all the inhabitants of the garden, hold the first place in our affections. Not so beautiful as the blue Pelopaeus [mud dauber wasps], nor so industrious as the little red-girdled Trypoxylon [mason wasps, which stock their nests with spiders], their intelligence, their distinct individuality, and their obliging tolerance of our society make them an unfailing source of interest. They are, moreover, the most remarkable of all genera in their stinging habits, being supposed to use the nicest surgical skill in paralyzing their caterpillars; and few things have given us deeper pleasure than our success in following the activities and penetrating the secrets of their lives. In our garden we have two species of Ammophila, urnaria Cresson, and gracilis Cresson, both of them being very slender-bodied wasps of about an inch in length, gracilis all black, and urnaria with a red band around the front end of the abdomen. A. polita and A. vulgaris, which look much like urnaria, are common in the sandy fields west and south of Milwaukee.

During the earlier part of the summer we had often seen these wasps feeding upon the nectar of flowers, especially upon that of the sorrel, of which they are particularly fond; but at that time we gave them but passing notice. One bright morning, however, we came upon an urnaria that was so evidently hunting, and hunting in earnest, that we gave up everything else to follow her. The ground was covered, more or less thickly, with patches of purslain [*sic*], and it was under these weeds that our Ammophila was eagerly searching for her prey. After thoroughly investigating one plant she would pass to another, running three or four steps and then bounding as though she were made of thistledown and were too light to remain upon the ground. We followed her easily, and as she was in full view nearly all of the time we had every hope of witnessing the capture; but in this we were destined to disappointment. We had been in attendance on her for about a quarter of an hour when, after disappearing for a few moments under the thick purslain leaves, she came out with a green caterpillar. We had missed the wonderful sight of the paralyzer at work; but we had no time to bemoan our loss, for she was making off at so rapid a pace that we were well occupied in keeping up with her. She hurried along with the same motion as before, unembarrassed by the weight of her victim. For sixty feet she kept to open ground, passing between two rows of bushes; but at the end of this division of the garden, she plunged, very much to our dismay, into a field of standing corn. Here we had great difficulty in following her, since, far from keeping to her former orderly course, she zigzagged among the plants in the most bewildering fashion, although keeping a general direction of northeast. It seemed quite impossible that she could know where she was going. The corn rose to a height of six feet all around us; the ground was uniform in appearance, and, to our eyes, each group of cornstalks was just like every other group, and yet, without pause or hesitation, the little creature passed quickly along, as we might through the familiar streets of our native town.

At last she paused and laid her burden down. Ah! the power that has led her is not a blind, mechanically perfect instinct, for she has traveled a little too far. She must go back one row into the open space that she has already crossed, although not just at this point. Nothing like a nest is visible to us; the surface of the ground looks all alike, and it is with exclamations of wonder that we see our little guide lift two pellets of earth which have served as a covering to a small opening running down into the ground.

The way being thus prepared, she hurries back with her wings quivering and her whole manner betokening joyful triumph at the completion of her task. We, in the mean time, have become as much excited over the matter as she is herself. She picks up the caterpillar, brings it to the mouth of the burrow, and lays it down. Then, backing in herself, she catches it in her mandibles and drags it out of sight, leaving us full of admiration and delight.

How clear and accurate must be the observing powers of these wonderful little creatures! Every patch of ground must, for them, have its own character; a pebble here, a larger stone there, a trifling tuft of grass—these must be their landmarks. And the wonder of it is that their interest in each nest is so temporary. A burrow is dug,

Ammophila urnaria carrying a caterpillar to her nest. Illustration by James H. Emerton from Elizabeth G. and George W. Peckham's *Wasps: Social and Solitary.*

provisioned and closed up, all in two or three days, and then another is made in a new place with everything to learn over again.

From this time on to the first of September our garden was full of these wasps, and they never lost their fascination for us; although, owing to a decided difference between their taste and ours as to what constituted pleasant weather, all our knowledge of them was gained by the sweat of our brows. . . .

Just here must be told the story of one little wasp whose individuality stands out in our minds more distinctly than that of any of the others. We remember her as the most fastidious and perfect little worker of the whole season, so nice was she in her adaptation of means to end, so busy and contented in her labor of love, and so pretty in her pride over the completed work. In filling up her nest she put her head down into it and bit away the loose earth from the sides, letting it fall to the bottom of the burrow, and then, after a quantity had accumulated, jammed it down with her head. Earth was then brought from the outside and pressed in, and then more was bitten from the sides. When, at last, the filling was level with the ground, she brought a quantity of fine grains of dirt to the spot, and picking up a small pebble in her mandibles, used it as a hammer in pounding them down with rapid strokes, thus making this spot as hard and firm as the surrounding surface. Before we could recover from our astonishment at this performance she had dropped her stone and was bringing more earth. We then threw ourselves down on the ground that not a motion might be lost, and in a moment we saw her pick up the pebble and again pound the earth into place with it, hammering now here and now there until all was level. Once more the whole process was repeated, and then the little creature, all unconscious of the commotion that she had aroused in our minds,—unconscious, indeed, of our very existence and intent only on doing her work and doing it well,—gave one final, comprehensive glance around and flew away.

FURTHER READING

Mallis, Arnold. *American Entomologists.* New Brunswick, N.J.: Rutgers University Press, 1971.

Muttkowski, R. A. "George Williams Peckham, M.D., LL.D. (1845–1914)." *Entomological News* 25 (April, 1914): 145–48.

Peckham, George W., and Elizabeth G. Peckham. *Wasps: Social and Solitary.* Westminster, England: Constable & Co., 1905.

Who's Who in America. Vol. 8 (1914–1915): 1925.

9

Alice Eastwood

1859–1953

As a small child in her uncle's Canadian garden, Alice Eastwood was attracted by two wildflowers—partridge berry and wild raspberry. For her, seeing those plants provided an incentive to pursue botany for the remainder of her ninety-four years. So after eleven years of teaching in a Denver high school, when her astute real estate investments yielded a sufficient income, she retired from teaching at the age of thirty-one and became a full time botanist.

Up to that time, she had been collecting plants during every spare moment, spending her summers in the High Rockies, traveling alone on horseback and by foot—averaging a steady four miles an hour—and building a reputation as Colorado's most adept botanist. Because of her accomplishments, she was singularly honored when the famous English naturalist Alfred Russel Wallace visited Denver and spent three days with her exploring Gray's Peak. It was an adventure she recalled enthusiastically many years later.

Her fame even reached California, and in 1892 she accepted an offer from botanists T. S. and Kate Brandegee to join them as joint curator at the California Academy of Science's herbarium in San Francisco. The following year she became sole curator when the Brandegees retired. She spent the next fourteen years organizing the Academy's botanical collection and expanding it through her own extensive botanizing in the Sierra and Coast ranges.

On April 18, 1906, disaster struck. The San Francisco earthquake and several subsequent fires destroyed the Academy, but not before Eastwood rescued 1,211 irreplaceable type specimens she had stored in a central place in case of an emergency. With that nucleus, she started all over again, re-collecting what had been lost and adding still more.

Alice Eastwood and her assistant John Thomas Howell in the Mojave Desert in 1933. They traveled to Utah and Arizona on a botanical expedition accompanied by Ynes Mexia, who took this photograph. *Courtesy Special Collections, California Academy of Sciences, San Francisco.*

Fortunately, the Academy's new location in Golden Gate Park now gave her access to land that could be converted into public gardens. Working with the park superintendent, she used gardening to educate the public about foreign and domestic garden plants and was eventually dubbed the "gardener's botanist." She loved all people who loved plants, and she worked tirelessly to promote interest in the horticultural use of California native plants.

But her interest in pure botany never wavered. At the age of sixty-eight, she reported to botanist Merritt Fernald that she had taken a collecting trip through Eldorado County and had walked twenty miles the first day, ten miles the second, and six miles the third. For many years she steadfastly insisted that only by botanizing on foot could she gain a true knowledge of the plants. Nevertheless, during the 1930s, she joined forces with the much younger John Thomas Howell, who had become her assistant at the Academy in 1930. Together they bought an open top Ford and nicknamed it "Leucy" for *Leucocoryne,* a Chilean genus. Howell drove the car on long collecting trips through California, Arizona, and New Mexico. While Eastwood collected near the car, he ranged farther afield. Eastwood also did the cataloging and cared for the pressed plants. "My days of exploring on foot are over, but one can do a good deal from autos, supplemented by one's legs," she wrote to a friend when she was seventy-five years old.

Like her good friend agrostologist Agnes Chase, she worked at the Academy far beyond official retirement age until she was ninety. Honors were heaped upon her by both horticulturists and botanists. Two genera were named for her—*Aliciella* and *Eastwoodia.* Botanists also honored her with species' names, such as "her" grass, *Festuca eastwoodae.* Because she helped to found the American Fuchsia Society, nurserymen named a fuchsia for her in addition to a lilac and an orchid.

What most pleased her, though, was renaming the herbarium to the Alice Eastwood Herbarium of the California Academy of Sciences. To her the herbarium and library of the Academy was "my child . . . dearer to me than life." At the end of her tenure, she had added a total of 340,000 specimens to it and had built up a fine botanical library with her own funds.

Probably the greatest thrill of her lifetime occurred in 1950 when she flew to the Eighth International Botanical Congress in Sweden. There she was made honorary president and seated in the chair of Carl Linnaeus, father of modern botany.

Eastwood published two small books—*A Popular Flora of Denver, Colorado* and *A Handbook of the Trees of California.* She also founded, with Howell, *Leaflets of Western Botany.* She published over three hundred articles in a wide variety of journals and magazines, including semi-popular articles on California gardens. But she never completed the autobiography she started, although she did cooperate with her biographer—Carol Green Wilson—shortly before she died.

Her letter in *Science,* which gives her account of the San Francisco earthquake and fire and her rescue of the type specimens, shows the spirit of a woman who never let convention stand in the way of what she wanted to accomplish. She was not easily discouraged and had no qualms about starting to collect all over again. In fact, she welcomed the challenge.

"In Portu Bodega" is one of her few published accounts of a collecting trip. Her lively interest in people and plants was a recurrent theme throughout her life, and her special talent was persuading people to allow her to do the unusual. Robert C. Miller of the Cali-

Alice Eastwood, at age eighty, studying a lupine specimen at the Academy in 1939 with the help of a mounted hand lens. *Courtesy Special Collections, California Academy of Sciences, San Francisco.*

fornia Academy of Sciences captured her personality best when he described Eastwood as "young at ninety-four because all her life she was studying, inquiring, learning, exploring . . . a blithe, ageless spirit living in a world of discovery forever new."

LETTER: MAY 7, 1906

[written after the San Francisco earthquake and fire]

I do not feel the loss to be mine, but it is a great loss to the scientific world and an irreparable loss to California. My own destroyed work I do not lament, for it was a joy to me while I did it, and I can still have the same joy in starting it again. The botanists of the University of California have given me the use of their library and collections and even a room which for the present I can call mine. The kindness of my friends has been great. I did not know that I had so many or that their affection for me was so warm and sincere. I feel how very fortunate I am; not at all like an unfortunate who has lost all her personal possessions and home.

To me came the chance to care for what was saved from the ruin of the academy, and with the help of my devoted friends I was able to do it. Nobody knew where the safe place was to be; for it seemed as if the whole city must go. . . .

The earthquake did not frighten me as it was felt less where I lived than in other parts of the city. . . . After getting breakfast, I went down to the academy. I could not get in. The store next door was open and they were taking things out, and I knew there was a door of communication with the front building. It was still as death. I had to climb over the demolished marble staircase at the entrance of the museum, but found the stairs going up the front building all right. When I reached the top a yawning chasm stretched between the two buildings as the bridge had been thrown down. I tried several doors but every one seemed to have deserted the place. I got out again and walked up and down Market St. . . . Everywhere buildings were in ruins. Presently Robert Porter [lawyer and friend from the Sierra Club] came along, and when I told him my trouble he went back with me, but the door was still locked. We went to the back and saw that the fire was on Mission Street, and the police were driving the people from their homes. We again entered by the store next door and when we came to the front hall found Mr. [Leverett] Loomis [Academy Director], Mr. von Geldren, General Foote, Mrs. Newell [Academy curators and staff members], and John Carlton [Academy caretaker]. Miss Hyde [Academy librarian] was in the library getting out the records, etc. Porter pulled me up the ruins of the marble staircase and we entered the museum, the door of which was now open. The marble staircase leading up to the top was in ruins and we went up chiefly by holding on to the iron railing and putting our feet between the rungs. Porter helped me to tie up the plant types, and we lowered them to the floor of the museum by ropes and strings tied together. Not a book was I able to save, nor a single thing of my own, except my favorite lens, without which I should feel helpless. We got all the things to the street and then it seemed as if we might have to leave them. The building next door was on fire, the military was in command, and nobody was allowed on the street. I rushed across to the safe deposit opposite, where I have a box, to implore them to take the things. There was a line of men there a block long and my place would be at the end, so with the permission of the officer in charge I dashed back. Porter then went and came back with word that an expressman on the corner of Stockton and Ellis would take them, but we had to carry them over as no vehicles were allowed on Market Street. I asked the man how much it would be and he said 'A high price.' I possessed $14.00 and feared it might not be enough. When he said 'Three dollars' I almost fell off the seat. I paid him four and took all the things except a few to my place of residence, and thinking it as safe as any. In the afternoon I went down to reconnoitre and see what the academy looked like. The back building stood, the staircase was still there, or rather the banisters, but everything within seemed burned up. . . . The fire was threatening from two directions and I decided to move the 'academy' to Russian Hill that evening. With the help of friends this was done, though everything had to be carried. The plants were the heaviest and largest bundles. There were some boxes of insects, some bottles of reptiles which Dr. Van Denburg [Academy's Curator of Herpetology] had saved, the heavy record books of the academy, and several things I did not know about. It was hard work. I packed my own things when I returned to my home and laid down to rest, but not to sleep. It was bright enough to read by the red glow in the sky, and it might be necessary to leave at a minute's notice. Only what one could carry could be saved, for there was either no chance to hire any kind of a conveyance or the charges were extortionate. Nobody seemed to be complaining or sorrowful. The sound of the trunks being dragged along I can never forget. This seemed the only groan the ruined city made. I took my things up to Russian Hill the next morning, and in the afternoon was able to have 'The Academy' removed to Fort Mason, where it was put in the care of Mrs. Hahn, whose husband is a captain there. I felt easy at last, for it seemed the safest place in the city, and returned to Russian Hill. Mr. John Galen Howard [Professor of Architecture at the University of California, Berkeley] invited me to take refuge in his home [at Berkeley], and I was glad to accept.

All my pictures and books are gone and many treasures that I prized highly; but I regret nothing for I am rich in friends and things seem of small account. I have since moved the academy things back to Russian Hill, as it was saved by the great effort of the few people who live there. My only regret is that I left for Berkeley Thursday evening instead of staying to help them, but I never dreamed it was possible to save it. It is an experience I am not sorry to have had if it could have been without the terrible loss. *There is not a reference library left in San Francisco.* I am afraid that in the rush of rebuilding the city such essential, but apparently immaterial, things will be neglected.

I am beginning already to recollect and intend to go to type localities as much as possible. I expect the academy will be able to give me but little aid for the present, but have a tiny income of my own and can get along, I feel sure.

IN PORTU BODEGA

Bodega Bay lies to the north of San Francisco and beyond Pt. Reyes. The actual distance is not to be measured by miles but by the time taken for the voyage, since that is dependent on the weather. During the occupation of the Russians, their ships were anchored in this safe haven. Even before the colony at Fort Ross was established, as early as 1812 when they sought otter and beaver along the Pacific coast, this was their harbor. It is a small body of water, somewhat triangular in shape, about two miles long and at the widest part about one and one-half miles wide. The extreme width of the entrance is only about 200 yards; but sufficient for the vessels of that time.

On the ocean side, a promontory known as Bodega Head rises at its greatest elevation to about 240 feet above the ocean and slopes on the east to the bay. On my visits in 1899 and 1900, there were the remains of an old wooden wharf with a large iron ring to which perhaps the Russians had fastened their boats. From the entrance towards the east, the bay is bounded by a sand bar of varying width culminating at the head of the bluff in an enormous dune of aerial sand. This dune cuts Bodega Head off from the mainland on the north and so makes it almost an island with water on the other three sides.

Bodega Head is made up almost wholly of biotite diorite, a type of granite. To the north, beyond the dune and along the east side of the bay, the formation is entirely of Franciscan sandstone. The diorite forms the steep cliffs rising from the ocean and extending almost to the entrance. It weathers badly and in the rainy season, landslides occur owing to the friable nature of the soil. When I first visited it in the spring of 1899, a fence along the bluff cut off these dangerous areas, protecting the cattle from being precipitated to the ocean below, and incidentally preserving in all its variety, beauty, and abundance the original vegetation. At that time, it was a dairy ranch run by Mr. and Mrs. William Caughey and their son, Frank. . . .

Bodega Point was the type-locality of several species in which I was particularly interested because of some confusion as to their identity. My desire to visit that locality by sea, following the probable route of the Russians was irresistible. I learned that a gasoline launch made trips back and forth to transport pastoral and agricultural products from the adjacent farms to San Francisco and return with what the farmers wanted in exchange.

At first the captain flatly refused to take me there, saying that he never took passengers and had no accommodations. I persisted, however, explaining my purpose and at last he reluctantly consented. Jim Caughey, the engineer, may have had some influence, because he knew that my visit would be a welcome change in the monotony and isolation of his mother's life.

At the stern of the boat there was quite a space for livestock, calves, hogs, etc., the bow was about as long as the stern, and between was a small cabin and engine room. As I remember it, I thought it to be larger than the common fishing boats at Fisherman's Wharf in San Francisco. At the time of the Russians, ships as large as the *H.M.S. Discovery* under George Vancouver could anchor in the outer harbor and in 1837, Captain Beechey of *H.M.S. Sulphur* landed there on the way to Monterey from exploring voyages in the Pacific. We were eight hours going up and I realized what "no accommodations for passengers" meant. The cabin reeked with the odor of gasoline, besides I liked being outside and to intrude on the privacy of the men was not to be considered at all. The alternative was standing in the bow of the boat and sitting flat on the deck when I was tired of standing. This didn't matter, nor the dry lunch which I had brought along. This was before the time of vacuum jars.

The welcome of the Caugheys was warm and I was very comfortable and happy. Part of an original Russian habitation had been added to and Mrs. Caughey had a little silver bell that she had found in some debris. Outside that protecting fence were all the species that I had come for. There was no shelter on that promontory and the winds were very strong, so it was difficult to collect and put my plants to press while I was out and I had nothing to take the place of a vasculum. On the return trip, I was given a box on which I could sit and the captain never again objected to me as a passenger. On one return trip we had a storm. While passing Pt. Reyes, we went so far out on the ocean that we lost sight of land. Garbed in a yellow slicker and cap, I was allowed by the captain to stay out until he, too, had to go in. Entering the Golden Gate, the boat rolled so that I could see the Sausalito Hills from the skylight of the cabin. I am a good sailor.

It was during the July Fourth holidays in 1900 that I was again on Bodega Head. The spring vegetation had gone but it was then that I collected plants that to me were undescribed and also two species that had been collected by Richard Brinsley Hinds on the Voyage of the *Sulphur*, namely *Phacelia distans* and *Monardella villosa*. The former grew on the bluff near the entrance and the latter on a rocky outcrop in the interior. The species that I described as new were related to well-known species but differed from the types as did some also collected by the Russians, undoubtedly a result of the peculiar soil and the insular environment. They resemble plants on Pt. Reyes where in some parts the soil is the same and the environment almost as insular. Insular varieties are always puzzling and interesting. Never do taxonomists agree as to their varietal or specific rank. A specific name enlists them in the Index Kewensis [repository of flowering plant names published by Kew Gardens in London] where the reference to their publication can be found, while a varietal name is not recorded there and generally is almost lost. Two species of *Platystemon* grew outside the fence. One was *P. leiocarpa* similar to a species from Fort Ross, and the other *P. villosa,* named by E[dward]. L[ee]. Green [Professor of Botany at the University of California, Berkeley] in Pittonia vol. 5. The collection of *Platystemon* from the Academy herbarium had been loaned to the National Herbarium at Washington before 1906 and was therefore saved from the San Francisco fire.

Since, at that time, all my notes on the peculiarities of the Bodega species were lost, as well as my collections there, with the exception of the types, I have to rely on my memory. Some species stand out vividly. The *Orthocarpus versicolor* was uniformly rose-colored, differing from the same species in San Francisco that formerly made large areas white. Along the coast of Mendocino near Fort Bragg, this rose-colored variety is common. The yellow bush lupine, *Lupinus arboreus,* as it grows along the coast, is a spreading bush, while at Bodega all were little trees with distinct, slender trunks and the yellow flowers, when they faded, turned rose-color. *Godetia grandiflora* formed a little garden all by itself in one place and there seemed to be no two plants with flowers of the same shade, varying from white to pale pink and with different markings. Indeed almost every plant showed some deviation from the mainland plants as I knew them.

In late summer, 1915, I made an attempt on a Sunday to reach Bodega Head by land. I took the train to Bodega station and was fortunate to have transportation to the town of Bodega. On Sunday there was no stage. At the hotel I learned that it was again a dairy ranch run by a Portuguese who lived there with his wife and small children. He happened to be in town and was in the saloon near by. When I inquired for him at the door, he came out and agreed to take me back in the buckboard on which he carried his milk cans. This was good luck that I had not hoped for. The bay was not then filled by sand but the change on the promontory was great. The fences were all gone, very little left of the vegetation as I remembered it, the house seemed dilapidated, and the evident poverty was about the worst I had ever seen. They did their best for me. I did a little collecting and was brought to the bay shore along the road early Monday morning. There I was stranded to await some means of returning to Bodega whence I could go by stage to the train. That road is but little traveled. My first chance was with a junk collector and I was glad of the lift. I held his solitary horse when he stopped for junk. It was at the beginning of the first World War and he seemed most desirous to get old rubber tires. My troubles were over when I reached the town. Later, with the help of friends, who gave me clothing, bedding, and canned food, I sent a box to these poor people.

Returning from Mendocino by the Coast route in 1937, I was astonished to see that the harbor had become filled with sand. This was probably at low tide. I learned that in 1935 the harbor was closed to all boats. What a change in 35 years! It seemed incredible. The winds must have been shifting those sands from the big dune for ages and at last transformed a beautiful bay into a sandy sink. A channel has been excavated since then so that small fishing boats can enter.

I am hoping during this spring to make another trip, and two different friends have offered to take me there in their cars.

Further Reading

Bonta, Marcia. "Alice Eastwood." *American Horticulturist* 62 (October, 1983): 10–15.

Dakin, Susanna Bryant. *Perennial Adventure: A Tribute to Alice Eastwood.* San Francisco: California Academy of Sciences, 1954.

Eastwood, Alice. "In Portu Bodega." *Leaflets of Western Botany* 5 (April, 1949): 162–67.

———. "Letter." *Science* 23 (May 25, 1906): 824–26.

———. Letters. Gray Herbarium, Harvard University, Cambridge, Mass.

———. Letters to Agnes Chase. Smithsonian Institution Archives, Washington, D.C.

———. Papers. California Academy of Sciences, San Francisco.

Fletcher, Maurine S., ed. *The Wetherills of the Mesa Verda: Autobiography of Benjamin Alfred Wetherill.* Cranbury, N.J.: Associated University Presses, 1977.

Howell, John Thomas. "I Remember When I Think." *Leaflets of Western Botany* 7 (August, 1954): 153–76.

Munz, Philip A. "A Century of Achievement." *Leaflets of Western Botany* 7 (August, 1953): 69–78.

Pyne, Stephen J., and Karl G. Grove. *A Great Engine of Research.* Austin: University of Texas Press, 1980.

Wilson, Carol Green. *Alice Eastwood's Wonderland: The Adventures of a Botanist.* San Francisco: California Academy of Sciences, 1955.

———. "The Eastwood Era at the California Academy of Sciences." *Leaflets of Western Botany* 7 (August, 1953): 58–64.

10

Florence Merriam Bailey

1863–1948

FROM THE TIME SHE WAS A CHILD living in western New York state, Florence Merriam Bailey watched birds. Encouraged by progressive parents and her older brother, C. Hart Merriam, who was himself a budding naturalist at an early age, Bailey never imagined that her sex might hinder her aspiration to be her brother's chief field assistant.

Plagued by ill health in her early adulthood, Bailey frequently traveled to the western United States in search of an open air cure, most notably in Utah, California, and Arizona. But she never ventured outside without her "opera glasses" for birdwatching.

By the time she made her first trip west in 1889, she was already the author of numerous articles for the fledgling *Audubon Magazine* on which she based her first book, *Birds through an Opera Glass,* published that same year.

Previously, after being elected the first woman member of the newly founded American Ornithologists' Union in 1885, Bailey had founded a chapter of the Audubon Society at her alma mater, Smith College, and soon had learned how to arouse interest in birdwatching among the general public. According to the preface in her book, "It was my good fortune when in college to be able to study the perplexities of nearly forty young observers, and this book is virtually the result of what I learned of their wants and the best ways to supply them."

She continued to write prolifically. She followed her first book with *My Summer in a Mormon Village* (1894) and *A-Birding on a Bronco* (1896), based on her western trips. In 1895, after her chronic tuberculosis was finally cured, she settled into the Washington, D.C., home

Portrait of Florence Augusta Merriam, circa 1886. *Courtesy Smith College Archives, Smith College, Northampton, Massachusetts.*

of her naturalist brother, his wife, and children. By then, he was head of the U.S. Biological Survey. Three years later she published her fourth book, *Birds of Village and Field,* also aimed at beginners, in which she again encouraged the use of opera glasses instead of shotguns for bird watching. Another strong interest, to which she devoted a good deal of time, was helping to found in 1897 the Audubon Society of the District of Columbia, where she also conducted bird classes for teachers for many years.

At the close of the century, she married Vernon Bailey, the chief naturalist of the U.S. Biological Survey and longtime friend of her brother. For the next thirty years they embarked together on biological surveys throughout the western United States for the federal government. They usually spent spring and summer camping in tents and collecting in the field and fall and winter residing in their comfortable home in Washington, D.C., where they wrote up their observations. The team of Bailey and Bailey complemented each other: he specialized in mammals and their life zones, along with reptiles and plants, and she continued her study of birds.

In 1902 Houghton Mifflin published her *Handbook of Birds of the Western United States,* which, through many revisions, remained a standard manual for nearly fifty years. She also wrote numerous entertaining and scientifically accurate articles about their western field work in such publications as the *Condor, Auk,* and *Bird-Lore.*

One of the least-explored areas of the Southwest was New Mexico, so the Baileys spent many field seasons there. Thus, when Professor W. W. Cooke, who was writing an ornithological study of New Mexico, died unexpectedly, Bailey was the logical person to take over the project. She was even named a special assistant by the U.S. Biological Survey, allowing her to work in its offices. Her *Birds of New Mexico,* published to general scientific acclaim in 1928, put her firmly into the ranks of professional ornithologists. Because of that book, she was made the first woman fellow of the A.O.U. in 1929. In 1931 she received the A.O.U.'s Brewster Medal, which acknowledged her as the author of the most important work related to birds of the Western Hemisphere published during the preceding six years. She was also awarded an honorary LL.D. degree from the University of New Mexico in 1933.

By that time she and Vernon had slowed down slightly but still continued to take shorter trips west most years and to collaborate on books and articles—most notably, his book *Cave Life of Kentucky* in 1933 and her last book *Among the Birds in the Grand Canyon Country* in 1939. The latter was based on her field notes from the summer of 1929 and the fall of 1931 and was supplemented with accounts of Vernon's solo trips to Havasu Canyon in 1929 and Chuar Creek in 1931. As usual, she referred to him in her writings as either the "Mammalogist" or the "Mapper of Life Zones." What appeared to everyone to be an idyllic marriage between "two devoted naturalists" ended abruptly in June of 1942 with Vernon's death.

Over the fifty-year span of Florence Merriam Bailey's writing career, her emphasis shifted, but her subject matter—birds—and her readable style never changed. From beginning to end, her work was based on careful field observations in a variety of settings—from her home grounds in New York state and the Smith College campus in her earlier books to the many under-explored areas of the western United States in her later writings.

Reading Bailey's *Birds through an Opera Glass* is pure delight, even today, for anyone who genuinely likes birds. Full of whimsy and delightful accounts of her own and other naturalists' observations, many pieces also illustrate her field techniques, such as "Ruffed Grouse: Partridge," which is reprinted here. "Long-Billed Marsh Wren" from *Birds of Village and Field* includes an evocative description of a day in a marsh and portrays Bailey's obvious joy at experiencing both the setting and the birds. The excerpts from her last book—*Among the Birds in the Grand Canyon Country*—describe the Baileys' living conditions afield as well as several of the most interesting western bird species, such as rock wrens and black-chinned hummingbirds. This account includes Bailey's usual keen observations and reflects her sympathy for her subjects, even the predatory Cooper's hawks.

Ruffed Grouse: Partridge

The partridge, or ruffed grouse as he is more properly called, is our first true woods bird. His colors are the colors of the brown leaves that lie on the ground, and as he crouches close to the earth it is no easy task to discover him. The one thought of the poor persecuted bird seems to be to keep out of reach of his enemies.

Here, one of his favorite covers is in a quiet spot where I go to gather ferns—a grove that "fronts the rising sun" and is full of dappled maple saplings interspersed with the white birches that gleam in the morning light and keep birch-bark scrolls rolled up along their sides ready for the birds to carry away for their nests. At the foot of the trees, and close to the moss-covered drumming-log, ferns stand in pretty groups of all growths from the tiny green sprays and the soft uncurling downy balls to the full grown arching fronds whose backs are dotted with brown fruit; while, as a protecting hedge along the front of the grove, great masses of the tender green mountain fern give their delicate fragrance to the air. But pass by this hiding place, and a sudden *whirr* through the bushes, first from one startled bird and then another, tells you they have flown before you. Approach the drumming-log when the air has been resounding with exultant blows—the noise stops, not a bird is to be seen.

As we feed the partridges in our woods and never allow any hunting there, in winter the birds venture about the house for food. The Norway spruces by the garden afford a warm shelter, and there, under the boughs, corn is kept for them on barrels and boxes. On the other side of the house, in front of the dining-room window, is a similar store for the blue jays and gray squirrels; and as they sometimes visit the partridges' table, the latter often fly around the house to see if the squirrels' corn tastes any better than theirs.

The first snowy morning they appear we have to peek through the shutters very cautiously, for they are painfully shy, crouching in the snow, listening tremulously to the least sound from the house, looking about every time they pick up a kernel of corn, and whirring off back to their evergreens if a window or blind chances to be thrown open. But they soon lose their fears, and some mornings we find their pretty footprints in the snow on the piazza.

One winter they seemed to show a fondness for music, often coming close to the house as I was playing the piano. Indeed they and the squirrels must both have followed the Pied Piper of Hamelin—the squirrels not only nibble their corn with complacent satisfaction when the music box is wound for them, but have even let themselves be stroked when a peculiarly pathetic air was whistled! Who dare say what forest concerts the pretty creatures may get up on the long winter evenings when they are tired frolicking on the moonlit snow!

Still the partridges seem to like the bright red berries of the cranberry-tree even better than they do music, and we have been much amused watching their attempts to get the berries from a bush by the garden. Sometimes they stand in the snow underneath and jump for them; but one day when the bush was covered with ice one adventurous bird flew up on a branch and nearly turned a somersault in trying to lean over and pick off the berries and at the same time keep hold of the slippery perch.

But our chief pleasure is in watching the partridges from the bay window of the dining-room. The young men are as proud as turkey-cocks of the handsome black ruffs for which they were dubbed "ruffed grouse," and when they strut before the ladies, raising their crests, erecting their spread tails, and puffing out the ruffs over their shoulders they remind one forcibly of the lordly cock. In matter of fact they do belong to the same family,—that of the gallinaceous birds,—and many of their mannerisms betray the relationship. Their way of scratching in the snow, resting their weight on one foot and scratching with the other, is like that of the common hen, and their drumming is the finished performance that is caricatured by Chanticleer. Drumming with the partridge is a joy. He beats the air with his wings till it must needs sing for him, and the music is full of refreshing pictures of green mossy logs, arching ferns, and the cool shade of the woods.

LONG-BILLED MARSH WREN [MARSH WREN]

When woods and fields have lost their relish, spend a day in a marsh and the world will seem young again. The expanse of the great level stretch, 'its range and its sweep'—a dark green sea interrupted only by its narrow winding river, seemingly bounded only by the horizon where treetops meet the small round clouds bordering the soft June heavens—both the expanse and solitude of the great green plain under the sky are infinitely restful.

But, aside from this, the marsh is a little world apart, offering keen, peculiar pleasures to those who know nature only in her more familiar forms. As you wade through the reeds, the long blades make pleasant music in your ears, seething as they bow before you and rise behind you. Even the unexpected plunge into deep water takes its place along with the first taste of sweet-flag and the moment when you sight the blue patch of iris down the marsh. As for birds, they pervade the margins of the plain and give it life. At one moment you are remonstrated with by Maryland Yellow-throats, small yellow birds who whip in and out of the reeds, peering up at you anxiously to make out if you would really harm their brood; at the next you are encircled by excited Red-wings, who fancy their fledglings in danger; and then, overhead, the Bobolinks, absorbed in their own happiness,

> " . . . meet and frolic in the air
> Half prattling and half singing."

But however much you are prepared for it by the other members of the choir, the first outburst of the Marsh Wrens is almost paralyzing. You feel as if you had entered a factory with machines clattering on all sides. Perching atilt of the reeds, with tails over their backs, the excited little music-boxes run on chattering and scolding almost in your very face, diving out of sight in the cat-tails only to reappear near your hand as you search for their nests.

Search for their nests? Yes, but only with gentle thoughts. The stilt-houses of these little lake-dwellers surely merit the attention of ornithological tourists. As you examine the round green balls of nests high up on the reed-stalks, what marvelous workmen the little builders seem! They bend down the tips of the long blades and weave them in together as if basket-making were an easy matter to them. Difficult work it seems to us to be done for the pure joy of doing, but nest after nest is made around the one which is actually to hold the chocolate eggs. One covets the pleasure of seeing the Wrens at work on these stilt-houses, and the added pleasure of seeing them bring out a brood of chattering brown mites upon the world of marsh. If all their nine eggs hatch, surely they will be kept busy hunting food for the hungry little folk! But they are quite equal to the task. Along the southern coasts where the rice grows, they take the opportunity to pick up the destructive weevils that feed upon it, and wherever they are they busy themselves hunting out the small worms of the earth that cumber the ground; for that is a trait of the Wren family.

CAMPING UNDER THE STARS ON THE WAY UP

In the mouth of the canyon, well off the trail, flanked by sunny green cottonwoods, stood the cabin for which we were bound, remote from tourist travel, facing the compelling view—cabin and cirque ours—undisturbed by the noise of the world far away. Overhead on the rim 3,500 feet above us our nearest neighbor, the Yavapai Observation Station, though equipped with a telescope for seeing fossil trilobites at our level, did not make us conscious of observation but served to emphasize our isolation and add to our serene satisfaction in being a part of the quiet landscape. . . .

When ready to make ourselves at home we had a happy surprise. One of our favorite birds, the friendly little rock wren of many camps in the arid, rocky country of the West, came out unconcernedly from under the cabin piazza as if it too were making itself at home—perhaps finding it good collecting ground for insects for its brood. After a few housekeeping preliminaries in the cabin such as arranging our outfit in its shelter, improvising a broom with a piece of burlap tied to half an agave stalk, and bringing up clear delicious water from Pipe Creek Spring near the cottonwoods below the bank, we were ready to look for birds.

In the canyon mouth a rock wren, perhaps the very one that had met us at the cabin, was found hunting on a shelf-like sandstone ledge nearby and a large family, perhaps its family, was found in the first boulder-strewn gulch below camp. An alert competent-looking parent that I called the mother was watched hunting for food for them over the sandy ground and among the rocks whose colors she matched so well that as she ran up a boulder she seemed little more than a swiftly passing shadow. Once she took a short cut down the

101

steep side of a rock to a hungry fledgling below. Another youngster had a red skunk berry in its bill, perhaps provided in a harried moment when insects, the more proper infant bird food, could not be found quickly enough. A fluffy little body with the yellow bill corners of a nestling, evidently fed to satiety, was seen resting quietly in a miniature niche between stones. How could it ever be found, silent and motionless?

The rest of the large brood were scrambling about up and down and in and out of crannies over the confused piles of rocks in the gulch. How could they all be kept track of? Their low chirring notes were doubtless of use to their parents, but when making their short flights their flitting wings, and when alighting their characteristic rock wren dipping and bobbing motions, must also have helped to locate them. Nature had need to help, for no time could be lost hunting for mouths when so many had to be filled.

While the small rock wrens had been busy raising families of young below camp, a pair of the large Cooper's hawks had apparently nested above camp in the cottonwoods of Pipe Creek Canyon. Our first hint of their presence was when a sudden heavy wind sent one of the old birds dashing down to shelter between narrow rock walls. After that, from our sleeping bags early one morning we heard young Coopers calling, and on my first round through the cottonwoods I was pleased to discover an adult with its reddish horizontal barring and wide white tail bands.

Later, when camp was quiet, the quickly repeated whistle of an antelope squirrel made us look up from our notebooks, and when the cries of a hawk followed we hurried off to investigate. At sight of us an old Cooper flew up the canyon, but an inexperienced one, with the vertical breast stripes of immaturity, instead of properly following, flew to the top of a huge mass of rock that had fallen from the cliff above, where he made an excellent mark—for the field glass. When approached he opened his broad wings and flew off across the stony slope, doubtless to strike terror to many small mammalian hearts. Here in the national park, where shooting was prohibited, his family was not called on to end the suffering of those crippled by guns, but by eliminating the weak and diseased still might help to keep up the hardiest stock.

On the stony ridges leading down from the canyon wall few birds or mammals were in evidence although once one of the little antelope squirrels, with tail straight up at its back, made a dash along the slopes. A few black-chinned hummingbirds caught sight of as they whizzed by were found about the opening flower stalks of the agaves or mescals here blooming later than in the warmer bottom of the canyon, the little hummers, wings whirring so fast they were visible only as two films. The spirited prairie falcon that makes his home in cliffs and has been found on both North and South Rims, was appropriately seen here in passing, and a migrating Bullock's oriole caught sight of by the Mammalogist. The familiar cliff-dwelling white-throated swifts chattered so loudly below camp, in the narrow clefts Pipe Creek had cut through the Tonto on its way to the Colorado, that we suspected they were arguing over nesting sites.

Two small birds found not only on the blackbrush cover of the main Tonto Platform but on the tongue extending up to the amphitheater of Pipe Creek were the black-throated desert sparrow [now the black-throated sparrow] and the blue-gray western gnatcatcher, the two sometimes seen in the same bush. The talkative little gnatcatcher, uncommon enough in the canyon to be eagerly welcomed, as it flipped nervously through the bushes crying *tsang' tsang'* seemed almost to propel itself along with its black, white-bordered tail. Sometimes its familiar *tsang' tsang'* ran into a song, one phrase of which suggested *tsang-set-tah-say'-tsee*, a song of brightness and delicacy, intricacy and charm. Two of the amusing little birds were seen coquetting one day, switching their tails so extravagantly that the black and white stood out in surprising contrast.

After watching gnatcatchers, the desert sparrow seemed positively phlegmatic, but it was nevertheless a cheery little songster gratefully enlivening the wide stretches of blackbrush. As is its custom it sang heartily with head thrown back as if thoroughly enjoying its tinkly, jumbled, and musically unimportant, albeit pleasing, production. In full face its black throat and contrasting snowy head and neck stripes stood out so strikingly that when seen standing in profile on a bare tree it was hard to believe that this was the same bird. Its brownish back and dull under tones made it almost disappear in the dull-colored desert landscape.

In spite of being desert sparrows whose name suggests that they should be content with juicy insects and moisture-producing seeds, two flew down through camp one morning to drink from the brook like thirsty inhabitants of well-watered regions. . . .

Our sleeping bags under the sky afforded us rare moonlight and sunrise pictures and also enabled us to hear choice nocturnal calls and the first morning bird songs. The soft-voiced Nuttall's poor-wills [poor-will] were heard by moonlight calling almost continuously, two often answering in rapid succession. One of them, so early one morning that he was unaware that anyone else was awake in camp, actually brought out a loud *poor-wil-low* from the floor of the cabin piazza, after which he dropped to the front steps and then to the ground by the campfire.

On another early morning of happy memory, from a distance up the amphitheater came the incomparable song of the cañon wren. After hearing only characteristic desert calls and songs—the harsh notes of the ash-throat [ash-throated flycatcher], the grating song of the rock wren, and the tinkling note of the desert sparrow—it was a singular pleasure to hear the sublimated chromatic scale of the cañon wren; beginning high, its pure bugling notes dropping down, each note rich in musical quality, full of poetic fervor.

One night after a thunderstorm over the North Rim, while the stars were still hidden, the moon gave a soft light through which the large landscape features could be discerned. Under the turreted South Rim our amphitheater walls led down in gigantic dark silhouetted steps lowering to the mesa; and beyond across the width of the great chasm was faintly seen the far-away familiar level of the North Rim. But as I gazed around dreamily, the soft, soothing voices of little toads, the drowsy chirring of crickets, and the faint distant poorwill, poor-will soon lulled me into peaceful sleep.

On waking the next morning I watched the sunlight coming into the canyon. First the Coconino cliffs at the top of the South Rim were lit up, their buffy turrets, battlements, and castellated walls rising and glowing as the sun illumined them. Then the light spread down the red wall till the great temples between us and the North Rim caught the light. Another morning, as the red wall was lit up, the illumination was celebrated by the musical cries of awakened piñon jays above.

Further Reading

Bailey, Florence Merriam. *Among the Birds in the Grand Canyon Country.* Washington, D.C.: U.S. Government Printing Office, 1939.

———. "Birds of the Humid Coast, Part I." *Condor* 19 (January, 1917): 8–54.

———. "Birds of the Humid Coast, Part II." *Condor* 19 (May, 1917): 95–101.

———. "A Drop of Four Thousand Feet." *Auk* 28 (April, 1911): 219–25.

———. "Meeting Spring Half Way, Part I." *Condor* 18 (July, 1916): 151–55.

———. "Meeting Spring Half Way, Part II." *Condor* 18 (September, 1916): 183–90.

———. "Meeting Spring Half Way, Part III." *Condor* 18 (November, 1916): 214–19.

————. "Notable Migrants Not Seen at Our Arizona Bird Table." *Auk* 40 (July, 1923): 393–409.

————. Papers. Smith College Archives. Northampton, Mass.

Bonta, Marcia. "Florence Merriam Bailey." *Bird Watcher's Digest* 12 (March–April, 1990): 106–13.

Horner, Elizabeth B., and Keith B. Sterling. "Feathers and Feminism in the Eighties." *Smith Alumnae Quarterly* (April, 1975): 19–21.

Kofalk, Harriet. *No Woman Tenderfoot: Florence Merriam Bailey, Pioneer Naturalist.* College Station: Texas A&M University Press, 1989.

Merriam, Florence A. *A-Birding on a Bronco.* Boston: Houghton Mifflin, 1896.

————. *Birds of Village and Field.* Boston: Houghton Mifflin, 1898.

————. *Birds through an Opera Glass.* Boston: Houghton Mifflin, 1889.

————. *My Summer in a Mormon Village.* Boston: Houghton Mifflin, 1894.

Oehseor, Paul H. "Florence Merriam Bailey: Friend of Birds." *Nature Magazine* 35 (March, 1950): 153–54.

————. "In Memoriam: Florence Merriam Bailey." *Auk* 69 (January, 1952): 19–26.

Stone, Witmer. Collection. Library of the Academy of Natural Sciences, Philadelphia, Pa.

11

Anna Botsford Comstock

1864–1930

"INSECTS," ANNA BOTSFORD COMSTOCK WROTE in her best-selling *Handbook of Nature Study,* "are among the most interesting and available of all living creatures for nature-study . . . the study of them is a fruitful field for intellectual growth." And Anna Botsford recognized early that nature study interested her more than any other field.

After the two years she spent as a modern languages and literature major at Cornell University, she married John Henry Comstock, entomologist and teacher at the same university, and redirected her intellectual focus toward nature. An interest in nature nurtured by her mother during her rural New York state childhood was now actively encouraged by her husband.

Shortly before they were married, Harry, as she called him, had presented her with India ink, pens, a drafting board, and a T square so she could draw insects to illustrate his research papers. After their marriage in October, 1878, she assisted him with his projects both at Cornell and during his brief tenure as Chief Entomologist for the U.S. Department of Agriculture. But both Comstocks preferred academia to political life and were relieved to return to Cornell to devote the rest of their lives to research, writing, and teaching about nature, specifically insects.

First, however, Harry insisted that she finish her education at Cornell, and in 1885 she received a bachelor of science degree. She then took up the art of wood engraving so that she could better illustrate Harry's *An Introduction to Entomology.* Once that textbook was published in 1888, Comstock's engraving work was fully recognized. Not only was she one of the first four women to be initiated into Sigma Xi, the national honor society of the sciences, but she was also

Anna Botsford Comstock's whimsical illustration of treehoppers, which originally appeared in Harry Comstock's *Insect Life*.

the third woman to be elected into the American Society of Wood Engravers.

Their next joint project, *A Manual for the Study of Insects,* was published in 1895 to general acclaim. In that book Comstock received full credit from her husband in the preface when he referred to her as the "Junior Author," for she had prepared the engravings and assisted in the writing. Two years later Harry published *Insect Life,* a more popularly written book, which contained many of the same illustrations as the *Manual.*

Many critics suspect that more than just some of the text for those books was written by Comstock, since portions read much like her later books. For instance, one of her most humorous illustrations, that of treehoppers, appeared in the *Manual, Insect Life,* and in her *Handbook.* No doubt it was the "Junior Author" who wrote in the *Manual:* "Nature must have been in a joking mood when tree-hoppers were developed, for these little creatures are most comically grotesque in appearance. . . . If the young entomologist wishes to laugh, let him look at the faces of tree-hoppers through a lens. Their eyes always have a keen, droll look, and the line that separates the head from the pro-thorax gives them the appearance of wearing glasses."

The same year that *Insect Life* was published, Comstock was swept up into the Nature Study Movement, a project initiated to encourage New York state youngsters to stay on the farm instead of migrating to the city. Under the direction of Cornell's Liberty Hyde Bailey, Comstock worked to educate rural school teachers about nature so that they, in turn, could teach their students. Out of that effort came Comstock's 1911 *Handbook* which has gone through twenty-five editions and been translated into eight languages. Packed with information on every natural subject, it provides teachers with a wealth of information as well as 232 meticulously planned lessons, field trips, experiments, and questions to ask their students.

Yet despite Comstock's budding career as a nature study lecturer, both at Cornell and throughout the state, she and Harry continued to help each other on a variety of book projects aimed at popular audiences, such as Harry's *How to Know the Butterflies* and *The Spider Book* and Comstock's *Trees at Leisure, The Pet Book, How to Keep Bees,* her thinly veiled autobiographical novel *Confessions to a Heathen Idol,* and *Ways of the Six-Footed.*

"Partners in science as in life," Cornell students called the Comstocks when they dedicated their yearbook to them in 1929. By then Harry had been retired fifteen years and Comstock eight, after she had attained full professor status for her role in developing the Department of Nature Study at Cornell. In 1923 the League of Women Voters named her one of the twelve greatest women in America for her contributions to natural science.

Although Comstock was thoroughly scientific in her work, her nature writing for children was purposely romantic, poetic, artistic, and anthropomorphic because she believed such an approach would be more appealing to them. Still, she did not oversimplify her writing for her youthful audience. For example, in *Ways of the Six-Footed,* she used such words as "auto-cannibalistic" without explanation. Originally published in 1903, her book is a collection of ten articles she had written for children's periodicals on the habits of some of the more common and interesting insects.

She claimed in her preface that "the object of the volume is not to give new facts, but rather to give another standpoint for viewing the facts already known." Such views included her ideas about social justice; for instance, in "Two Mother Masons" she writes that "it is safe to assert that in the insect world the question of 'woman's rights' is settled in the affirmative," and in "The Perfect Socialism" she contrasts the apparent altruism of social insects with the acquisitiveness and competitiveness of humans. But she did choose subjects that she had personally observed so that she could "here and there . . . add something not before recorded."

"A Dweller in Tents," from *Ways of the Six-Footed,* discusses the basswood leaf-roller in Comstock's delightfully readable style and gives readers an insight into her methods of studying and illustrating her subjects. Her sense of humor, empathy with the caterpillar, and careful replacing of it beneath the same tree where she originally found

Portrait of Anna Botsford Comstock. *Courtesy Division of Rare and Manuscript Collections, Cornell University Library, Ithaca, New York.*

it indicate Comstock's lifelong reverence even for nature's humblest creatures.

A DWELLER IN TENTS

Near one of my favorite woodland paths stands a young basswood tree. Every summer, during the months of July and August, this tree presents a very strange and, if truth be told, a decidedly dishevelled appearance. At first glance it would seem as though each individual leaf had become dissatisfied with its form and had concluded to re-model itself according to its own caprice. Close inspection reveals but few leaves on the entire tree that retain their normal shape; and what is true of this tree is, I fear, true of many basswood trees each summer throughout the northern United States.

The cause of this ragged appearance of these handsome trees is, however, not to be attributed to rebellion and anarchy on the part of the leaves. The real agent is a lively little " worm," which cuts the leaf half across and makes the flap into a roll, wherein he lives and feeds, safe from the sharp eyes of hungry birds and from the vicissitudes of rain and wind.

This little householder has no doorplate to announce his name to the world; possibly because his house would afford scant room for the dignified name *Pantographa limata*. From this omission on his part to vaunt his real name he is commonly called the "Basswood Leaf-roller," that being our rather crude way of distinguishing his cater-pillarship from others of his kind which take possession of our forests in happy summer time.

One August day I plucked one of these rolled leaves with the in-tent of studying the inmate. I found the little tent-ropes of silk that fastened the roll down to the leaf were quite strong, requiring con-scious effort to tear them asunder as I made my way into the green tube. It was not until the leaf was entirely unrolled that I discovered the tenant. He was a handsome little creature according to caterpil-lar standards of beauty; his green body had an opalescent sheen that was most gemlike; and his head and thorax were vividly, aggressively black and shining. Notwithstanding my admiring glances he was not at all pleased to make my acquaintance and evinced his displeasure by twisting and wriggling most spitefully. He hurried this way and that, never taking the trouble to turn around, for he was quite as adept in "backing" as he was in going forward.

Finally he buried his head under a corner of the leaf and remained motionless. Evidently the beautiful philosophy of the ostrich was his also. However, he was soon made aware of the fallacy of this reasoning, for I proceeded to examine him in detail through my lens. I noted the shining tubercles, six on each segment, as seen from above, four in front and two behind, each one adorned with a bristle. I noted the alertness of the highly polished black head and the thoracic shield shining like ebony. I was interested to find that his six true feet were apparently encased in patent leathers, after the most approved and latest fashion in gentlemen's boots.

I found him so interesting that I rolled him up in his leaf and took him home and placed him in a box, intending to sketch him very soon. Alas, must I confess it? That very day I began a new and absorbing piece of work that crowded out all thoughts not relating to it, and I forgot all about my little leaf-roller for a week. I suddenly remembered him with a pang of remorse and hastened to him. I fully expected to find my prisoner a wasted corpse. But no! he had fastened his broken tent down again with silken ropes; then, finding the pasturage getting dry, had abandoned his old home and folded over and fastened a corner of the leaf, in vain hope of finding there fresher food. In this lesser tent I found him a little pale, it is true, but with spirit still undaunted. He greeted me with a spiteful jerk; this time his scornful rejection of my advances seemed justified. I sent immediately for fresh leaves and transferred him to one of them. In a very short time he had folded an edge of the leaf over himself and secured it with a web of silk. But he had concluded, evidently, that eating was not a safe indulgence in this uncertain world, for he refused to take even a nibble from his new pasture. It may be, however, that he had so far matured that he no longer needed food; possibly he was ready to seek a nook under leaves or earth in which to spend the winter, and was meditating upon the fact that the hand of fate which swept him from his native tree had placed him beyond the reach of earth in which to hide.

I first made a full-length portrait of him; a performance on my part which he manifestly regarded as an unpardonable liberty. I then made a detailed study of the head and thorax. To do this I placed him in a watch-glass, while I studied him through a compound microscope. While I looked he lifted his second booted leg in a deprecating way as if to say, "Is there then in this wide world no justice to be meted out to mortals who outrage the rights and persons of innocent caterpillars?"

I tried to put on paper this deprecatory attitude, but it was too subtle for my clumsy powers of delineation. In fact, he was from first to last a very bad "sitter" and very exhausting to the artist's patience. However, he was well worth the trouble he cost, for he was as interesting as

111

a harlequin in his vivid costume of black and green. The black face was made grotesque by ten little eyes of assorted sizes, placed in circles, each one shining like an opal. His black legs were adorned at the joints with what a costumer would call "slashes" that revealed a lining of green; on the segment nearest the body the black band was cut into gay points.

When I finished the sketch I rolled him in his leaf and took him out into the woods. Then, asking his pardon for inconveniencing him, wishing him a comfortable winter, a successful pupahood in the spring, and a final glorification into mothhood in June, I placed him under his own basswood tree.

The adult of *Pantographa limata* is a very pretty moth, with wings of delicate buff marked with olive-green. There is a beautiful purplish iridescence to the olive-green, which is a delight to the eye that loves delicate, suggestive color.

The interesting thing about this species from a scientific standpoint is that it has broken away from family traditions and become a leaf-roller. Most of the leaf-rolling caterpillars belong to the *Tortricina*, although rarely they are found in other families. Our little friend belongs to the *Pyralidina*, and has developed his leaf-rolling habit entirely independent of his ancestors or near relatives. If the individual which I studied fairly represents the species, I am not surprised at this original line of development; for in all my dealing with insect kind I have never met one of the "little brothers" who knew his own mind more clearly and conclusively than the subject of this sketch.

Further Reading

Comstock, Anna. *The Comstocks of Cornell.* Ithaca: Cornell University Press, 1953.
———. [Marian Lee, pseud.]. *Confessions to a Heathen Idol.* New York: Doubleday & Company, 1906.
———. *Handbook of Nature Study.* Ithaca: Cornell University Press, 1911.
———. *Ways of the Six-Footed.* Ithaca: Cornell University Press, 1977.
Comstock, Anna Botsford, and John Henry Comstock. Papers. Dept. of Manuscripts and University Archives, Cornell University Libraries, Ithaca, N.Y.
Mallis, Arnold. *American Entomologists.* New Brunswick, N.J.: Rutgers University Press, 1971.
Smith, Edward H. "Anna Botsford Comstock: Artist, Author, and Teacher." *American Entomologist* 2 (Summer, 1990): 105–13.

————. "The Comstocks and Cornell: In the People's Service." *Annual Review of Entomology* 21 (1976): 1–25.

12

Cordelia Stanwood

1865–1958

IN THE VOLUMINOUS FIELD NOTEBOOKS SHE KEPT from 1906 until 1956, Cordelia Stanwood called herself a "Watcher in the Woods," an apt term for the solitary and sensitive naturalist that she was.

After eighteen years of teaching elementary school in Massachusetts and New York state, she suffered a nervous breakdown, which forced her to return to her childhood home in Ellsworth, Maine. There she recovered her equilibrium by observing the birds that lived on the forty-acre property she called Birdsacre. Her newfound peace of mind was evident when she later wrote, "The find of a new bird always fills me with enthusiasm," and "the discovery of a rare and uncommonly handsome bird is an occasion for unwonted jubilation." During her first three years as an amateur ornithologist, she located the active nesting sites of a hundred species, compiling more observations on nesting life than any previous researcher. Although she rarely left her home grounds, she corresponded with most of the renowned naturalists and ornithologists of the time, such as John Burroughs, Edward Forbush, Albert O. Gross, Ralph Palmer, and Frank Chapman. In addition, her writing and observational abilities were championed by Althea Sherman, who also made certain her material was paid for and published in the *Wilson Bulletin*.

When Arthur Cleveland Bent began his monumental *Life Histories of North American Birds* series, he asked Stanwood to contribute chapters on the warblers, thrushes, and other songbirds she specialized in. Instead, she sent him her extensive notes, which he used to produce the bulk of the nesting observations for at least sixteen species, including the winter wren, red-breasted nuthatch, brown creeper, golden-crowned kinglet, olive-backed and hermit thrushes, and ten warbler species.

Despite her affectionate feelings for birds, she cautioned others of sentimentality, believing that "the scientific writer should be [careful] to verify all his surmises." In pursuit of this philosophy, she suffered torments from black flies and mosquitoes as she sat motionless for hours at a time in the Maine woods observing nesting songbirds.

She not only wrote about birds in both popular and scientific publications, but she also photographed them from a portable canvas blind she had designed and constructed. She then developed her own stunning black-and-white photographs of young red-breasted nuthatches, black-capped chickadees, broad-winged hawks, hermit thrushes, yellow-bellied flycatchers, magnolia warblers, and golden-crowned kinglets among others. She also photographed a wide variety of nests and used the photos to illustrate "What of the Nest?", an article she wrote in 1939 for *Nature.*

But no matter how hard she worked photographing and writing about birds and other natural subjects, she could not earn a decent livelihood. She spent long Maine winters weaving, dyeing, basket-making, hooking and braiding rugs, fashioning gloves, and constructing jewelry boxes and picture frames in burned woodwork, all of which she sold to increase her paltry income. She also raised chickens and bees, milked the family cow, and gardened, activities which led to "how-to" articles for such publications as *Farm Mechanics* and *American Poultry Journal.* Too proud to accept help from anyone, even her siblings, she was reduced in her old age to selling greeting cards from door to door.

Such activities, though, still remained peripheral to her central life among the birds. Even while her neighbors considered her odd and reclusive, the larger scientific world acknowledged her expertise in ornithology and photography. Edward Forbush, for instance, used thirty-eight of her bird photographs to illustrate his *Birds of Massachusetts and Other New England States,* and Francis Herrick, an expert on nest construction, asked her to supply nests for the museum at Western Reserve College in Cleveland, Ohio. Three years after her death in 1958, her work received a citation from the U.S. Department of the Interior, which acknowledged "the faithful service of Miss Cordelia Stanwood in reporting, for use in scientific investigations, observations on the distribution, migration and abundance of North American birds."

Hermit thrushes were Stanwood's special birds. She wrote: "When the thrush sings, I desire to live in a small, scrupulously neat camp, open to the sun and the wind and the voices of the birds. I would like to spend eternity thus, listening to the song of the thrush." "The

Cordelia Stanwood's homemade bird blind. *Courtesy Stanwood Wildlife Sanctuary, Ellsworth, Maine.*

Hermit Thrush: the Voice of the Northern Woods" was her first published bird study in 1910. It was accepted for publication by Frank Chapman, author of *Birds of Eastern North America* and then-editor of *Bird-Lore*, the official publication of the National Audubon Society. The piece begins poetically with a wonderfully evocative description of the hermit thrush's song and continues with a detailed account of her five-year study of nesting hermit thrushes. This pleasing blend

116

Photograph of black-capped chickadee feeding young, taken by Cordelia Stanwood. *Courtesy Stanwood Wildlife Sanctuary, Ellsworth, Maine.*

of popular and scientific writing set the standard for Stanwood's style over the decades to follow.

"Tenants of Birdsacre," written ten years later for *House Beautiful*, includes Stanwood's valuable observations of nesting black-capped chickadee behavior. It also displays some of the best examples of her photographic work, with an explanation of how she obtained the pictures.

THE HERMIT THRUSH: THE VOICE OF THE NORTHERN WOODS

In the Canadian fauna, the Hermit Thrush, the most definite Thrush to study, comes a month before the Olive-backed [now Swainson's] thrush arrives, while the snow-wraiths still linger in the shadowy forests, before the arbutus has begun its subtle task of transmuting decaying earth molds into rough leaves, waxen petals, and delicate perfume, and stands out against a background of well-nigh silent woods. It tarries as long after its congener has departed. Again it is in the foreground of a landscape, accented by dry rustling leaves and naked tree trunks, with but few birds to rival it in our attention.

When the Hermit Thrush makes its début in the spring, its song is wonderfully sweet, but it does not come into full possession of its voice until some time after its arrival. In early August, it is still in full song. It was in the gloaming, August 4, 1909, that I stole upon one of the most ethereal demonstrations of the Hermit Thrush I ever witnessed. My narrow footway lay through a stretch of evergreen woods, interspersed with a few birches and poplars. The birds were perched at different heights on the side of the woods illumined by the sinking sun, and seemed to vie each with [the] other in hymning its glories. Each burst of melody was more indescribably perfect. Before the last cadence of one song died on the air, a pure, serene exalted paean of praise burst forth from another golden throat. The air palpitated with Thrush harmonies. I paused and passed on unobserved in the quickly gathering shadows, my footsteps falling noiselessly on pine leaf and moss-tuft. By August 14, the song is thin, suggesting the imperfect attempts of a young bird. Later than that the Hermit Thrush seldom sings.

It is to be regretted that so many of the young fail to mature. A record kept for five years, containing the history of fourteen nests and forty-seven eggs, shows that only nineteen fledglings left the nest. The offspring of twenty-eight birds were nineteen. My notes on Olive-backed Thrush and Robin show even more fatal data, as their nests are larger and most of them so badly exposed. I wish to emphasize the fact that these very beautiful, insectivorous birds lead a most precarious existence, having to contend not only with wild foes but with the ever-prevalent, half-fed cat.

The Hermit Thrush usually nests in open spaces in an unfrequented wood, beside a wood-road or even a quiet street, and on the borders of pastures skirted by woodlands. The nest is placed, generally, under a low fir tree, occasionally under the tip of a long fir branch, rarely in a clump of ferns. A swamp appears to be a necessary concomitant. Seven nests were located in a knoll, two in a damp hollow, and six just above the swale in the dry earth of a hillside. In almost every case, the slight excavation for the foundation of the nest was made in the loam of a decayed log or stump.

The nests are very much alike. The outside of the structure is composed of moss, dead wood, twigs and hay; it is lined with a small amount of black, hair-like fiber, and pine needles. Once or twice the foundation of the nest consisted of more than the ordinary amount of moss. At another time it was made almost entirely of sticks or twigs. Fourteen were lined with pine needles, one with the red fruit stems of bird wheat moss, and bird wheat moss [itself]. The proportions of all nests are about the same. The one constructed entirely of twigs was about a half-inch thicker at the top than the others.

In two or three cases, I have found the Hermit Thrush very timid. Generally, the bird flies from the nest as a person approaches, or runs away over the leaves with head and tail drawn down, to appear less conspicuous, mounts a branch at a safe distance, regards one a few instants, while it slowly raises and lowers its tail, then glides from sight. One or two have been so tame that I have had to put my hand out, as if to touch them, to drive them from the nest.

In 1907, beginning June 14, I found five nests, the last on July 1. Each clutch of this year contained three eggs. Either the eggs or the young were destroyed in all these nests save one, and that, I believe, was the second nest of the bird that season. The fate of the other two nests was a great disappointment. In the hope of finding one more, I entered the next pasture, and turned over each small fir carefully, to see if its fragrant branches concealed one of the coveted abodes. Under almost the first fir, I saw a large beautifully made nest with the lining of the bottom and side torn out. Here was another defeat; but, behold! On the top of a knoll a few yards away was what appeared to be a freshly made nest. I concluded that these were both nests of the Hermit Thrush; that the first nest I found had been destroyed, that the bird went away a short distance and constructed a second, that the accident had befallen the bird so lately that she had barely succeeded in completing the new nest. I was exceedingly anxious to know if I had been wise enough to read a tragedy and its sequel aright from these few facts, so I visited the knoll each day; the fourth day, there was the egg of a Hermit Thrush. Two days later, at noon, the bird was sitting on three eggs. On the twelfth day, July 10, two birds were out of the eggs by noon. They were large birds, covered with a sparse growth of burnt-umber down about one-fourth long. On the fifth day, the birds had quills on the wings and pinfeathers on the back. The eleventh morning, July 20, the last nestling left the nest in the afternoon.

A space for the nest was hollowed in a bit of decayed root or log, under a fir tree, beside a stump in the top of a knoll, overgrown with bird wheat moss and boulder fern. For foundation, the nest had a mass of dead wood, dead leaves, moss, roots, and fern stipes; for lining, pine needles and black hair-like plant fiber.

The diameters within were two and one-half inches by three and one-fourth inches, depth three inches. The thickness of the walls at the top was one inch, at the bottom one-half inch. Nearly all these measurements were taken before the eggs were laid.

June 2, 1908, I flushed from the nest a most gentle Hermit Thrush, incubating four eggs.

June 7, there were three nestlings in the nest, burnt-orange in color, marked with long, very dark-brown down. On the third day the eyelids of the young Thrushes were parted in the center one-sixteenth of an inch. The feather tracts were of the hue of gunpowder, the spaces between the feather tracts a tone of burnt-orange.

The fifth day the eyes of the young birds were well open; very dark brown pin-feathers were beginning to show through all the feather spaces; the pin-feathers were longest in the center of the tract and shortest on the edges; they looked, at this stage, like horse-hairs slightly overlapping each other.

The sixth day the quills were longer and fuller. The seventh day the tips of the quills and pin-feathers had burst, so that in the morning the tips of the speckled, olive-brown and golden-buffy feathers showed.

The tenth day the young Thrushes opened their mouths wide for food, as usual, at my approach, but on the eleventh day, the nestlings did not attempt to open their beaks for food in the morning or afternoon. This was the first time they showed any indication of fear.

On the twelfth day. The young Thrushes were gone by 9 o'clock this morning. The nest was immaculate, save for the quill scales that filled the interstices. It was placed in a knoll, under a miniature fir, just off a street not much frequented, in an open space in a growth where firs, pines and spruces predominate.

Generally, I find my nests of the Hermit Thrush by turning over trees and looking under the branches. In such cases, or when the Thrush is flushed from the nest, if she is merely incubating, she usually disappears quietly. When the young are in the nest, the bird acts more disturbed, often mounting a stump or branch, and calling *chuck! chuck! chuck!* or sometimes *p-e-e-p! p-e-e-p!* This almost always attracts the attention of her mate and the other Thrushes, who respond in numbers, and join their calls to the chorus of *chucks* and *peeps.* I have known the bird, however, to fly away almost without a protest, even when the young were taken from the nest.

August 22, 1909, while gathering blueberries for the tame Thrushes, I flushed a Hermit Thrush from her nest, containing three eggs. This is the latest date on which I have found the Hermit Thrush nesting.

August 27, three young were hatched; twelve days later, September 8, the nestlings left the nest before 9 o'clock.

The time of incubation, as one can readily see from the above record, is twelve days; the young remain in the nest twelve days, and leave early in the morning, as a general thing. One egg is laid each day about ten o'clock in the morning, and the bird begins to incubate by 12 o'clock of the day the clutch is completed.

I have found the number of eggs in a set to vary from four to two. I should judge from the nesting dates I have gathered that the Hermit Thrush, like its cousin the Robin, raises from two to three broods during a season.

TENANTS OF BIRDSACRE

Of the many and varied tenants that lease a building-site at Birdsacre from year to year, no one of them is more beloved than the cheerful, little black-capped chickadee. The chickadee is the first love of all beginners in bird-study. The very fact that he is one of our earliest attachments in the bird-world endears him to us the more since it is proverbial that man loves his old friends best.

The popularity of chickadee is due in great degree to his accessibility. He remains with us the year round. He never changes his garb in youth or age, summer or winter, and he always announces his name in a gentle, confiding, cheerful way that is entirely captivating, as soon as he has the slightest opportunity.

> "... piped a tiny voice hard by,
> Gay and polite, a cheerful cry,
> Chic-chicadeedee!"

What more could the most obtuse novice in bird-lore demand of any bird?

During the bitter winter weather, a bit of suet draws this animated "scrap of valor" to the lilac several times a day where his joyful chatter, "*Suet-for-me! Chickadee, dee, dee!*" gladdens many a prosy hour. But chickadee does more than cheer the landscape with his plump presence, and brighten one's mental atmosphere with his pretty refrains. Chickadee renders valuable service these winter days. He eats the eggs of the moths that would destroy our fruit and foliage when he finds them hidden in the crevices of the bark and around the tender buds, and I have seen him attack the great, leathery cocoon of the Polyphemous moth on a frosty winter morning, tear a good-sized hole in it, and feast on the larva hidden so securely within. The mite of a bird that looks so helpless in the midst of a vast world of snow and ice, is doing the work it would take a wise man to accomplish, and he sings while he labors! How much we are indebted to this little friend in feathers!

Last spring a pair of chickadees continued to haunt the lilacs, the honeysuckle and the rosebushes around the house. On a morning in early May I heard one of them chittering so persistently, I glanced out the window of Birdsacre Cottage just in time to see a plump little bird with gray back, white wing-bars, black cap and chin, and white underparts tinged with the palest of buffy tints on the sides, busily shredding a bit of cotton wadding. This the bird held down with her feet while tearing off fragments with her bill until the fluffy mass bulged out all around her beak.

I say her, because the female bird is nearly always more gentle than the male bird, and rather more anxious to get the cradle ready for the pretty cream-white eggs with the minute brown freckles all over them. This jolly chickadee never ceased calling to her mate as she picked the cotton; therefore, I knew it must be Mrs. Chickadee. When she had gathered all her beak would hold, she flew to an apple tree near, and laid the cotton on a limb, where she again shredded it carefully. Would that cotton ever be sufficiently fine and fluffy to furnish her dainty abode?

By this time the mate was fluttering in and out of the apple tree, also, and the two twittering birds, the female bearing the cotton in her beak, flew away in the direction of some gray birches that grew along an old, stone wall above the cottage. There they disappeared.

Instantly I dropped my work, opened the door, and stole away in the wake of the birds. Before many minutes I had reached the wall and was greatly elated to quickly discover a dilapidated birch-stub that I thought might be the abode of the wee, brave homesteaders. Upon close inspection, however, it proved to have been occupied some previous spring. Nothing daunted, I continued along the wall, and a few minutes later came upon another stump, not unlike the first. The top of the bole was about five feet above the ground and slanted toward the rising sun. In the strong morning light, I could see that the birds had hollowed it to the depth of about ten inches, and were lining it with fern down, fine hair, and some moss. The tuft of cotton batting had been dropped into the bottom, and was ready to be pressed into place, but the birds were nowhere around. They had undoubtedly gone for more lining stuffs.

For a number of years I had been planning to photograph some young chickadees. Here was a nest so charmingly situated that it looked as if it had been made to my order! The old, weathered stump against the lichen-covered wall, presided over by two merry chickadees was indeed a subject worthy of the camera. So, very happy, I returned to my work, but said nothing of the pretty secret the old stub by the stone wall was guarding so carefully.

I had found chickadees nesting so many times, I knew about what their plans were. It was necessary to visit them only occasionally to keep in touch with their home affairs.

The nineteenth day of May, I peeped into the stub, but at first could discern nothing. The cavity was so small at the base, I began to doubt that the birds were really occupying it. As I grew accustomed to the dim light, however, I discerned a bright eye regarding me intently. The brooding bird filled the nest so completely that she held her tail flat against the wall of the hutch. It resembled a bit of weathered stick! The bird was incubating! Although I had visited the nest before, I never had seen an egg. The chickadees are so cautious that the female, after laying an egg, draws the lining materials over it carefully before leaving the nest. And not content with these precautions, although the nest is in a deep, dim hole in an old weathered stump, the last spot in the world where one would think of looking for a softly cushioned seraglio, the careful parent birds begin to brood soon after the first egg is laid, each taking his turn at the task. The chickadee mates share all burdens and pleasures as nearly equally as birds can.

Such rainy weather followed! Two days at a time, with only a break of a few sunny hours, the rain fell in sheets. Always I found one of them shielding the precious eggs without so much as a leaf to protect him from the storm. Could the chickadees survive this constant exposure to the severe weather, I wondered? Even if they lived, would the eggs keep dry and warm? The stump slanted to the southeast, the direction from which the storms came. I feared the small house would become flooded.

The last day of May, I happened to think of the lodge by the wall, and wandered in that direction. Seating myself on a granite boulder near the stub, I waited. Soon I heard "*Phee-bee!*" Then the sweet whistle drew nearer—"*Phee-bee!*" A faint, answering "*Phee-bee!*" and the waiting mate perched on the rim of the nest with a beakful of caterpillars and crane-flies. The sitting bird, after partaking of the dainties, flew away, and the fresh bird took up her duties. Before long, the female called her mate from a nearby apple tree, and both birds flitted away for a few moments.

I took this opportunity to peer into the stub. To my great joy I saw four, limp, pale-orange chicks about as large as bumblebees. The faithful parent chickadees had won out!

For the first time I was able to determine when I should be able to photograph the little family, if no foes discovered them. Young chickadees remain in the nest about fifteen days. In two weeks the nestlings would be large enough to have their photographs taken. How pleased the boy who helps me take pictures would be when he learned of the pretty family in the old stump!

At last the time was propitious! The birds were so gentle, the boy and I placed the camera near the nest without any screen to conceal it, but as the sun remained on the stub but a few minutes, we had to try several mornings before we secured prints of the mature birds. The boy and I were kept very busy placing the youngsters. As soon as we posed them in focus, one or both parent birds returned with immense caterpillars and moths in their beaks, and perching in trees behind and above the young birds, called "*Chickadee, dee, dee!*" vigorously, causing the youngsters to twist their heads around, flap their wings, and flutter off the perch into the grass in every direction, like so many bits of thistledown. The boy found them and returned them to the branch, I do not know how many times. It was also his duty to determine which babe posed most successfully that we might catch his likeness in different positions. At last, he selected one, a pert little chickadee who acted as if he would like to pose forever. Him, we snapped again and again. By the time we had exposed the last plate, most of the babes were very sleepy, and upon being put back into the nest, snuggled down blissfully, but the pert little chickadee hopped out of the nest as fast as we put him back. At last we decided to let him sit on a branch over the stump. He remained very quiet until a parent chickadee appeared with crane-flies, when he flew up into the tree to meet him, and was lost in the foliage. I knew that by the following day the whole family would be on the wing. The chickadees continued to twitter and gather food in the shrubbery round Birdsacre Cottage all summer.

FURTHER READING

Bonta, Marcia. "Cordelia Stanwood: Pioneer Student of Nesting Behavior." *Bird Watcher's Digest* 5 (May–June, 1983): 40–46.

Graham, Frank, Jr. "Squire of Birdsacre." *Audubon* 81 (November, 1979): 24, 29.

Hutchinson, Gloria. "Birdsacre." *Down East* 27 (September, 1980): 52–59.

Labbie, Edith. "The Lady of 'Birdsacre' Sanctuary." *Lewiston Journal* (November 19, 1977): 1A, 3A.

Richmond, Chandler. *Beyond the Spring: Cordelia Stanwood of Birdsacre.* Lamoine, Maine: Latona Press, 1978.

Stanwood, Cordelia. "The Hermit Thrush: The Voice of the Northern

Woods." *Bird Lore* 12 (May–June, 1910): 100–04.

————. Papers. Stanwood Wildlife Foundation. Ellsworth, Maine.

————. "Tenants of Birdsacre." *House Beautiful* 48 (October, 1920): 280–82.

13

Agnes Chase

1869–1963

BOTANICAL COLLECTOR YNES MEXIA ONCE DESCRIBED agrostologist Agnes Chase disparagingly after the two women had spent a couple days collecting together in Brazil. Mexia wrote that Chase was "almost a human grass . . . who lives, sleeps, dreams nothing but grasses and writing a book on them." Certainly, during Chase's two collecting trips to Brazil between 1924 and 1925 and again between 1929 and 1930, she claimed to have made "by far the largest collection of grasses ever brought out of Brazil"—4,500 species—adding at least 10 percent to the world's knowledge of Brazilian grasses. But she also collected thousands of other botanical specimens.

Chase had, after all, begun her career as a general botanical collector and illustrator for the first in a series of supportive male mentors—bryologist Rev. Ellsworth Jerome Hill. He had needed someone to draw the new species he had discovered, and Chase, a young widow in her twenties at the time, offered to assist him. She had originally taken up plant-collecting as a hobby after her teenage nephew, Virginius Chase, had urged her to join him. She became increasingly knowledgeable in various plant species and eventually specialized in the flora of northern Illinois, her native state, and northern Indiana.

Although Hill could not afford to pay Chase for what turned out to be excellent illustrations, he did share his knowledge of botany with her and taught her how to use a compound microscope. He also introduced her to her second male mentor, Charles Frederick Millspaugh, curator of botany at the Field Museum of Natural History in Chicago. Recognizing her artistic talent, he persuaded her to illustrate, again without pay, two botanical museum publications.

In 1903 Hill convinced Chase to apply for an opening as a botanical illustrator at the USDA Bureau of Plant Industry in Washington, D.C. She easily obtained the position because she scored the highest grade on the qualifying test. A short two years later she was already collaborating with Bureau agrostologist Albert Spear Hitchcock, her third and most powerful male mentor. She remained a botanical illustrator until 1907, when she was appointed as Hitchcock's scientific assistant in systematic agrostology.

For the next twenty-eight years Hitchcock and Chase worked closely together on his monumental *Manual of Grasses of the United States,* which was lavishly illustrated by Chase's drawings. In pursuit of information for the book, both Hitchcock and Chase collected extensively in the United States, but they also worked on classifying grass specimens sent to the USDA grass herbarium from all over the world.

Although Hitchcock did most of the foreign collecting, he did send Chase to Puerto Rico in 1913, to Europe in 1922, and to Brazil. Another trip to Europe in 1935 and Venezuela in 1940 completed Chase's periods abroad. Each trip was a source of joy and discovery to her, and she shared her experiences in letters and journal articles. During her second trip to Brazil, she briefly ventured farther south into Paraguay and Argentina. Although she found Brazil's Mato Grosso province to be the best place for grasses, she wrote to Hitchcock that "the midges and mosquitoes were something terrible and to go down into the marsh and stir up more of them, literally clouds of them, took all the nerve I had."

After Hitchcock's death in 1935, Chase inherited his position at the Bureau until her official retirement in 1939. She continued working without pay, however, for twenty-four more years. During that time she revised not only Hitchcock's book but her own popularly-written *The First Book of Grasses,* which had originally been published in 1922. She also wrote the preface for and consulted on the *1948 Department of Agriculture Year Book* volume, entitled *Grass.* She catalogued and filled insect-proof steel cases with the 10,031 grass-type specimens which she herself had first described, and she completed and revised a card index on grasses.

She received her first college degree, an honorary Doctor of Science from the University of Illinois in 1958, when she was eighty-nine years old. Reflecting on her newly acquired degree, she told *New York Times* reporter Bess Furman that "girls didn't get to go to college, when I was young. . . . I had to just pick up my education as I went along." She was also made the eighth Honorary Fellow of the Smithsonian Institution and a fellow of the Linnaean Society of London.

Portrait of Agnes Chase with herbarium grass specimens and a hand lens.
Courtesy Smithsonian Institution Archives, Record Unit 95.

At the age of ninety-one, she wrote prophetically to a niece, "If I had any sense I'd quit the herbarium and grasses, but it would be easier to stop breathing," which is exactly what she did when she finally resigned four years later. Agnes Chase, one of five children raised by her poor widowed mother and grandmother and fed a sparse childhood diet that occasionally consisted of only oatmeal, had become, by the end of her life, the "dean of American agrostologists" and the object of respect by fellow scientists from all over the world.

The following excerpt is a lively account of her first expedition to Brazil. In it she provides valuable information on several aspects of exploration and research. She describes her collecting techniques and her impressions of the people and the countryside. She tells her readers that she is not only a student of tropical North American plants but that she also has a special interest in the flora of eastern Brazil because of plant species it shares in common with Panama and the West Indies. She even provides a brief history of previous Brazilian scientific expeditions, then launches into the details of her own experiences. Her trip began when she arrived in Rio de Janeiro on November 1, 1924. From then until May 31, 1925, she traveled by foot, car, train, dugout canoe, muleback, and even hand-pushed trolley car to reach the inaccessible marshes, savannas, and mountain peaks in pursuit of new grass species. By the end of the account, the reader cannot help but marvel at her undaunting courage and limitless energy.

EASTERN BRAZIL THROUGH AN AGROSTOLOGIST'S SPECTACLES

Through the kindness of Dr. Campos Porto, Miss Bandeira[1] and I were able to visit Itatiaia, the great mountain that rises where the States of Rio de Janeiro, São Paulo, and Minas Geraes touch. The journey from Rio de Janeiro, to Barão Homem de Mello (Campo Bello—the nome[n]clature of Brazilian towns being like that of plants, with numerous changes of names and consequent synonyms) was through jungle-clad mountains and across rocky streams. From Barão Homem de Mello we started on horseback toward the towering mountain mass to the north, our collecting outfit following on a pack horse. We had charming views of Rio Campo Bello far down the narrow valley below and could hear its tumbling waters. The slopes were mostly forested with different species of palms, especially a very slender one that grows in clumps, suggesting gigantic clumps of sugarcane. We reached the Florestal on Monte Serrat about 4 o'clock. From Monte Serrat (816 meters altitude) to the summit of the mountain and for some miles beyond on the Minas Geraes side the country is a Federal reserve under the charge of the Jardim Botanico. The Florestal is a sort of forest station and experiment station combined, where scientific work is carried on under the direction of Dr. Paulo Campos Porto. The station is a long low building, with pleasant living rooms, a laboratory, library, and dark room, surrounded by gardens. There are great groves of *Araucaria brasiliensis,* beautiful against a background of blue mountains or white mist. From the Florestal there is a vast outlook up the mountains and down over a sea of lower hills.

The next morning we left shortly after 8 o'clock with two pack animals bearing camping and collecting outfits. It had rained during the night and masses of white mist hung between the mountains, the nearby araucarias outlined against them. The trail was difficult, up over stones and through deep mud or across streams. It was necessarily slow going so I did not have to give much attention to the horse, but could keep my eyes on the forested slopes above and below, with their palms, tree ferns and great masses of hanging bamboo, and on the trail border where *Panicum, Ichnanthus* and a silvery *Paspalum* promised rich collecting on the way back. Once we saw down the steep slope below a dark brown monkey up a palm tree so slender that it swayed under his weight, and a second running up the trunk. They looked at us and chattered—then one climbed down, while the upper one spread his little arms and sprang from the tree, sailing down (it must have been forty or fifty feet) into the top of another palm. A third, then a fourth monkey ran up the same palm, turned to look at us and made the same leap, while one, just glimpsed lower down, kept calling or scolding.

We stopped at a mud-hut resthouse at a place called Macieiras (the place of apples) because the Jardim has planted an apple orchard on the hillside here. It was a grassy and a mossy place and Miss Bandeira and I collected until called to supper at about dark. Macieiras is about 1,900 meters altitude and the grasses were northern or alpine genera, *Agrostis, Calamagrostis, Danthonia, Bromus,* and the like.

About 7 in the morning we started up the mountain on horseback, and in less than an hour were above the timberline. We passed glowing gardens of a big red *Ilippeastrum* (an ally of *Amaryllis*), three or four flowers in a cluster, often all open; lovely meadows of an *Erigeron* that comes out white and turns rose pink, and masses of a yellow composite. At Itatiaia Alta, a great stretch of gentle slope, full of boulders and with great clumps of *Cortaderia modesta*, we left the horses near two tiny lakes.

Above Itatiaia Alta the peak, called Agulhas Negras (the black needles), rises abruptly, composed below of steep, bare granite cliffs, deeply furrowed vertically. We climbed up the furrows on all fours and crossed from one series to another over steep slopes covered with a low bamboo (*Chusquea pinifolia*) most convenient to cling to. At the top of these furrowed cliffs is a great overhanging rock that seemed to stop all progress, but the way led through a crevice to one side and over and between boulders wedged in the crevice. The worst place was like a chimney flue, which we ascended with the help of a rope.

The view from the summit was magnificent, mountains everywhere, in all directions, from dark granite or green slopes near to wonderful blues in the distance. From under a cloud we looked out on the Minas side on mountains glowing in sunshine, as far as the eye could reach, like looking into the sunshine from under a vast parasol.

At the summit was dwarfed *Chusquea pinifolia,* the only grass, a pink *Oxalis,* a tiny cactus (*Epiphyllanthus candidus*), a little fern, bromeliads, an ericaceous plant resembling *Gaultheria* with lovely pink flowers, two carices, and a composite. In wet mossy rocks coming down I collected *Poa, Agrostis,* and *Bromus.*

Reaching Itatiaia Alta again an excellent hot meal awaited us by a clear cold streamlet—this was mountaineering de luxe. Here, above timberline, grasses were abundant. I made the return journey afoot, collecting as rapidly as possible, for night shuts down quickly in the Tropics.

The next morning I started down afoot with my portfolio. The way was long and grasses many, so I had to walk and collect at top speed, reaching the Florestal just before dark with bulging portfolio, a big handkerchief tied around a bundle, and an armful besides.

It rained hard during the night and in the morning the mountain tops were hidden by the mist, but the araucarias are at their best with white mist for background. I started again immediately after café to collect on the way down to Barão Homem de Mello, where we were to take the noon train.

Baggage regulations on Brazilian railroads are the despair of a foreigner. One's clothing goes on the train with the passenger, but other baggage follows on a later train. My clothing was of no consequence, while my precious collections would spoil if I could not take them with me to dry. By some kind of magic Dr. Campos Porto got all my collections on our train, and I heartily wished that I had more Portuguese than *muito obrigada* and *agradecida* at my command to thank him for the wonderful trip and for this crowning favor. . . .

On April 6 I left Bello Horizonte for Ouro Preto, the old capital of Minas, the "Villa Rica" of Martius[2] and other early travelers. Though only about 100 kilometers to the southwest the country was very different, being granite and red clay. One day in the Ouro Preto hills and the next by horse to Itacolumi, the high peak (1,752 meters) to the southeast, where again I had a rich harvest on high open campos and rocky slopes, and then I left the Zona do Campo for Viçosa in the Zona da Matta. Dr. P. H. Rolfs, formerly director of the Experiment Station at Gainesville, Fla., is building up a school of agriculture for the State of Minas Geraes at Viçosa. The country is much more fertile and more densely populated than the Bello Horizonte country. Here Ceiba and quaresma (*Tibouchina* sp.) were in bloom. I had missed them in Serra do Curral and Serra de Cipo. I was fortunate here in being the guest of the Rolfs family. The swampy places and borders of the second growth forests (chaparão) that clothed the hills afforded good collecting. Two days were spent at Anna Florencia to the northeast, and then with Doctor Rolfs and his daughter I made a trip to Serra da Gramma, some 60 kilometers east of Viçosa, in the Serra Sebastião. We stayed at a fazenda, two days' journey on horseback from São Miguel, stopping over night, going and returning, at Araponga. (This musical name is that of the anvil bird of the region.) The trail led through forested hills often hung with bamboos. We reached the fazenda in the middle of the afternoon and had time to botanize for a few hours. The third day we rode to the base of Serra da Gramma, then proceeded afoot—a man to cut the trail, the old fazendeiro to help him, the guide, three men from Viçosa, Doctor Rolfs and his daughter, and I. For some distance we followed the rocky bed of a stream then struck into the virgin forest. This was the real tropical jungle of the school geographies, dense and dark, with palms, tree ferns, vines, and bamboos all tangled together, with brilliant bromeliads up the trees, and multitudes of ferns. From about 1,500 meters altitude the bamboos made the climbing difficult and fatiguing. The very steep trail was cut but there was no time to clear it, and we tripped and stumbled or sank into soft humus, up and up, then slipping and sliding down into a deep ravine, then climbing up again. We were nearly exhausted when light appeared ahead and we knew we were nearing the open summit. But the "campo" we were expecting was composed for some distance of dense brush up to our waists—almost what we would term chaparral. It was nearly dark when we passed the brush and came to open, grassy ground. It was too dark to go down hill for water, so we made camp without it. When streaks of scarlet appeared in the sky I was glad to get up and start collecting. Everything was wet with dew and it was like working in ice water, but there was too much to collect to wait for the sun.

There are three peaks; we had camped on the lowest. We ascended the second through dense chusqueal (tangled *Chusquea*), but did not have time for the third, which appeared to be very like the second. On the way down the trail through the forest I found a single *Chusquea* in flower—it is always cause for rejoicing when one finds bamboos in flower—and a few other grasses.

On the return journey to Araponga and the following day to São Miguel the cavalcade halted when I wanted to collect, and it was frequently, for there were two bamboos with flowers, one a beautiful slender vine, *Chusquea capitata*, besides numerous other grasses.

A few days after our return from Serra da Gramma, Miss Rolfs and I left for a trip to Pico de Bandeira, the culminating point of Serra da Caparao, the mountain range which separates Minas Geraes and

132

Espirito Santo to the east. It is claimed by recent topographers to be the highest point in Brazil, 2,884 meters in altitude. The village of Caparaó, the railroad station nearest the peak, lies only about 150 kilometers east of Viçosa, but to reach it we had to spend two days on the railroad, stopping over night at Uba and again at Santa Luzia Carangola, covering two long sides of a triangle to reach the other end of a short base. It was this paucity of railroads that prevented me from carrying out the extended itinerary I had planned in Brazil. Doctor Rolfs sent with us a reliable youth from the school farm, and at Caparaó we hired three riding mules, a pack mule, and a guide, who had to go afoot, because another animal could not be procured. We bought food to last three or four days, and next morning, May 1, we started about half-past 10.

Caparaó is only 814 meters in altitude, lying in a hollow between two ridges. For an hour or so the trail led up through partly cultivated or pastured hills, then, as we rose higher, through virgin forests with palms and an occasional *Araucaria* standing out alone. A high-climbing leguminous vine, with brilliant scarlet flowers about 2 inches long in loose pendant racemes 6 to 10 inches long, was frequent in places, and the gorgeous purple quaresmas (*Tibouchina* sp.) were still in bloom—the last I was to see of them. The trail became obscure, and Miss Rolf's questioning brought out the fact that the "guide" sent with us had never been this far on the trail. There was a resthouse below the peak where we expected to spend the night; this we had been told we could reach in three hours and a half, but darkness came on with no resthouse in sight, so we camped on a shoulder of the mountain, with plenty of down timber, which enabled us to keep a big fire going all night—a great comfort, as it rained till midnight and then cleared and turned very cold. The barometer showed that we were at about 2,100 meters altitude. In the morning a herder hunting stray horses put us on the trail to the resthouse.

The resthouse was a low hut of upright sticks, partly chinked with mud, the roof a combination of wooden shingles and sheets of zinc. Horses had been in the hut so we had to clean it out; then we floored it with shingles we found outside, made a fire in the stone and clay mound designed for that purpose, and had dinner. It drizzled all afternoon but this mountain meadow was rich in grasses and compositae, so I collected, bringing armfuls into the hut to put in press and write up.

The night in this "resthouse" was less comfortable than the preceding night in the open, for the roof above the "stove" was of shingles, and in my efforts to warm the hut I had nearly set fire to it, so we had to discourage the fire and nearly froze. In the morning, leaving the useless "guide" at the hut, Miss Rolfs, José, the boy from Viçosa, and I started for the Pico. *Chusquea pinifolia* began some distance below our first camp and continued up the mountain, the plants becoming dwarfed at higher altitudes. This species was abundant on Itatiaia, but here I found it in flower for the first time. A second species of *Chusquea* (*C. tenuis*), with tall arching culms and narrow blades, was also in flower.

From the resthouse and for some distance below we had seen a high pyramidal peak, much the highest in sight. The trail led through a saddle between this peak and a ridge opposite, obscured in clouds. We deliberated as to which side we should climb (there is no detailed map of the region) and decided in favor of the towering pyramidal peak. It was a hard climb but presented no such difficulties as those encountered on Agulhas Negras, and this agreed with accounts of Pico de Bandeira. But at the summit the clouds lifted for a few minutes from the opposite ridge and it was higher than we were. We learned later that we had climbed Pontão Crystal, 2,798 meters high, instead of Pico de Bandeira, 2,884 meters high. There was no time to ascend the other ridge, nor food enough to allow us to remain another day. The botanizing on Pontão Crystal was probably as good as on the Pico so I probably did not lose much, still it was disappointing. We reached the resthouse about 2 o'clock, packed at once, and started back down the mountain.

At the clean little hotel at Caparaó the following day I got my great stacks of plants in press ready for the train at 3. After a night at Santa Luzia Carangola, where the hard beds seemed soft by comparison with our recent ones, we parted in the early morning, Miss Rolfs and José returning to Viçosa, I bound for Rio de Janeiro. . . .

May 31, rejoicing in what I had found and regretting what I had not (Doctor Rolfs says a botanist is never satisfied), I sailed for home. A compiled list of grasses known from Brazil contains about 1,100 species. In the few points of eastern Brazil visited I collected between 500 and 600 species. The grass flora of Brazil must be far greater than at present known and would well repay further exploration.

NOTES

1. María Bandeira, daughter of a prominent Rio De Janeiro doctor, had been educated in England. When Chase visited Brazil, María was studying mosses at Rio's Jardim Botanico and accompanied Chase on her botanical explorations nearby.
2. Carl Friedrich Philipp von Martius (1794–1868), German botanist

and traveler, was sent to Brazil to collect plants in 1817 by the king of Bavaria. He and J. B. von Spix traveled together from Rio de Janeiro through several of the southern and eastern provinces of Brazil and ascended the Amazon River to Tabatinga.

FURTHER READING

Chase, Agnes. "Collecting Grasses in Brazil." *Journal of the New York Botanical Garden* 26 (September, 1925): 196–98.

———. "Eastern Brazil through an Agrostologist's Spectacles." *Annual Report of the Smithsonian Institution 1926* (1927): 383–403.

———. *The First Book of Grasses.* 3d ed. Washington, D.C.: Smithsonian Institution Press, 1959.

———. Papers. Smithsonian Institution Archives, Washington, D.C.

———. "Studying the Grasses of Venezuela." *Explorations and Field-Work of the Smithsonian Institution in 1940.* Washington, D.C.: Smithsonian Institution.

———. "Visit to European Herbaria." *Smithsonian Miscellaneous Collections* 54 (1923): 80–82.

Fosburgh, F. R., and Jason R. Swallen. "Agnes Chase." *Taxon* 8 (June, 1959): 145–51.

Harney, Thomas. *The Magnificent Foragers.* Washington, D.C.: The National Museum of Natural History, Smithsonian Institution, 1978.

14

Ynes Mexia

1870–1938

"SHE WAS THE TRUE EXPLORER TYPE AND HAPPIEST when independent and far from civilization. She always made light of the privations and dangers," wrote botanist T. Harper Goodspeed in his book, *Plant Hunters in the Andes,* about botanical collector Ynes Mexia. Mexia would have agreed wholeheartedly with Goodspeed's posthumous assessment of her.

"I am not a dyed-in-the-wool scientist, I am a nature lover and a bit of an adventureress," she wrote to her mentor-doctor Philip King Brown, "and my collecting is secondary, even though very real and very important."

Mexia came to her love of nature late in life, following a series of tragic episodes. After an unstable childhood in the United States with her American mother, who refused to live with her philandering Mexican husband, Mexia moved to Mexico City to live in her father's hacienda for the next ten years. There she met and married a young German-Spanish merchant shortly before the death of her father in 1898. After only seven years of marriage, her husband died, but not until she had spent most of her brief married life in court defending her father's will against his scheming mistress and stepson.

By then she was only thirty-four years old and the owner of a thriving poultry and pet stock–raising business, which she operated out of her father's Mexico City hacienda. Four years after her husband's death, she remarried, this time to a man who was sixteen years her junior and who worked for her. Within a year, he had ruined the business and she had suffered a nervous breakdown. Fleeing both her marriage and business failures, she went to San Francisco seeking medical help. There she found Dr. Brown whose counsel and support gave her the impetus to end her marriage and begin a new life in San Francisco.

But it was not easy. Over the next ten years she was plagued by periods of emotional instability and feelings of worthlessness. But when she began hiking with the local Sierra Club, she discovered her interest in nature which led to her taking natural science courses at the University of California in Berkeley.

She quickly discovered her affinity for botany, and at the age of fifty-five she embarked on her first botanical collecting trip to western Mexico with botanist Rosanna Stinchfield Ferris. Despite fracturing her ribs and injuring her hand after a fall from a cliff, she returned with five hundred specimens, including *Mimosa mexiae,* named for her by botanist Joseph Nelson Rose. Such naming gave her an immortality she craved—"permanent exhibits under my name in the Herbaria of the world for all time to come," she told Brown.

Many of her friends and associates in California described her as spoiled, egotistical, quick-tempered, and overbearing. But she dealt firmly, kindly, and fairly with Latin Americans from all walks of life during her solo collecting trips into the remote areas of Mexico, Brazil, Ecuador, Peru, Colombia, Argentina, and Chile. Goodspeed credited "her intimate knowledge of native customs and psychology and the confidence which the Indians reposed in her" as being the key to her success. For instance, Palma, who accompanied her on two of her South American trips, was described by Goodspeed as a "short, stout, jolly young Ecuadorian" who "ranged far and wide to gather in armloads of miscellaneous vegetation which he would triumphantly deposit at Mrs. Mexia's feet." And her mentor Alice Eastwood called her "one of the most remarkable women of the world."

Before her death from lung cancer in 1938, Mexia traveled widely and wrote extensively. In a series of articles she wrote about several of her collecting trips, she was able to convey her sense of excitement and wonder. "Camping on the Equator" is an account of her 1934–35 expedition to Ecuador and Colombia under the auspices of the U.S. Department of Agriculture's Bureau of Plant Industry and Exploration. During the expedition Mexia searches for a rare wax palm as well as the Indians' plant sources for the fish poisons they used. The account describes the daunting conditions Mexia endures and how she takes charge, pushing her guides beyond their limits, then finally pitching in to set up camp when they are defeated by bad weather. Even while she complains about their lack of resolution, she seems to understand their psychology, poking gentle fun at their weaknesses and her own. After a full year, she emerges with five

Ynes Mexia collecting on horseback. *Courtesy Special Collections, California Academy of Sciences, San Francisco.*

thousand plant specimens.

"Three Thousand Miles up the Amazon" is even more enthralling. Mexia's love of the outdoors, her adventurous spirit, and her fearlessness under conditions others would find unbearable come through clearly. Vivid descriptions show her floating serenely along on a flimsy balsa raft through a raging Amazonian gorge or dining willingly on toucans, monkeys, and parrots while she is marooned by heavy rains in the Upper Amazon rain forest. The following excerpt concludes her two and a half years in Brazil and Peru from 1929 to 1931, during which she collected sixty-five thousand plant specimens as well as several birds she had skinned herself for ornithologist Joseph Grinnell, whose "eyes grew big as [he] looked at the birds."

CAMPING ON THE EQUATOR

Ecuador, the Land of the Equator! There my life-long shadow would dog my step no longer, but, vanquished, would grovel beneath my feet. At last I would stand on the earth's great belt, nearest the beneficent sun. But would it be beneficent, or would it strike me down with its invisible power or burn me with its intense rays? . . .

On this particular trip I was on the trail of a certain Wax Palm, said by early travelers to grow on the Volcan de Chiles, one of the lesser peaks over whose crest runs the boundary line between Ecuador and Colombia. The sketches and description show it to be a tall, slender-trunked palm, sometimes reaching 200 feet in height, the stem covered with a whitish wax-like substance. Its great interest to us lies in the fact that it is said to grow at greater altitudes and to endure greater cold than any other known palm, hence more adaptable to our California climate. The locality had been given as only "Volcan de Chiles," so it was up to me to find it.

The railroad went no farther than Ibarra, where a letter of introduction brought me much assistance from Mr. Tamayo. From there an automobile took me, Palma, my faithful helper, and my equipment to the little town of Ángel (misnamed), where I had my first experience of the cold of the high Páramo. A side trip to lower levels took me on a search for Cinchonas, or quinine-bark trees, then on to Tulcan, the border town of northern Ecuador. I carried a letter to Señor Augusto del Hierro, the customs officer, a tall, severe gentleman who later thawed out and became most genial. To him I explained my pressing need for Wax Palms. He informed me that the Volcan de Chiles was a snow-peak, that the upper reaches consisted only of rocks covered with eternal snow and ice, that below this extended the Páramo, which was far above tree-line, and that if I wanted trees of any description I would have to circle the mountain to the north along the Páramo belt and on the eastern side drop down to tree-level, where possibly that palm might be found. This sounded reasonable, so I requested the means of transportation. There was difficulty in securing horses and a guide for the trip, but after several days' search an *arriero,* or packer, with two saddle- and two pack-animals was found, who said he had been over the trail some years before. He claimed it was a terrible trail, and he was right!

The next morning Palma and I were ready by seven o'clock, but along came the animals about eleven, and in three hours we reached the little village of Tofiño, close to Chiles, where we made a hasty cold lunch. Here José, the *arriero,* insisted that we pass the night, as he said there was no shelter farther along. To this I vehemently objected, for surely a three hours' ride was not a day's journey. Finally, I rode on, driving the pack horses so that José and his son followed perforce. After all it was bluff on my part, for I did not know the way; but it worked! Soon the trail dipped to a deep, boggy hollow and we had a taste of what was to follow. Riders and packs had to come off and while the horses wallowed through the ooze the loads were carried across by the men and the animals repacked. It was drizzling, with a cold, biting wind, regular *"paramo"* weather, on that mountain-side, and José insisted we would have to spend the night up there, so at dusk we came to a stop on the wet, bleak upland. The only vegetation consisted of the coarse Páramo grass and Frailejones, tall, woolly-leaved thick-stemmed composites, and of these José said he could make some kind of a shelter after he unpacked the horses and staked them out.

A more dreary campsite I have never seen. The ground was boggy and very wet underfoot, yet there was no available water, no shelter, and, of course, no wood. The drizzle settled down into a cold rain while José and his son cut some of the tall Frailejones and piled them into a clumsy windbreak, then sat down, supperless, in the cold and wet to shiver the long night through.

"But," I objected, dismayed, "we can't stay out in the rain all night at this altitude; we will all be frozen or sick from exposure with no shelter."

No, there was nothing to do about it, they gloomily insisted.

Well, I thought of a lot of things to do, and that speedily. The old man would not turn a hand, just sat hunched up shivering in his poncho, but Palma and the boy hustled under my orders, stretching a pack-rope between some tall Frailejones, making a sort of fly out of my two blessed "alligator-skin" ponchos, filling in the holes in the windbreak, putting less-damp Frailejon leaves as mitigators of the wet ground underfoot, and getting my cot up under the improvised shelter. It continued to rain steadily and the wind whistled and snatched at the frail fly which, though it did not leak, was rather inadequate. Finished, the old man moved in.

Hot food seemed the next desideratum, but the Frailejones were all dripping wet, and Palma and the boy wrestled for an hour trying to coax a blaze, while I prowled around in the dark and rain hunting for the undermost, drier leaves. Finally, with many matches and bits of our precious candle, a faint blaze was nursed to life. There was a little water in my canteen, and in that we heated some boiled potatoes and some of the familiar pea-soup powder that luckily I had along; and did it taste good! I crawled into my cot, Palma lay down on a pack-cover, and the two men huddled up beside him. The rain pattered fitfully on the taut "alligators," and we slept, doubtless the only human beings on that vast Páramo.

In the chill, overcast morning the old man complained that he had slept under a drip all night, but I did not care; why didn't he get

140

up and fix it? There was no hope of a fire, so we ate some cold bread and saddled up (luckily the animals had not broken loose) glad of the exercise to warm up.

As we picked our way, for trail there was none, the horses slipped and plunged and went down in the Alpine bogs along the steep hillsides. Horses and riders were soon covered with mud. We slithered along for hours. We were working along the north face of the mountain, in Colombian territory, but never a glimpse did we get of old Chile's snowcap, for he had wrapped himself in his customary cloud-blanket, through which we were groping our way. In the late morning we came to the steepest ascent of all and, climbing upwards through the drizzle, came to a cleft at the crest called the Portazuelo, which let us through to the descent beyond.

Cutting through the Portazuelo we commenced a terrifically steep descent—how the men got those horses down I do not know. The trail has been used by the Indians for centuries and is worn down until it is a miniature box canyon ten to twenty feet deep. Of course a stream has appropriated this inviting, ready-made bed, and there are small waterfalls and boulders in the course. Riding was not to be thought of, and Palma and I jumped from tussock to tussock of grass or slid into the boggy ground, collecting a few plants as we went, until a valley opened out between the stark hills, and our eyes were gladdened by some gleams of sunshine. Not far away was a little mud hut, called the Tambo, which we reached at two o'clock. There, the women made us some hot soup and boiled some potatoes, their only crop, and, believe me, it went to the right spot.

Again disregarding José's pleas that we "call it a day," we rode on down the valley, now with only occasional boggy places, and about five o'clock reached another adobe hut, just below tree-line, where *aguardiente* was sold and a lot of drunken natives were shouting. This time José was sure we could go no farther, but I pushed him along and as the afternoon advanced he really got a move on. The trail was wide and well marked, but crossed with *camellones,* the wash-board-like humps and depressions that form in the soft muck of Andean trails. Each animal puts his feet in the tracks of his predecessors, and deep grooves are formed, filled with mud and water and with rounded ridges between them. It was the first experience of my young horse with this phenomenon and he did not like the deep holes. He tried to walk on the humps, from which he slid, or else insisted on crowding up to the banks, where overhanging branches worked havoc with the rider. It grew rapidly warmer as we descended, and the forest thickened. We collected as we went. It was not until after dark that we reached a bamboo hut in a warm, pleasant valley, where we hap-

141

pily camped. Next morning we went on to the hamlet of Myasquer, where we had been told the coveted palm might be found.

Myasquer was a disappointment. The natives were stupid and would not guide us or help our search, so, perforce, we continued in a now beautiful forest, recrossing the line into Ecuador, to a house in a deep, watered valley, where a friend of José lived. One Wax Palm, or *Palma Real*, as it is called here, we saw, but it was on an inaccessible cliff overhanging the river. Such a disappointment!

José's friend received us hospitably, as the natives usually do, and when approached on the subject of Wax Palms, said he knew of but one and that it was half a day distant by rough trail. He finally agreed to guide us to it, so the next day, we started, but not as early as I could have wished.

That trail! It went up the side of a mountain so steep that in places I had to be hauled up, and then through choked forests and along precipitous slopes, apparently endless, where the sun shone tirelessly. Our progress must have been under a mile an hour, but eventually we rounded a spur and from afar saw the beautiful palm, its slender trunk white against the dark forest and its spreading crown waving above the forest canopy. We reached it—a photograph—and with a pang (unfelt by my companions) I gave the order. The ax bit in, and the great tree crashed to earth.

Unluckily, it was not in fruit so no seeds were available, but at least it was in flower. I photographed the great spathe and flower-cluster, so heavy the two men could hardly lift it; made measurements and notes; and took portions of the great arching fronds. Then we started on the long journey back, arriving after dark, very tired, very hot, very dirty, but very happy that the long quest had at least produced the desired herbarium specimens of this little-known palm tree.

That evening, after being fed, a bath seemed the most desirable thing in the world; but the only available water was a small pool directly in front of the house and bathing suits were far away. As it was dark, the difficulty was solved by the owner herding the family to the back premises while I gratefully waded in. Unluckily for my peace of mind the numerous and rather ugly dogs discovered the queer white apparition in their home-pool and threatened to eat it up.

The next day we started on the return journey, collecting along the way. By good luck, not far from the trail, well up towards timberline, I found some desired Cinchonas. Late in the afternoon we had climbed to the lower reaches of the Páramo, where the trees had dwindled to shrubs and where tempting blueberries grew abundantly, much as they do in Alaska; so as I rode along I snatched handfuls of them and ate them. Presently I began to feel sick and dizzy and wondered whether the altitude was affecting me, although I had not felt it before. Reaching the little Tambo at dusk, I nearly fell off my horse and violent chills and pains assailed me. The kindly natives declared that I had eaten poisonous berries instead of blueberries and they dosed me with molasses-water, which I was too ill to resist. The much-frightened Palma carried me to my cot, but of course doctors and drugs were days away. As the chills and pains increased, a chicken was chased, a feather extracted and, unwashed, was poked down my choking throat. After repeated applications of this homely remedy I lost those berries and everything else besides, and gradually the pains subsided. Later I was told that children are often poisoned, sometimes fatally, from eating the berries, but soon learn to distinguish them from the harmless ones. Next morning, to my relief, I was all right again.

We wallowed back along the flanks of old Chiles in a driving rain. The horse Palma was riding slipped and went down, but he leaped nimbly to safety as it fell. The horse rolled over into a hollow with all four feet in the air, whence it was extracted with difficulty. Without further accidents we reached the little Village of Tofiño, and, as I had had all I wanted of that particular volcano and the road was good and the moon full, Palma and I rode on to the town of Tulcan, where we arrived rather late.

THREE THOUSAND MILES UP THE AMAZON

Most of us, I think, have felt the fascination of the Amazon region. So much have we heard of its rivers, its tropical beauty, its luxuriant forests, the wild life and wilder Indians that lurk in its depths, that the pictures drawn by our imagination are vivid and unique. This vision of the unspoiled wilderness drew me irresistibly, and from this tale of how I went and what I found you shall judge what there is of fact and what of fiction in the old stories.

With some letters of introduction, a knowledge of Spanish, and a quantity of botanical-collecting equipment, I left San Francisco in October, 1929, taking a steamer that went through the Canal and landed me in Rio de Janeiro. From there I went to the highlands of Brazil, in the State of Minas Geraes, and collected at various points there for a year and a half. [She met and collected with Agnes Chase on one trip.] Returning to Rio, I decided that if I wanted to become better acquainted with the South American Continent the best way would be to make my way right across it. Inquiry developed the fact that it was possible to cross the Andes from the west coast and then come down the Amazon River. But I was already on the east coast, so why not from east to west? No one had ever heard of its being done, so they did not know. Also, I heard about the Pongo de Manseriche, the Iron Gate of the Upper Amazon, which few had seen, but reputed to be magnificent. Well—why not?

A comfortable motorship took me up the Brazilian coast to Pará, at the mouth of the Amazon, where the staff of the Goeldi Museum did much to assist me in my preparations. On August 28, 1931, with a truckload of equipment, I boarded the river-steamer "Victoria" and started up the famous river. Surely there was no roughing it on the steamer. Screened cabins, electric fans, ice plant aboard, as well as fresh meat "on the hoof."

The river itself is a tawny flood, looking more like an inland sea, "El Rio Mar de las Amazonas," than a river. Everywhere it is island-sown, and these islands divide it into *paranás,* or channels, each of which may be several miles wide. Vessels ascending the river follow these side channels, often bringing the boat sufficiently close to island-shore or mainland to enable one to see many interesting features. Every foot of *terra firma* is heavily wooded, and these forests of the Lower Amazon are truly magnificent. From the center of a channel they may look like a heavy dark line on the otherwise watery horizon; but when approached they take on the appearance of tall walls of living green—crowded, impenetrable, composed of innumerable varieties of ever-verdant trees, among which are conspicuous many species of graceful palms towering above the green canopy.

Our steamer was a wood-burner, so daily it would tie up at some tiny clearing in the otherwise unbroken forest where huge piles of cordwood awaited us, and where bronzed half-naked *caboclos* (Indian or negro half-breeds) toiled like demons to fill the capacious maw of the "Victoria." These stops gave me a chance to go ashore, where a few airy thatched houses, a dozen or so inhabitants, some chickens and pigs constituted the settlement. Everywhere the forest crowded the scanty clearings, hemming them in darkly.

The sixth day up the river brought us to the town of Óbydos, perched on low pink cliffs, a rare sight in this flattest of alluvial basins, and remarkable as one of only two points where both banks of the Amazon can be seen without intervening islands.

After leaving Óbydos the wild life became more abundant. Huge *jacarés,* or caimans, slid off sand-banks as we chugged along. Numbers of the beautiful white aigret herons were outlined against the green of the forest bank, while flocks of chattering parrakeets [*sic*] flashed green and silver as they wheeled above the river. Everywhere are seen the dugout canoes, some holding half a dozen persons and carrying produce, and others, mere shells, with a single paddler. The latter, in this country, where the water-path takes the place of the trail, are significantly called *monterias,* or "mounts." Most numerous, of course, are the canoes around the little clearings, where the dwellers run out eagerly to watch the "Victoria" pass—a man or two, half a dozen ragged children, the chocolate-colored naked babies, and, in the background, the thatched house built on stilts as a precaution against the floods.

Eight days up the river the map shows a "Santa Julia." It consisted of two forlorn-looking shacks standing apart. From the farther one issued an official. He entered a canoe displaying the yellow-and-green Brazilian flag, and accosted the "Victoria." When he came aboard I discovered that we were just entering the vast State of Amazonas, and needed his official permission. After another day or two, we arrived at Manaos, on the Rio Negro, just above its junction with the Amazon. It is the capital of the huge and little-explored State of Amazonas. Certainly a surprise, for this city, in the heart of what is generally considered a howling wilderness, is a very modern place, with wide, tree-shaded streets, electric trams, hospitals, splendid public buildings, and a beautiful opera-house of Italian marble topped with a gold-tiled dome.

Four days at Manaos, and we were on our way. The vast river, however, is of many moods and has many names, here being known as the "Solimoes," from a now vanished tribe of Indians which once lived along its banks. The river's course lies but a degree or two south of the equator, and I had dreaded the heat, only to be agreeably surprised as to the temperature. It is hot at times, but nothing like the heat found in our own Southwest, for example. Sunstroke is unknown, for the moisture in the air is so great that the sky is generally cloudy, while the daily afternoon thunderstorms cool the air appreciably. Great was my amusement, after one of these showers, to see the ship's pilot emerge from his cabin in overcoat and muffler!

The ever-present forest changes somewhat as we progress. Palms, while present, are no longer a dominant note. The "Imbaubas" (*Cecropia* sp.) take their place, with their slender white trunks and enormous leaves, so down-covered that they gleam silver-white under shining sun or tropic moon. The forest trees in this section are so covered with vines and *lianas* that they look like verdant columns or queer un-tree-like geometrical forms, while perhaps a two-hundred-foot "Ceiba Pentandra," or silk-cottonwood tree, spreads a perfect dome above the forest roof.

The "Victoria" is a fine vehicle from which to become acquainted with the country, or, I should say, with the river (for the land in this

145

region is but a varying combination of silt and water), as she is always stopping for some interesting performance. She sidles up to the bank covered with ten-foot *capim* or tall grass, and the crew go ashore to cut fodder for our hungry beeves [cattle]. I jump into boots and khaki (much to the amusement of the passengers) and walk the plank to investigate the forest.

Beautiful as is the forest seen from the river, it is repelling to enter. The canopy is so dense that it cuts off all sunlight, prohibiting undergrowth. There are no trails; it is dark and dank, with crowding tree-trunks, tangling *lianas,* rotting logs everywhere, and oozy, treacherous soil. No flowers are to be seen; such trees as are in bloom keep their color and fragrance for the forest roof where the real life of the forest displays itself.

Again the boat stops, the men drop into a canoe, paddle to a cove, casually cast a net, and back they come with the dugout piled high with gleaming, silvery fish, which we find very good eating at dinnertime. Like the exuberant growth above ground, the *cafe-au-lait* waters of the Amazon are seething with the life hidden in its opaque depths; but of this we catch the merest glimpse. Most conspicuous of the water-dwellers are the "Bôto Preto" and the "Bôto Vermelho," the black and red porpoises, known only in this great fresh-water system. They leap and play as do their cousins of the salt water.

Time seems to have no meaning in this world of sky and water; but after twenty-two days of river life we reach the Rio Javary coming up from the south, which marks the boundary between Brazil and Peru. The hamlet of Tabatinga shows but a tiny guard-house, a few lounging soldiers, and an old bronze cannon, to which the "Victoria" tied fast. Crossing the Javary we entered the territory of Peru, the guard-house here consisting of a thatched hut in the jungle. But on the northern shore there is a little cluster of huts until lately in Peruvian territory. Old boundary treaties were vague; this pathless wilderness never knew surveyor, and Peru, Colombia, and Brazil each claimed this hitherto unwanted jungle. It was awarded to Colombia by an International Boundary Commission, to give an outlet through the Amazon and to the Atlantic. Thus, in this obscure corner of the wilderness the three great countries meet—Brazil, Peru, and Colombia, with Ecuador clamoring for entrance—and this junction is fraught with danger.

At Chimbote, our first station in Peru, our wood was loaded by the Iahuas Indians in native costume, consisting of a full short skirt of split palm-leaves, cape, armlets and anklets of the same, dyed an orange-red that shaded into their smooth brown skins. Rather stunning they were, and quite willing to pose for their pictures in exchange for a few crackers.

On the twenty-fourth day we approached Iquitos in Transandean Peru, and my long, lazy, delightful voyage of 2500 miles on the "Victoria" was over. Iquitos is quite a lively town, sitting like a spider in the center of its web, whose silken strands are the shining rivers which come from north, west, and south, traversing this wilderness. The *lanchas,* or river boats, which ascend these rivers and their affluents, carry simple necessities to exchange for skins of beast, bird, and snake, for rubber and mahogany, for vegetable ivory, and for monkeys and parrots.

Here, repacking my equipment, I laid in three-months' supplies, and hiring three men, I embarked on one of those *lanchas,* which wandered up the much-named river (now the Marañon) for another week, until we reached Barranca, where the "expedition" was dumped ashore. The "Alberto" whistled thrice, turned, and slid down the river.

José, the guide-hunter, with some difficulty hired a large dug-out canoe, with four Indian paddlers, which would carry half the baggage. He was to follow with the rest as soon as he could secure another canoe. With me, in this first canoe, went my two *cholos,* or civilized Indians—and fine fellows they turned out to be. I gave the word, the men dug in their paddles, and we were off on the last leg of the journey west to the famous Pongo de Manseriche.

If the voyage on the steamer was full of interest, that in the canoe was enthralling. We crept along the river-bank, often under the overhanging trees to avoid the current, the men poling in the shallows along the generous curves of the meandering stream, or bending to the paddles as they stemmed the swifter current. I sat amidships under a little palm-leaf shelter, forgetting my rather hard "box-seat" in watching the river and its life as it unfolded before me.

The second day out we passed the last hut in its tiny clearing. We took on huge bunches of green plantains and a supply of the sweet manioc roots for food. From there on there was no sight of human beings—only the shining, shimmering, cream-brown river, stretching from sunrise to sunset, confined by living green walls on the right and on the left, and above all the high-arched sky, delicately clouded at dawn, its intense blue relieved as the sun rose higher by fleecy white clouds, which soon piled aloft in huge cumuli, and turning black and threatening as they tore down upon us in a torrent of blinding rain, with thunder and lightning, for the afternoon storm. The deluge lessened, passed us by, traveling Andes-ward, and left us crawling in its wake refreshed and enlivened under a cloudless sky until we headed into the burning heart of a tropical sunset.

And, as dusk came swiftly, we would search out a sandy beach, often tracked by jaguar and tapir, and camp for the night. Valentino would deftly light the fire and have his pots simmering in no time. I would roam around watching the bird life and the vegetation. Neptalí would put up my cot and mosquito-net, spread large musa-leaves for a rug, bring water for my bath—for no one dare bathe in the Father of Waters; his spawn are too voracious. Up at dawn, and another day of inching the heavy canoe past monstrous stranded trees, battling the current, or poling cheerfully in a world of naught but river and forest and sky; at last the long-desired wilderness, untouched and unmarred by the hand of man. Then one day, as we started ever westward, a blue mist hung low on the horizon athwart our river highway, which, unlike other morning mists, did not dissipate with the rising sun, but took on a dim outline and a deeper blue until it dawned upon us that it was no mist, but the eastern-flung chain of the mighty Andes, the barrier that would end our journey.

Day by day the blue outline rose higher and grew clearer, the seemingly impassable barrier of the Sierra del Pongo. On the ninth day it towered above us, densely tree-clad. As we reached its foot, we found ourselves surrounded by the Aguaruna Indians, who live in this region. Our first reception was rather dubious, for copper-headed spears and twelve-foot blow-guns with their tiny darts were much in evidence. The Aguarunas had long since spied our large canoe ascending the river, and were prepared to meet the Wambisas, a tribe of their blood enemies, who live on the Rio Morona below them. When they found we were "Christianos" instead of the dreaded Wambisas, they were greatly relieved and received us with rejoicing. I had come prepared, and solemnly presented each woman with a needle and each man with a small fish-hook as good-will gifts. The Indians took us to their *moluca,* or thatched communal house, and were delighted to have their pictures taken. The men wear a sort of skirt made from the wild cotton which they spin and weave, or, lacking this, they use a fibrous bark beaten thin. The women have a kind of garment tied over one shoulder. The boys go naked. The roar of the waters came to our ears, the clouds hung low over the blocked iron gateway of the Amazon, and the end of the water-trail was near.

The Marañon has its source some 170 miles north of Lima and but a hundred miles or so from the Pacific. It flows northwest for hundreds of miles, cutting deep cañons between the Cordillera Occidental and the Cordillera Central of the Andes, then, turning abruptly eastward, it escapes from the central chain and cuts through the Cordillera Oriental by a *pongo,* or gorge, here named from the Manserisse Indians, who inhabited this region at the coming of the Spaniards.

148

The nearly perpendicular walls of the Pongo are estimated to be about 600 meters high. The Sierra del Pongo is composed of hard sandstone and limestone from which ammonites and cycads have been recovered. It is buckled into an anticline through which the river cuts at right angles. The length is only some seven miles; but when a river normally from one to several miles broad tries to get through a jagged cut at one point but thirty meters wide, quite a good deal happens.

The Pongo cannot be passed by launches or by boats larger than canoes which can creep from rock to rock or can be hauled up by ropes. It cannot be passed by any craft when the river is rising or in flood. Luck was with me, for the river was falling. My *cholos* were experienced river men and we entered the gloomy gorge, with its towering walls densely clothed with vegetation from top to bottom. Although I took many snapshots, the constant rain precluded clear results. The depth of the water in the gorge, said to be 330 feet, is too great for rapids, but the zigzag course of the raging flood, dashing from side to side of the narrow cañon causes terrible whirlpools; the water wells up from beneath in great domes and standing waves and rushing cross-currents. However, aided by the unusually low water, we crept up along the jagged rock-walls safely and came out at the embayment beyond. As we looked behind, the Sierra del Pongo apparently cut off our retreat, for no passage is visible until one is actually within the portals.

I established camp a few miles above the Pongo, at the mouth of the Rio Santiago, which heads in the Ecuadorean Andes. José joined me in a few days, the canoes and paddlers were sent down the river, and, as if awaiting that, the rainy season began with unprecedented violence and the rivers rose and rose until the roar of the Pongo could be heard for miles.

For three months I camped there, collecting botanical specimens and making short excursions, always by canoe, except one, when I climbed to the crest of the Sierra del Pongo. There were friendly Aguaruna Indians living in the vicinity, and José knew a little of their language. We bartered trade-goods with them for chickens, plantains, hearts of palm, and manioc roots, to supplement our dry provisions, as well as for articles of their dress and their feather and shell ornaments. The "boys" hunted toucans, monkeys, and parrots—I can assure you, they are not bad eating. There I passed Christmas of 1931, setting up a little palm-tree under my thatched shelter, trimming it with wild red peppers and poinsettias, and hanging on it some simple presents for my three boys and the mystified but delighted Indians.

We were effectually marooned by the deluges of rain and the flooded rivers; but if we were to get out some day, arrangements had to be made for it. So we bribed the Indians to bring us logs of balsa, the lightest wood known, and with these Neptalí constructed a large raft, binding the logs with tough *lianas,* and raising on it a platform of palm bark. In January there was a pause in the downpours, and the floods subsided temporarily. We loaded the raft with my precious collections of plants and birds and insects, the remainder of the equipment, our four selves and a tiny baby monkey that José had acquired, and, with the Indians looking on, loosed the vine rope that held us and swung out of the Santiago into the Amazon. Valentino and Neptalí stationed themselves at the big oars, and we were swept into the Pongo. The raft was caught by the racing current and was tossed about like a straw. The upper whirlpool, the "Ullco Huacanqui" ("Thou shalt weep bitterly") of the Indians, caught us, whirled us around thrice, then spewed us out, and we sped on our way safely past the second great whirlpool and through the constricted neck. In twenty minutes we had raced through the most dangerous part of the course and the gorge widened. Here we were carried into a circling backwash which swung us around and around in spite of the boys' efforts. The rocks were jagged and it was with difficulty that the raft was fended from them until a lucky thrust pushed us out into the current once more and we floated down the river at good speed.

Rafts are extensively used on the river system of this Upper Amazon basin, especially for freight, and while they are eminently practical, they have some disadvantages. They are unwieldy, their course can only be roughly directed, and, if swept down with the force of the current against one of the many huge stranded trees, the lashings are apt to be burst asunder and the balsa logs scattered wide with results easily imagined. Or they may be washed ashore by the current, and a raft cannot be backed. Our raft, however, was well made, and we swung merrily down the stream. A palm-leaf thatch was built over the platform and our "houseboat" was most comfortable. A chicken-coop in the back held our remaining poultry, and at a fireplace built at the rear Valentino prepared our meals en route. While the smoke was annoying when the raft drifted tail first, that was the only drawback to the most delightful mode of transportation that I have encountered. I wrote notes, watched the river birds, the beautiful islands and forests, and the great river, and prepared my collections. José's baby monkey insisted on being petted and mothered, and if shut up would cry pitifully. It was a terrible nuisance, but it was so tiny and amusing that one could not help loving the little thing.

150

At dusk the boys would gradually work the heavy raft toward the shore, but good landing-places were scarce, and we would often be swept down quite a distance before Neptalí could manage to snub us to a tree. A curtain and my cot would be put up, the boys would lie on the uneven floor, we would hear queer wood-noises and would gradually drift off into peaceful sleep. Near Barranca a boat came out to meet us, bringing a huge packet of accumulated mail, some of which was dated August—this was January! Thus for two weeks we floated down the Marañon, and my heart grew heavy as we drew near Iquitos, for my ideal journey on a raft was over.

At Iquitos I packed my collection and started it on its long journey down the Amazon and through the Canal to California, while I continued my journey to the west coast. I took a hydroplane up the Amazon and the Ucayalli rivers to Massesea, an airplane across country to San Ramon in the lower Andes, mule and automobile to chilly Tarma at 10,000 feet in a valley of the Andes, then the Transandean Railroad, which, after crossing a pass at nearly 16,000 feet, drops down a steep incline to Lima and Callao and the Pacific. I had fulfilled my wish to cross South America at its greatest breadth. A steamer brought me up the west coast and back to the bay region, very glad to see familiar faces and places once more.

FURTHER READING

Eastwood, Alice. Letters. Gray Herbarium. Harvard University, Cambridge, Mass.

Goodspeed, T. Harper. *Plant Hunters in the Andes.* New York: Farrar and Rinehart, 1941.

Mexia, Ynes. "Botanical Trails in Old Mexico: The Lure of the Unknown." *Madrono* 1 (1929): 227–38.

———. "Camping on the Equator." *Sierra Club Bulletin* 22 (February, 1937): 85–91.

———. Letters. Missouri Botanical Gardens, St. Louis, Mo.

———. Papers. Bancroft Library. University of California, Berkeley, Calif.

———. Papers. University Herbarium. University of California, Berkeley, Calif.

———. "Three Thousand Miles up the Amazon." *Sierra Club Bulletin* 18 (February, 1933): 88–96.

15

Mary Sophie Young

1872–1919

FEW NATURALISTS, MEN OR WOMEN, kept a journal as detailed, anecdotal, or humorous as Mary Sophie Young's account of her first major botanical collecting trip into Trans-Pecos Texas back in 1914. Instead of merely a dry listing of botanical specimens, the account presents a fun-loving, intrepid naturalist whose appreciation of the beauty around her was tempered with a fine sense of the absurd.

Four years after she received her Doctor of Philosophy degree from the University of Chicago at the age of thirty-eight, Young, a native of Glendale, Ohio and a Wellesley College alumna, was not only an instructor in botany at the University of Texas but also in charge of the university's herbarium. Although she had had little taxonomic training, she had learned enough to rapidly expand the university's collection both by her own collecting in the Austin area and by exchanging her duplicate specimens with other botanists and herbaria.

To accomplish this task, she spent her spare time and money organizing field trips and enlisting students to accompany her on her rugged walks near Austin. Her efforts culminated in *A Key to the Families and Genera of Flowering Plants and Ferns in the Vicinity of Austin, Texas,* published by the University of Texas in 1917, and "The Seed Plants, Ferns, and Fern Allies of the Austin Region," which appeared posthumously as University of Texas Bulletin No. 2065 on November 20, 1920. Both were impeccable works of scholarship written in acceptable, but dry, academic prose.

Not so her journal. She probably never expected it to be published forty-eight years later by the older brother of the young male student—Carey Tharp—who had accompanied her on the trip.

Mary Sophie Young with her collecting rig. *Courtesy Texas State Historical Association, Austin, Texas.*

Otherwise, she might not have confided so much that was not botanical—her struggle with the recalcitrant burros she had purchased to pull the roofless buggy carrying her camping gear and plant presses; the time she spent cooking monotonous but cheap food; her attempts to keep their camps tidy, their shoes intact, and their clothes mended; and even her meticulous and time-consuming removal of weevils from the cornmeal. Through it all she remains cheerful and optimistic, even when she and Carey are mistaken for tramps because of their torn and dirty clothing or jeered at by people who know she is a professional but question her unconventional life.

Primarily, though, her journal presents a graphic picture of her botanical work in the ruggedly beautiful Trans-Pecos area. Through her journal Mary Sophie Young emerges as a determined, brave woman, undismayed by weather, insects, heat, or dirt. In contrast, friends described her as quiet, modest, and hard-working, deceptively frail in appearance, and suitably attired in high button shoes, a long skirt, long-sleeved blouse, and wide-brimmed hat. But she concealed in her skirt pocket a .25-caliber Colt automatic along with her .22-caliber six-shooter revolver, both of which she had the ability to use to bring down the rabbits she needed to supplement her meager field diet.

Good students remembered her as a teacher who insisted that they think for themselves, yet generously gave them both her time and money if they needed help. Several, in fact, were offered free room and board in exchange for very little work so that they could afford to attend the university. When she died prematurely of cancer at the age of forty-eight, she was mourned by a host of friends, students, and colleagues who regretted that she had not had time to finish either her life's work or all the notes she had assembled on later botanical trips to the Chisos and Guadalupe Mountains and the Panhandle area of Texas.

The following excerpts from her journal recount repeated efforts to climb Mount Livermore, the second highest peak in Texas. It also demonstrates her doggedness, her appreciation of the countryside, her practical side, her dry sense of humor, and, most of all, her fascination with botany.

MARY S. YOUNG'S JOURNAL OF BOTANICAL EXPLORATIONS IN TRANS-PECOS, TEXAS, AUGUST–SEPTEMBER, *1914*

AUGUST 14

This was the day that we went to Livermore. We started up the gully back of the house somewhere around nine A.M. carrying two canteens, two knapsacks, two guns, and a botany can. For lunch we had a can of baked beans, four teacakes, and two cakes of chocolate.

The other canyon is wide and it was easy going after we struck the road. There is a tank some distance up and considerably further along a cement trough with the water from a spring piped into it. We might have left our canteens at home if we had known how much water we should find everywhere, but it is not usually safe to be without a canteen in this country.

We finally lost the trail and, as we had no idea which was Mt. Livermore, aimed for the most attractive looking mountain. We certainly did some climbing, and Carey with the two canteens must have had a hard time. We went up a very steep long slope, then around the top of that small mountain, only to find ourselves cut off from the next mountain, the one with high rock bluffs topping it, by deep ravines. We made our way partly around the canyons then crossed them where they were not so very deep.

Of course, there are no trails in these mountains, but what makes them so hard to climb is the fact that long grass and shrubby plants cover the rocks and loose stones in many places so that one is very much impeded and beside cannot tell where he [is] going to put his foot. The tales one hears of rattlesnakes on rocky slopes are a little disturbing too. We were tired enough to rest several times. Really we could not have finished that climb without. We reached the base of the first rock bluff and found ourselves quite able to walk along on the level. We climbed a little more, reached another bluff, to discover that we could go no further. Back of us was a cliff several hundred feet high, almost if not quite perpendicular, below, which continued into the bald rock top of the mountain. This bluff is broken more or less in places that look easy to climb. Botanically, it was quite different from anything else I have seen. It was beautifully painted with orange, yellow, and gray lichens, and decorated in every crevice with very many plants, ferns, selaginellas, liverworts, beside more hardy crevice plants. Pine trees appear in some of the more broken portions as apparent crevice plants. The talus slope at the base was a tangle of grapevines, wild tobacco (?) mentzelia, composites of various kinds that concealed the rocks and made passage difficult. We found the best place we could and sat down on a narrow ledge, our backs to the bluff, and ate our dinner. The view before us was certainly magnificent—the foothills in the foreground, with our canyons winding out through rolling green hills to the plains beyond. *There* was space; wide, brown, hazy, spotted with the shadows of the clouds, the plain lay before us, stretching out miles and miles to the mountains, which like gray clouds skirted the horizon.

After lunch, Carey found a place under a clump of *Quercus hypoleuca* and began to do math problems. I started collecting. As I passed around the clump of trees climbing from rock to rock, there was a commotion among the weeds and a black animal ran into Carey's shrubbery. He had a hairy back, and by the color I knew he was not the skunk we had known was somewhere about. I called to Carey, and just then the beast, seeing another enemy ahead, snorted like a hog and rushed out of the bushes. It was a young black bear. I might have shot him if I had had time to get out my gun, but he made tracks around the mountain side at the rate of about twelve miles an hour. He was too far to shoot by the time Carey got around the bushes. We regretted deeply that we could not have bear meat to eat and a bear rug to take home with us, but are glad to have seen a real live wild bear in his native haunts. (Those in Glacier Park are almost tame.) There must be a lot of wild animals in those mountains, they are so hard to climb that probably very few people come.

We saw some chimney-like affairs down in the canyon that we think the hunters use to cook deer.

Carey beat around in the bushes, hoping to scare up another bear, but without success. At least, however, he can say that he has been on a bear hunt.

There is a beautiful gorge in our mountain with a small stream of water running down it in a broken waterfall. After you climb the first flight of stairs it opens up with a much more beautiful cut than it looks from below. It is, in vegetation, like the streams of the northern Rockies. I found several old acquaintances. It looked possible to climb higher, but I came to one place where my courage was not quite enough. More trips in that region would pay, but those places are so inaccessible!

We started back at 3:45. We decided that it would be much easier to come by way of Goat Canyon [actually Pine Canyon], so started down the mountain toward the southwest. The canyon proved to be very beautiful. We went down a branch first. It went down, down, and down, over waterfalls, and more waterfalls. When we reached the larger canyon, we found it an almost impenetrable thicket, largely of *Quercus hypoleuca,* with much arbutus, an occasional willow, walnut, ptelea, and what looks like ash. We found a single, leafless, red-purple orchid in the moist soil of one thicket. When we were tired of stooping to go under trees, we would try the bed of the stream for awhile, stepping from stone to stone and slipping once in a while. The canyon continued for an unreasonably long time just as bad. Then it grew a little wider and kept on endlessly like that. Finally the bluff began to show signs of widening and I was sure that the next opening would bring us to the forks of the canyon. But it didn't. After another unreasonably long time, I found we were coming to the forks and told Carey it was only about a mile home. But it wasn't the forks. On and on went that endless canyon and the trouble of it was it kept looking less and less the way it ought near the forks. Another thing that troubled me was the position of the sun. I thought it ought to be in our faces, and instead it was decidedly to the right. We went on and on, and still no signs of the forks. I was considerably worried; it did not seem possible that we could be in the wrong canyon, and yet what was the matter with it that it kept on so long, and what was the matter with the sun? It is such lonely country and the ranches are so far apart and so hidden in hollows that it would be next to impossible to find one if we were lost. The idea of going without supper or breakfast and sleeping in the open without a blanket was not attractive. We discussed climbing the ridge, but I saw an opening and kept on a little longer. We came to the opening. There was a branch canyon—but extending in the wrong direction, and there was no north branch. Up the big branch was something white, two windmills, that looked like ours, but they were against a background of great mountains not like ours at all. Windmills usually suggest a house in settled countries but not here. It was the lonely time of the evening and up the other valley was an outcrop of that uncanny white rock.

We were sure we were lost then. The sun was not more than an hour high and we never could make our way ten miles over the hills home, even if we could see where home was. We started up a ridge as fast as we could go. I felt rather weak. All of a sudden I noticed that the valley with the white rock looked remarkably like the south branch of Goat Canyon and it flashed over me that perhaps instead of the main canyon, we had been in the north branch. Then over the ridge ahead of us loomed up a familiar and most welcome sight, a pyramidal top of a mountain, our mountain, the one just across the canyon and downstream a little way from our home.

We were weary and hungry when we reached our house. Carey stopped in the orchard and he said, ate five half ripe peaches. As they are as big as a tin cup, that is no small quantity. . . .

AUGUST 18

It was a fine morning and we started on our trip at about 9 o'clock, with one canteen, two knapsacks, and the botany can. The first part was in the level through the canyon, but soon we began to climb, and there the road changed to a trail. It was a good deal like the Montana trails, except that they were through the open, or oak woods, instead of pine, fir, and spruce, and there was no mud.

The mountains and canyons are very pretty—of course everything is on a small scale. The mountains are pretty well wooded—oak on the summits and pretty well down. A sprinkling of cedar and pine beginning on the high slopes and increasing toward the bottoms of the canyons where, in the high, moist valleys, they form the dominant part of the tree vegetation. The alligator cedars can be recognized at a distance by their silvery blue color. The trail is cut out of the side of the mountain, so one gets a good view. In places it zigzags back and forth and once or twice goes down for some distance, then up, but most of the time it was a pretty steady climb.

We finally came in sight of the cement tank we had been on the watch for. It was really two cement dams across the narrow canyon. There was good water to drink which we appreciated. Here Carey satisfied his sporting instincts by catching all the tadpoles in a small pool. They did not put up much of a fight, so it was not a hard task. We used up half an hour or so at the tadpole pool and as much more time trying in vain to find the trail. It was supposed to go all the way to the top of Livermore. At last, giving it up, we started up a slope we thought must be the right direction hoping to see where we were, but the farther we went the less we could see of where we were. We tried to keep going northwest, so as to be able to find our way back. We found a rock bluff with a new species of pine tree just below it (It must be *P. ponderosa*). After climbing that, still more upward slope. Coming finally to the top of the ridge, however, we saw Livermore before us, and recognized the rocky bluffs we had seen the last time.

The vegetation here is most interesting—a pine tree with cones the length of this page, with the other pine. Campanulas, Menarda, and an entirely different, moist undergrowth. We did not think we were going to reach the top of Livermore, but we ate our beans and chocolate and peaches and felt better.

Down the slope and up the next one gave a complete change from the pine vegetation of the north facing to the thicket of oak brush of the mouth facing mountain side. Whenever we thought we had reached the top there was always another climb ahead of us, and when we really did reach the top there was Livermore peak itself farther off, connected with our peak by a ridge. There was a trail, however, which was comforting, and we followed it, always finding we had farther to go than we thought. We saw our rock bluff around which the little bear fled last Friday. The view of the plains is grand, also of the mountains to the north. There is a sort of a rock pinnacle that stands up sharply and I suppose is the very highest point. We made our way over loose, broken rock to it, and started to climb it—almost straight up—but the black clouds and the thunder scared us back. We thought we were in for a soaking and wanted to find our tank with the plain trail home before we got lost in a fog. We followed the trail back, over the ridge, but lost it again and got a whole canyon out of our way. We crossed it to the right canyon and Carey finally found the trail way below the tanks. It rained some but very little.

Near home a fine young jack rabbit crossed our trail. Carey hit him first shot, but he ran into the brush squealing. The second shot went through his body too, and he still squealed. Another shot made him jump straight up in the air and fall kicking vigorously—but he still squealed. Another shot in the head didn't phase him—he still kicked and squealed. We couldn't stand the squealing, and one more shot did stop that. He was such a young tender-looking jack rabbit that our hearts were softened toward him. His meat looked very dark red when we skinned him. It looked tougher than any tough steak I ever saw. Well, we had jack rabbit for supper! It is good exercise to eat jack rabbit—gives you an appetite. Jack rabbit should always be served with tooth picks. Jack rabbit is economical, one piece two inches in diameter and half an inch thick will last an average man all day if he chews constantly and his jaws stand the strain. Jack rabbit meat would make good sole leather. We are going to put a new heel on Carey's shoe from some of our jack rabbit that is left. I am going to try stewing some of what is left. (We have had four meals already and it isn't half cooked yet and we threw away some.) Maybe if we soak it all night and boil it all day we shall be able to chew the juice, but I don't know. I do not like jack rabbit. This was a young jack rabbit—only about half grown. I wonder what an old patriarch of a jack rabbit would be like. No, I don't. I don't want to know.

We were homesick for our house that night. If it had not been so late we would have come on home, but when I thought of leading Nebuchadnezzar [a mule] through the creek fifty-seven times in the dark, my courage gave out. So we stayed another night. It threatened rain some, but the morning was fair. . . .

AUGUST 21

Friday I started shortly after eight o'clock for another tramp to Livermore. The only available lunch was one huge pancake and some bacon. It was not an attractive lunch and I did not in the least enjoy eating it. Cold pancake is not, at best, very appetizing, nor cold bacon either. O, for one grocery store!

I went over the ridge between Merrill and Goat canyons, but probably lost time by so doing, for I had to leave the ridge below the flat-topped rock bluffs. I went up the canyon by way of the bed of the stream and found it much better than our first climb. There are many rock falls that help one out, like staircases. It was on one of these slopes that I found my rattlesnake. He was lying in a crack between two rocks, taking a nap with his head and upper part of his body sticking out. I thought, from the cross stripes on his body, that he might be a rattler. I thought at first of shooting him, but decided that, as rocks were bigger than bullets, the chances of hitting him were greater with rocks, so I gathered an armful and opened fire. At the first shot the snake awoke with a start—but he wasn't hurt. The next time, tho, he got it in the neck and began to squirm. When he squirmed his tail into view, there were his rattles. I was afraid he would squirm himself down the crack, so I couldn't get his rattles, but was also afraid to put my hand near for fear he might squirm his head into view. Of course they can't bite without coiling, theoretically,

159

but I don't want my hand near their heads even when they are dead. Another rock anchored him securely and I finally screwed up enough courage to reach down the crack and saw off the end of the tail. The end—about an inch long—when cut off entirely, asserted its independence by waving the rattles defiantly in the air. It was most uncanny. I was almost afraid of that tail after I had wrapped it in a piece of paper to take home to Carey. It was rather too bad—when Carey has been longing for a rattlesnake, and I have been scared to death that I might see one, that I should be the one to find it.

I wanted to go home after that—but decided that the chances of rattlesnakes on the way back would be just as great as those ahead, so went on. The base of the big bluff is very much like what we saw the first time, but faces north or northwest and there were aspen and buckthorn and "white oak," beside false Solomon's-seal in addition to the usual things. I made my way around the rocks, across a little ravine to the pass, from there to the top of a small peak. The other side of the pass is a canyon, sloping to the north that looks as if it would have the new pine in it. If I can learn to ride Nebuchadnezzar I want to go once more and visit it.

There was water in the canyon part of the way, but I forgot to put any in the canteen, and the little pink oxalis on the bluff was the only relief from thirst. It did very well, too.

Coming down on the opposite side of the canyon would have been easy except for those abominable thickets of oak. I started at two or quarter past, and at four was opposite the flat-topped rock bluff.

At a quarter of six I arrived at home just in time to see Carey jump from his window sill and rush madly in the direction of the barn. His errand, however, was not too urgent to let him stop for some green apples. Nebuchadnezzar and Balaam were galloping up the canyon in the company of a bunch of cattle. Balaam's wound is doing so well that she evidently feels skittish.

FURTHER READING

Tharp, B. C., and Chester V. Kielman. "Mary S. Young's Journal of Botanical Explorations in Trans-Pecos, Texas, August–September, 1914." *Southwestern Historical Quarterly* 65 (January, 1962): 366–93.

———. "Mary S. Young's Journal of Botanical Explorations in Trans-Pecos, Texas, August–September, 1914." *Southwestern Historical Quarterly* 65 (April, 1962): 512–38.

Young, Mary Sophie. Papers. Eugene C. Barker Texas History Center. University of Texas, Austin.

16

Edith Clements

1874–1971

EDITH CLEMENTS WAS EIGHTY-SIX YEARS OLD when she published *Adventures in Ecology: Half a Million Miles from Mud to Macadam.* It was, she wrote, "the story of two plant ecologists who lived and worked together for four decades, traveled hundreds of thousands of miles in the study of natural vegetation and grew hundreds of species of plants in greenhouse and garden and then cooperated with conservationists, foresters, agriculturists and cattlemen in putting the knowledge so gained to practical use." The book is, in fact, autobiographical, starring Clements as chauffeur, cook, all-around handy person, photographer, artist, stenographer, and translator for her eminent husband, Dr. Frederic Clements, one of the world's pioneering plant ecologists.

But Edith Clements had her doctor's degree too, the first ever granted to a woman at the University of Nebraska. She received it after completing her thesis on the "Relation of Leaf Structure to Physical Factors," based on "about 300 species collected in the Colorado foothills and mountains of the Pikes Peak region." Significantly, though, her undergraduate degree was in German, and she became a teaching fellow in German at the University of Nebraska after her graduation. The following year she married Frederic Clements, and he influenced her to enroll in botanical graduate studies. But she also minored in Germanic philology and geology, and Frederic joined her in her comparative philology course as "together we traced modern Germanic languages from Indo-European roots, through Sanskrit, Greek, Latin, Pre- Germanic, Gothic and Old English, to modern English and German." Later, she used her language abilities to translate books and articles into several foreign languages and to cite them in the bibliographies of their publications.

Frederic Clements called her Cherie and no doubt admired her athletic, intellectual, and artistic abilities. A Phi Beta Kappa undergraduate, she had also been captain of the midget basketball team, president of her junior class, and had participated in exhibition fencing and tennis. Frederic, on the other hand, was a chronic diabetic as well as a workaholic. "Before I 'humanized' Frederic . . . he would forget to eat or sleep, sometimes to an extent that produced hallucinations. Someone had to remind him." She was that "someone."

She was also a full participant in his work. On their honeymoon they first conceived the idea of an alpine laboratory on Pikes Peak. It was to be an experimental mountain testing station for plant acclimatization. Together they spent several summers collecting plants with the help of relatives and friends. They sold them to scientific institutions to raise enough money to buy their first cabin, which they called Pinecroft, for their laboratory. During that period Frederic taught botany at the University of Nevada and wrote *Research Methods in Ecology* in 1905, based partly on his work at the laboratory. Then, from 1907 until 1917, he was head of the University of Minnesota's botany department. During his tenure at both universities, Edith Clements was an assistant in botany.

After the publication in 1916 of what Paul B. Sears called a "work of profound scholarship"—*Plant Succession: An Analysis of the Development of Vegetation*—Frederic became a research associate at the Carnegie Institute of Washington, D.C. He was now free to study during the summers at the Alpine Laboratory, which the Institute took over, and during the winters at the Carnegie-owned Tucson Institute and Coastal Laboratory at Santa Barbara, California. At the same time, Edith Clements was made a field assistant by the Institute. In pursuit of his research the two Clementses also traveled to remote areas throughout the United States.

In addition to driving ornery cars over non-existent roads and fixing stalled cars during frequent breakdowns, Clements bought all their supplies, took Frederic's dictation in the field, and put her "skill with pencil and brush" to good use by illustrating his many publications as well as her own *Rocky Mountain Wildflowers* and *Flowers of Mountain and Plain*. Her paintings in *National Geographic* accompanied her "Wildflowers of the West" and their co-authored "The Flower Pageant of the Midwest." Both were republished in book form, with supplementary text, as *Flowers of Coast and Sierra* and *Flowers of Prairie and Woodland*.

Clements seemed to not only accept but cherish her role as supportive helpmate, judging from one story she recounted in

162

Edith Clements with "Billy Buick," which she drove on research trips with her husband. Photograph from *Adventures in Ecology*.

Adventures in Ecology: A young female friend wondered aloud to Clements how much she would have to know to travel about like her and Frederic. When Clements gave her a long list of subjects to study and books she would have to read, the friend replied, "I believe I'd rather get married." Clements responded, "That's the idea. . . . It's much easier to marry someone who knows it all and if you know some, yourself, and can draw and paint and take photographs and drive the car, and typewrite and a few things like that, you can go along the way I do."

And go along she did. According to *Adventures in Ecology:*

> Not only were the slopes steep and slippery, but the deep soft shale made climbing them almost impossible, since every step forward was followed by a slip backward. Of course, some of the tiny pioneer plants that were to be photographed, seemed to be in especially inaccessible situations. Once in a more or less favorable position, however, the tripod must be kept from slipping or blowing over by my frantic grabs as the wind blows my hair into my eyes and my hat from my head. The camera cloth flaps and flutters; it is a struggle to keep it in position, to hold the tripod, insert the film pack, pull the slide, snap the shutter. Perspiration pours into my eyes and down my nose, and every fresh gust threatens to send the entire outfit, including myself skittering down the steep slope. By this time I am a wreck; by the end of the day I am several wrecks. I tell Frederic that I am offering myself a burnt sacrifice on the altar of his love of work. He looks at my peeled nose and red neck and assents as calmly as though a mere wife were a small price to pay for the rewards of scientific research. . . . So, it's get a bath and a night's rest and keep on!

Still, after reading her breezy, often tongue-in-cheek account of their life together, written many years after Frederic's death in 1945, Clements emerges as a competent, take-charge person with a bumbling and aloof, albeit brilliant, husband.

The following excerpt from *Adventures in Ecology* describes their experiences as she and Frederic, accompanied by a male graduate student, nicknamed Ginger, set out on a collecting trip through the southwestern United States. The account clearly illustrates her knowledge and ability to describe plants, her enthusiasm for Frederic's successes, her organizational abilities, and, especially, her coolness under fire.

Edith Clements typing up notes in the field while husband Frederic Clements looks on. Photograph from *Adventures in Ecology*.

ECOLOGY AND WORLD WAR I

It is springtime in Tucson. A golden mist of blossoms veils the pale green of the palo-verde trees; balls of yellow down gleam among the feathery leaves of mesquite and cat's-claw; torches of flame-colored flowers sway on the ends of the slender branches of ocatillo [*sic*], and the desert floor is spread with a carpet of many hues among which golden-hearted cactus blossoms reflect the sunlight from silken petals of pale yellow, pink, burnt-orange and deep crimson.

It is a wonderful day in Tucson. It is a wonderful day in our lives! The Dream is on its way. The Alpine Laboratory is under the wing of the Carnegie Institution of Washington, with a budget, with a staff, with a future and Frederic is Director as Research Associate of the Institution. He calls himself an "escaped Professor" with full time for research! His book on "Plant Succession" is published and has placed him in the front ranks of the ecologists of the world!

Our earlier experience with the ideal winter weather of Tucson, together with fellow workers and friends among the staff of the Desert Laboratory and the faculty of the University of Arizona, settled the question of where we would have our own winter home. The coming summer would be spent in carrying out a special assignment connected with the war effort, and the time was near for the start. One of Frederic's brightest students from the University of Minnesota would "do his bit" as field assistant. I would serve as chauffeur, typist, photographer, mechanic, commissary-general and second field assistant.

The project was to be a study of the western and northwestern ranges, with a view to determining how efficiently the sheep- and cattle-men were carrying on grazing practices, and suggesting improvements where these could be made. The general idea seemed to be to "make two blades of grass grow where only one grew before." My mind was a little hazy as to just how this would help toward "winning the war" until "Ginger" undertook to explain in the condescending way he had when imparting knowledge to the "inferior feminine intellect."

"More grass, more grazing, more cattle and sheep, more boots, more buttons, more blankets, more mutton, more beef, more 'corn-willie.' But I don't like 'corn-willie'," he added after a pause: "Perhaps we'd better not have more of that!"

"But that's what the army lives on," I said teasingly, "and when you are called to the colors, you will have to eat it or die."

"If I'm willing to die for my country," he said thoughtfully, "I'll eat 'corn-willie' if it kills me."

But we couldn't spend time talking. We had to get ready for the trip. Frederic showed me a map with the prospective route outlined on it.

"My goodness!" I gasped. "What a lot of 'great Wide-Open Spaces'! Suppose we get lost, or the car breaks down?"

"It isn't all lonesome and uninhabited," he reassured me. "We have road maps as well as the Automobile 'Blue Book' to use where there are no maps."

"Nothing to it!" boasted Ginger. "Dr. MacDougal says that people travel in cars nowadays who do not know whether the radiator holds gasoline or water."

"Yes, and maybe they got into trouble and maybe they didn't. As for me, I'm going to be ready for emergencies."

Our earlier experiences with automobiles in prairies, sand-hills and badlands, had failed to make us exactly enthusiastic about this mode of travel. However, it had very definite advantages over trains, wagons and horses in ecological field work or surveys, especially since now we had our own car. "Billy Buick" had become the pride of my heart and I not only liked to drive, but I knew what made Billy go. To be sure, I had backed into a few telegraph poles and fences, and taken the garage-door off its hinges, while learning, but I did not run into the roadside ditch as Frederic did because he was much more interested in the vegetation than the road. I even learned how to start on a hill which the instruction book says is "very hard to do, but can be done with practice." So I was elected not only chauffeur but chief mechanic for I knew the difference between the transmission and the differential. I could diagnose most of the unexpected sounds in Billy's interior that indicated trouble, and occasionally could make the necessary adjustments or repairs. I certainly knew how to clean spark-plugs and connect the cylinders in proper order, ever since the day I connected them wrong and created a commotion by going down the street with explosions beneath the hood like a bunch of fire-crackers! I actually enjoyed getting under the car and shooting grease-cups full of gooey black grease. Our neighbor disapproved of this, and after watching the operation declared that I was "no lady."

So, these essential preliminaries accomplished, it remained, on the morning of the day set for the start of the great adventure, to bring Billy from the shop where the Tent-and-Awning man had been commissioned to evolve a fascinating "Pullman berth" from the seats so that we could sleep in comfort instead of on the ground in any emergency that made camping out necessary.

Leaving Frederic to finish packing and closing the house for an absence of several months, Ginger and I proceeded to the shop. We found Billy lying dismembered all over the floor, while the Tent-and-Awning man sat among the wreckage, calmly smoking a cigaret.

"Good Heavens!" I gasped. "You promised the car would be ready for an eight o'clock start!"

"Humph!" grunted the Tent-and-Awning man, surveying the scene with a gloomy eye. "I had to have a honeymoon, didn't I, since I up and got married. I just got back."

Here was a crisis to arouse the fighting spirit of anyone engaged in winning a war. Ginger and I advanced upon the enemy with all the ammunition we had. Pleadings and arguments weakened his defences and an offer of extra financial rewards brought about his capitulation as he began to put poor Billy together again. Ginger and I brought up all necessary reserves of praise and encouragement or handed him tacks and things whenever he showed a tendency to sit and rest some more.

Victory at last, although I doubted its completeness as I surveyed the lumpy expanse achieved by cutting through the back of the front seat and attaching hinges which permitted it to join horizontally with the rear seat. Ginger was of the opinion that this had weakened the car; also that quite possibly the hinges would give way at some inopportune moment and precipitate the driver into the laps of rear-seat passengers.

Considerably chastened by these reflections and the fact that it was already one o'clock, we reached the house to find the Director patiently waiting amid piles of luggage. Friendly neighbors stood around, offering advice, warnings and gloomy prophecies as well as bets on the impossibility of finding space in one car for the appalling number of things that seemed to be absolutely indispensable for the venture. I won the bets for I had a diagram that showed a "place for everything" and finally I had "everything in its place." That is, everything except a pile of sugared and buttered pancakes, left from breakfast. Ginger had planned to have them for lunch, but there was absolutely not a vacant spot for them, and when he wasn't looking I put them on the shelf in the garage.

"Cora," the portable Corona typewriter, perched on a small shelf attached to the "dashboard" where Frederic could type field-notes as we rode. However, desert dust collecting in her little "insides" brought on peevish fits which made it necessary for me to take notes in the field. "Baby Ben" gazed at me from a hole cut in the instrument board, to fit his round, chubby face, and at unexpected moments, startled us all with sudden shrill alarms.

Extra cans of gasoline, oil and water were fastened to the running-boards, together with a box of tools and the suitcases. Beneath the seats were side-curtains, tow-chain, mud chains, tire-mending outfit, tire pump, and my precious "Pull-me-out" complete with "dead man," crank and chain!

On the rear bumper were strapped a collapsible cot, and a canvas roll of sheets and blankets, for emergency camping-out. In the tonneau were scientific instruments, field glasses, the camera, tripod, film packs and a refrigerator lunch-box with compartments for ice and supplies of food for field lunches.

Two o'clock! Ginger inserted his six feet two among the articles on the rear seat. I tooted the horn; the assembled "multitude" shouted and we were off! To a start; and then a sudden stop as a tire went flat! Three o'clock and on the way again. Up and over Paso Robles in the Tucson mountains, and the world lay before us! A world of sand and mesquite, of giant cacti and creosote bushes. The Santa Ritas and Sierritas rimmed the horizon to the left of us; the Silver Bell Mountains to the right of us; lonely Baboquivari Peak pierced the sky ahead of us, and beyond lay unknown mountains, an undiscovered country—and a white road. And presently a fork in the road. I turned left.

"I think you should take the right fork," said Ginger, who cherishes the conviction that, no matter which road I take, it is the wrong one.

"Look in the Blue Book and find out," I said, backing the car.

"I am looking. It says: 'Fork at corral and windmill; two miles of very rough dusty road across a dry lake. . . .' Oh! I've got the wrong page—that's the way between Phoenix and Blythe. There aren't any directions for this road to Ajo."

So the Blue Book had failed us! That Bible of the motorist, put out by the Automobile Club of Southern California, for the aid and comfort of bewildered travelers where any road looked like a "main road" and as often as not ended in a farmyard! Here were minute directions such as: "end of road, turn right," "left turn beyond schoolhouse," "road dangerous but passable: travel at your own risk," and the like for many pages and many routes. Without it—we were lost! But at that moment of anxiety and indecision a good angel in the form of a swarthy Indian appeared, chugging stolidly along in an old Ford! What luck! He too was on his way to Indian Oasis on the Reservation and at his suggestion we followed as he unerringly steered a course among the maze of roads and crossroads and forks which marked the way across the "trackless desert!"

More good fortune in the way of an invitation from the doctor stationed on the Reservation, to share his supper and lodging in an unfinished cabin! Good-byes in the morning and instructions to follow the "main traveled road" sent us happily on our way. And then a fork at two equally well-traveled roads. Ginger said it was just as difficult to choose the correct fork on the desert as at a banquet table, and Frederic, after consulting his map, favored the right fork, since we were supposed to keep Mount Copeka on our left—the big mountain ahead—moreover the left one led suspiciously towards Mexico!

"Hold it!" said Ginger who had been looking hopefully to the rear. "Here comes a car!"

Another rescue party! Such luck! Bad luck, as it turned out this time, for the occupants of the car were four rough and tough-looking characters who, although they claimed they were going to Ajo and would show us the way, took the left fork. Frederic continued to look worried and to scan his map, while I had doubts about guides who careered crazily along and threw a whiskey bottle out of the car from time to time. And presently, the car stopped some distance ahead and the men got out and started to walk back towards us!

"Quick!" said Frederic, "take this road to the right!"

"Hurry!" said Ginger, "They are going to shoot."

Sure enough: hardly had I turned Billy in the other direction and tried frantically to get up speed, when I heard a shot, which fortunately went wild, and we were soon out of reach of more! Ginger reported that the men had given up the chase, after shaking their fists threateningly in our direction, and then he added calmly:

"I expected something like that. I read in the paper about a couple of old folks who had been lured toward the border, that same way, robbed of their car and left in the desert. The robbers then crossed the border into Mexico where our law cannot get them. And not only that," he continued, "a woman was killed and her husband, who was driving, wounded when bandits tried the same trick."

"Good gracious!" said I indignantly, "why didn't you tell us earlier and we wouldn't have followed them."

"Oh, I didn't want to make you nervous," was the serene reply that made me too furious even to speak as I shakily continued to urge Billy to get us to some safe distance. He did, and we all were thankful indeed to see houses and people again as the last of the bumps and chugs of the fifty miles through the Indian Reservation ended in the little mining town of Ajo. But I could not help thinking as I fell into an exhausted sleep that if our first day was an example of what lay ahead in the next five months, and we survived, Uncle Sam would surely give us medals for bravery in the line of duty!

FURTHER READING

Clements, Edith S. *Adventures in Ecology.* New York: Pageant Press, 1960.
———. Papers. Nebraska State Historical Society, Lincoln, Nebr.
Ewan, Joseph. *Rocky Mountain Naturalists.* Denver: University of Denver Press, 1950.
The National Cyclopedia of American Biography. New York: J. T. White, Co., 1946.

17

Edith Patch

1876–1954

LONG BEFORE IT BECAME ACCEPTABLE TO QUESTION the widespread use of pesticides, Edith Patch did so and was ridiculed for her efforts. Patch was basically a naturalist, however, who found insects so fascinating and their habits so complex that they provided challenging puzzles for scientists to solve. Her own insect specialty was aphids, and her most important scientific contribution, the *Food-Plant Catalogue of the Aphids of the World including the Phylloxeridae,* published in 1938, is still the only extensive record of aphids and their host plants.

That work was the culmination of her thirty-four years as an entomologist for the University of Maine's Agricultural Experiment Station. Before she was hired as the first woman scientist in an agricultural experiment station, Patch first had to prove her commitment to her profession. She was offered an unsalaried position, working for then-director Charles Dayton Woods, in hopes of becoming head of the entomology department the following year. Her first task, however, was to organize the department. Patch accepted the responsibility readily. Disregarding the advice of well-intentioned friends, she immediately resigned her high school teaching position in Minnesota and moved to Maine. Impressed by her determination, Woods arranged for her to teach entomology and agricultural English at the University of Maine on a salaried basis while she fulfilled her unsalaried agreement with the station. Woods often had to defend his hiring of a woman for such a position to male entomologists and agriculturalists. When one critic declared, "A *woman* can't catch grasshoppers," Woods replied, "It will take a lively grasshopper to escape Miss Patch."

A native of Worcester, Massachusetts, Patch moved with her family to Minnesota when she was eight years old. She was an unusually determined little girl, who was fascinated by nature, so her family's ten acres of prairie land between Minneapolis and Anoka provided a continuing stimulus for her interest. Monarch butterflies were her special favorite, and, as a high school student, she wrote a prize-winning essay about them. Impressed by her abilities, her teacher urged her to spend at least some of her adult life writing accurate and entertaining nature stories for children. So, led by what was later described as "the mind of a scientist, the soul of an artist," she entered the University of Minnesota and majored in English. She won more prizes, this time with her sonnets and romantic stories. But she also studied entomology under Professor O. W. Oestlund, who introduced her to the study of aphids.

In 1904, the year after she was hired, she was named head of the University of Maine's Department of Entomology, just as Woods had promised. Twenty years later she was made director of the experiment station, the first woman director in the United States. During her early years, while building an enviable reputation in economic entomology, she received a master's degree from the University of Maine and a doctorate from Cornell University, where she had studied under John Henry Comstock.

Patch also kept her promise to her high school teacher. Like Anna Comstock, who encouraged her, Patch spent her off-hours writing anthropomorphic yet scientifically accurate stories and books for children. Altogether, she produced seventeen children's books and one hundred stories. She also wrote more than forty periodical articles on popular science and nature subjects for such publications as *Scientific Monthly*.

Her scientific output was equally prolific. She was Fellow of the American Association for the Advancement of Science and the first woman president of the Entomological Society of America. Of her eighty published scientific articles, fifty-four concerned aphids. Two genera (*Patchia* and *Patchiella*), five species, and one subspecies of aphids were named for her by other scientists. Her description of one aphid genus, *Microparsus*, is still valid today, and, of the thirty-five aphid species she described, ten are still valid as she first described them, and nine remain valid in different genera.

As a scientist she was a careful, conscientious worker. She studied aphids by watching them through every generation of their life cycle and kept detailed notes on their dates, food habits, and behavior patterns. For instance, she discovered that melon aphids overwintered in the live-for-ever weed and potato aphids in wild rose bushes.

In the following excerpt from "Marooned in a Potato Field," Patch

Edith Patch at her microscope. From the Edith M. Patch Papers. *Courtesy Special Collections Department, Raymond H. Fogler Library, University of Maine, Orono.*

explains how her assertion about the host plant of potato aphids (*Macrosiphum solanifolii*) was challenged by male scientists, at a time when potato mosaic was wreaking havoc on the lucrative seed-potato industry of Aroostook County, Maine. The article describes how she spent the entire potato-growing season both in Aroostook County and in New Brunswick, Canada in search of evidence to prove her theory. The piece illustrates her scientific thoroughness and field work techniques as well as her sense of humor and ability to tell a good story.

Patch also takes the opportunity to advance a few of her own ideas regarding the altering of the natural environment by humans. She laments the loss of forests in favor of potato fields and asks, "Would the Pine Tree State . . . not have done well to conserve a grove here and there?" She also describes the frantic desire of potato growers to spray. This "epidemic of solanimania," which everyone suffered from, causing growers to "rush to potato fields like mad dogs to water. . . . The call of the hour, 'Let us spray,' was observed by all; but the baptismal creeds for potatoes proved as numerous and varied as those for people." Finally, she regrets that in her role as a "servant" to the "interests of agriculture," she will be a "hangman to the rose. Surely agriculture is a cruel and exacting mistress." And that may be the very reason that, when she retired in 1937, she stopped working on aphids and devoted all of her time to nature observation, traveling, writing for children, and raising flowers.

Marooned in a Potato Field

The circumstance of my exile was in accordance with the rule of contrasts, by which life whets her sense of humor. For it is given even to those who, following the traditions of eight generations, were born within forty miles of Boston to will to go the way of the winds when spring beckons their gypsy instincts; and I confess to taunting visions of elephants dancing in the jungles of one continent and tadpoles named Guinevere disporting in the southern pools of another— glimpses of desire that blurred my eyes a bit as I reached the end of my own so different journey and found myself marooned in a potato field. . . .

It came about thus. A few years previously the plant doctors who spent their summers hobnobbing at Aroostook Farm had informed me that my pet aphid, *Macrosiphum solanifolii,* was spreading their pet potato disease from sick plants to well ones. Said disease (spelled m-o-s-a-i-c but popularly known as "mozik") is not so especially disastrous in the north in potatoes grown for the table; but the south looks to the north for seed, and a tuber with a taint of mosaic in its substance grows, after being transported to the south, to a miserable plant, indeed. Now there is this similarity between the egg business and potato growing—there is no excess profit in the product grown for the table, but for the man who can dispose of his product for purposes of propagation there is a possible fortune. The seed-potato industry, actual and potential, means a great deal to the state o' Maine. And it was threatened, they told me, largely because my "pet aphid,"

174

a million or a billion strong, was inserting its beak into the tissue of sick plants and, after imbibing mosaic juice, dispersing to other parts of the field and inoculating healthy plants with the disease.

Their question as to what I would advise under the circumstances made me feel a bit responsible for my insect charges, albeit with something of a lump in my throat, as I replied, "Remove the wild rose-bushes from the border of fields where certified stock is desired for seed purposes."

My suggestion being met with a sceptical frown from my phytopathological colleagues, I recalled to them the story of *Macrosiphum solanifolii:*

This insect is a migratory species. During the summer it produces viviparous generations abundantly upon potato and certain other herbaceous growths that it accepts as "summer hosts." In late summer and early fall, winged individuals are developed which migrate from potato and other summer hosts to the rose-bush, where subsequently appear, as progeny of the winged migrants, wingless egg-laying females and winged males. The eggs of these apterous oviparous females are deposited on the rose-bush, and remain there unhatched until spring, this plant accordingly being termed the "over-wintering host." About the time the new growth of the rose is in its tenderest and most succulent condition in the spring, the aphid egg hatches and the young insect grows into a wingless viviparous form—the progenitor of all the succeeding generations for the season and hence called the "stem-mother." The daughters of the stem-mother grow up on the rose, part of them with wings and part without. The winged daughters fly forth to seek their pleasure (i.e., a summer host, not hard to find in a land over-run with their favorite sap) and start on the potato vines, the summer colonies, which are augmented a fortnight later by the advent of their nieces from the rose—for their wingless sisters, remaining on the rose, produce winged daughters which migrate in their turn to the potato fields in the vicinity. Thus the cycle runs—the spring migrants going from rose to potato, their progeny unto several generations dwelling on the potato as a favorite summer host; fall migrants winging their way back to the rose where the fall generations, the over-wintering egg and the spring forms reside.

But this recital did not dispel the sceptical frown before alluded to. In fact there was nothing new in the story, for I had told it first as long ago as 1915. The plant doctors had, indeed, but one comment to make. When I wound up with "Obviously the destruction of the wild roses in the vicinity would break the aphid cycle," they remarked quietly, "Of course we may have overlooked them, but we have never observed many wild roses in northern Aroostook."

That was their challenge. It was admirably done, I think. A courte-ously constrained statement bearing directly on the point under con-sideration and characteristically conservative, as is the habit of one scientist (if he be discreet) speaking to another. But that brief guard-ed sentence was charged and I knew it questioned whether I was sure that *Macrosiphum solanifilii* overwintered on the rose, wholly on the rose, and nothing but the rose? As an aphid detective working out the life cycle of this species in Penobscot County, what did I know about the conditions in northern Aroostook where, according to res-ident observations, wild roses are, at least, comparatively rare?

Certainly that much of professional criticism was implied and possibly a running personal stricture may have been included. At any rate, I found myself wondering whether my colleagues were reg-istering a disappointed conclusion that in failing them at an hour of need I was demonstrating some inherent disability leading to an in-ference that entomological work in general and the task at Aroos-took Farm in particular was after all a man's job! There was, perhaps, a personal "dare" as well as a professional challenge in their signifi-cant suggestion that a recommendation to uproot wild roses where wild roses had not been observed to be rooted down seemed hardly in order. Obviously there was but one thing to do either on profes-sional or personal score. The various due official sanctions having been all registered by November, 1920, the next May I laid aside the garb of a laboratory entomologist and donned the khaki of a field scout.

Naturally, first came an intensive quest for wild roses within dan-gerous proximity to potato acreage. For, as I had taken my "pet aphid" on rose annually since May, 1904, and in seventeen years' collecting had never found the spring generations on any other vegetation, there must be no data overlooked in this particular. How many miles afoot this quest led me, I can not state, but it was as far as one could explore in the days of a fortnight, down one side of the hedge rows and lane rows between farms, and up the other; in and out and round about the bordering woodlots; wading beside marsh fringes in rub-ber boots; and tramping forth and back along the length and breadth of hillside pastures. And in none of these places did I find a wild rose-bush. News of wild roses in river thickets reached us by way of botanists and fishing men; but (fortunately for one in sympathy with wild life conservation), it did not, in the localities visited, seem nec-essary to seek them out.

For without that we found rose-bushes, plenty of them, and that along the broad highway! There were dooryard roses near Aroostook Farm, thousands of stems of them, in both directions, within short walking distance. The wheel of the field assistant helped add to the same sort of data; and later by automobile route we saw them at Fort Fairfield, Caribou, Van Buren, Frenchville and all along the roadways between them and Presque Isle. Surely the life-cycle of *Macrosiphum solanifolii* is in no danger of breaking in northern Aroostook for lack of rose sap. That became evident to us all before the summer was over. . . .

. . . in the immediate vicinity of northern seed-potato fields, the rose will go. How otherwise? For the man from Bermuda will still come seeking "certified bliss," and the gold of southern states will demand healthy tubers. The northern growers will voluntarily attend to a matter that bears so directly on their purses. They have troubles enough without those borne by the wings of migratory aphids.

These were a part of the composite reflections of ninety days that conversed with me as I took a solitary walk across Aroostook Farm the night before I left. The skies were rich with sunset radiance and the glory of rainbow. Under their beauty spread out for interminable miles the potato fields in which I had been marooned for three months by the calendar. As I looked across as much of the green-leaved sea as my gaze could cover, a shiver of revulsion swept over me—a feeling more nearly akin to weary hate than I would think possible to have for any growing plant. There was something hideously manufactured about the landscape, artificially colored with prescribed baptismal dopes; and I detested the whole sprawling amorphous brood of *Solanum tuberosum*.

Was I then at last cured of my attack of solanimania? Had I shaken off the delirious taint of the potato kingdom? Ah, no, no one ever recovers. And a day or so later, when sitting before my long deserted desk at Orono, I drew into place a blank sheet of paper and headed it:

Maine Agricultural Experiment Station
Bulletin No. 303
"Rose-bushes in Relation to Potato Culture"

And the things written under that caption brand the writer as a faithful servant of agriculture or, if you prefer, a servile slave of the spud.

FURTHER READING

Adams, J. B., and G. W. Simpson. "Edith Marion Patch." *Annals Entomological Society of America* 48 (1955): 313–14.

Brockway, P. J. "Dr. Patch of America." *Maine Alumnus* 18 (April, 1937): 5–11.

Gibbes, Elizabeth. Interview with author. Orono, Maine, November 18, 1986.

Mallis, Arnold. *American Entomologists.* New Brunswick, N.J.: Rutgers University Press, 1971.

Olson, Cheryl. "Edith Patch: Receiving Credits Long Past Due." *Bangor Daily News*, September 3–4, 1983.

Patch, Edith. "Marooned in a Potato Field." *Scientific Monthly* 15 (August, 1922): 166–80.

———. Papers. Special Collections Dept. Raymond H. Fogler Library, University of Maine, Orono.

———. "Tour to the Entomological Congress." *Journal of Economic Entomology* 31 (February 20, 1939): 775.

Stoetzel, Manya B. "Edith Marion Patch: Her Life as an Entomologist and a Writer of Children's Books." *American Entomologist* 2 (Summer, 1990): 114–17.

18

Ann Haven Morgan

1882–1966

WHILE SHE WAS A PH.D. CANDIDATE AT CORNELL UNIVERSITY, Ann Haven Morgan was dubbed Mayfly Morgan because of her intense devotion to the taxonomy and biology of mayflies. For her dissertation work she had studied the mayflies of Fall Creek, near Ithaca, New York. From the first of April until the first of August, she carefully reared mayflies in small wire cloth cages that she had designed herself. She placed these cages into the creek, held them in place with stones, then began long hours of careful scientific observation. Altogether she observed representatives of seventeen different mayfly genera.

Throughout her forty-one years as a teacher of general zoology at Mount Holyoke College in South Hadley, Massachusetts, mayflies remained her favorite preoccupation and their watery environs her special passion. She was an authority on water zoology and developed the field of winter biology, pursuing her twin interests, even in the coldest weather, at her outside laboratory—a little pond near the top of Mount Tom. First by trolley from South Hadley, then on foot following the car tracks from Northampton, Massachusetts, she waded through deep snow to reach her pond. When she arrived, she chopped holes in the ice, then searched the traps she had set for water bugs in an effort to observe the beginnings of their annual cycle.

Morgan credited her interest in aquatic biology to Professor James G. Needham, director of Cornell's Limnological Laboratory and her advisor first as an undergraduate then as a Ph.D. candidate. Needham had first showed her "how to look for things in the water," she wrote in her classic *Field Book of Ponds and Streams: An Introduction to the Life of Fresh Water*, published in 1930. He also proposed her name for

Ann Haven Morgan dredging for stream creatures, circa 1945. *Courtesy Mount Holyoke College Library/Archives, South Hadley, Massachusetts.*

membership in the Entomological Society of America in 1908, four years before she received her Ph.D.

A native of Waterford, Connecticut, Morgan learned at an early age to love the woods and streams near her home. She pursued her interest at an academic level and spent her professional life rapidly moving up the academic ladder at Mount Holyoke. She advanced from instructor to associate to full professor within eight years, then chairman of the zoology department, a position she held for thirty-one years. But Morgan also reached out beyond academia, first with her *Field Book of Ponds and Streams,* aimed at "both beginners and seasoned investigators—an angler's favorite," then with her *Field Book of Animals in Winter* (1939). In her preface to the latter, she wrote, "It is hoped that [this book] may show how much there is to be learned of animals in winter and above all how invigorating is the job of finding it out." She had written the book during holidays and in "odd hours here and there."

Both field books are amply illustrated by her own meticulously rendered drawings and photographs. In the winter book she includes drawings of the ovaries of gyrinid beetles in January. One photograph shows thousands of beetle larvae that have crawled over the soft snow in an open field during a January thaw near South Hadley, Massachusetts, in 1930. Another photograph, taken by Patch to observe underwater winter life, depicts an ice-filled stream at below-zero weather.

In the 1933 edition of *American Men of Science,* Morgan was designated among the country's 150 most important zoologists. She was also a Schuyler Fellow at Cornell, a visiting fellow at both Harvard and Yale, and a fellow in the American Association for the Advancement of Science.

After she retired from Mount Holyoke in 1947, Morgan shifted her interests more strongly toward conservation. She joined the newly formed National Committee on Policies in Conservation Education, sponsored by the Izaak Walton League, and worked to reform the science curriculum in schools and colleges by giving summer workshops in ecology for teachers. In 1955 she wrote her last book—an introductory zoology textbook with a strong conservation ethic—*Kinships of Animals and Man: A Textbook of Animal Biology.*

Her talents and interests were best summed up in a memorial written one year after her death by Charles P. Alexander in *Eatonia.* He described Morgan as "a true pioneer in the taxonomy and biology of mayflies [and a] distinguished conservationist and authority on many branches of aquatic ecology."

The following excerpts, "Mayflies" from *Field Book of Ponds and Streams* and "Fresh-Water Sponges in Winter" from *Scientific Monthly,* show her careful field methods and her ability to record her observations in a lucid, pleasing style. The mayfly excerpt discusses points of interest to fishermen without neglecting scientific accuracy. This excerpt also has inherent interest to the general reader. Through lyrical descriptions of mayflies and discussions of their brief lives, Morgan exposes her own sensitive feelings about insects.

A chapter on freshwater sponges in her *Field Book of Animals in Winter* describes how she had collected young colonies of *Spongilla fragilis* from a stream in South Hadley in late April and even as late as the second week in November. During her research she also found the gemmules on the undersides of rocks in streams, as "Fresh-Water Sponges in Winter" explains. This excerpt illustrates the efforts she expended in the depths of winter to observe the humblest of living creatures.

MAYFLIES—EPHEMERIDA (PLECTOPTERA)

Many persons have seen mayflies even though they have not recognized them as such. They may have watched great swarms of "flies" over a lake at twilight, or come upon dead insects strewn upon the lake shore or beneath streetlights, or have fished with the artificial bait-flies, many of which are modeled after mayflies.

Nymphs.—Mayfly nymphs are of many shapes and sizes; some have flattened heads and bodies and their sprawling legs are held akimbo as in *Heptagenia.* Active runners, like *Callibaetis,* are set high on spindling legs, while the little creeper, *Leptophlebia,* almost drags its low slung body. But all mayfly nymphs agree in having seven pairs of gills on the abdomen, and with rare exceptions have no gills anywhere else. They have two or three long slender tail filaments, or setae, and but a single claw on each foot. Stonefly nymphs, sometimes confused with mayflies, have two claws on each foot and nearly all their gills are on the thorax. Their differently shaped bodies reveal much about the places where they live and their way of getting a living. Many are well fitted for particular habitats but are helpless when they are out of them. *Epeorus* is so flat and its gills and claws such efficient holdfasts that it can cling to a rock no matter how strong the current, yet it is quite helpless among slender plant stems where *Callibaetis* is thoroughly at home.

Adults.—Mayflies spend nearly all of their lives as nymphs in the water. During this time they eat a great deal and in a few weeks, or in the case of some species, in a year or more, they emerge into the air as subimagos or "duns" with pale gray wings. Subimagos soon shed their skins again and become fully matured imagos or "spinners." As winged insects their lives last only a few hours or days at most, during which they do not eat at all. For a long time the fishermen have called them "duns" and "spinners." Fishermen of England have given them other picture names, like "the silver gray," "the evening spinner." Many of these fishermen have made their own "dry flies," wrought of silk and fur and feathers like those described in that most charming of guides, Ronald's "Fly-Fisher's Entomology."

Adult mayflies are delicately beautiful insects, soft gray, and brown, or pale and translucent, fragile and short-lived, as their name, *Ephemerida,* implies. They have large front wings and small hind ones except in some very small species such as *Caenis* in which hind wings are altogether absent. The adults have either two or three tail filaments, which are much longer than those of the corresponding nymphs. Their mouth parts are shrunken and useless; so that in the mayfly countenance the whole mouth region is like a receding chin. Their legs are weak and little used for walking; the front legs of the males are long and often held forward with a reception-line cordiality. Dr. J. G. Needham has aptly named one mayfly the "white-gloved howdy."

As soon as they emerge from the water the subimagos fly upward to overhanging trees or shrubbery. They molt but move about little until the mating flight which in some species occurs almost immediately, in others within a day or two.

The mating flight usually takes place in late afternoon or twilight. Then hundreds of spinners, mostly males, swing up and down through the air in a rhythmic dancing flight over streams or lakes. With their rudder-like tails stiffly extended they drop downward in swift descents of thirty feet and more and then bound upward with the lightness of springing thistledown. Hundreds or even thousands of them move up and down together. In half an hour they have disappeared into the trees as suddenly as they came, or they are strewn upon the water to become the food of eager fishes. During the flight a dozen or so from the hundreds of males mate with the few females which almost immediately lay their eggs in the water and then die upon its surface.

The little mayflies of the genus Baetis fly in a low compact mating swarm and the female literally climbs down into the water to lay her eggs. The following description is taken from my notes on her habits.

Flying close to the surface of the water, the insect alighted on a stone projecting slightly from the water and well protected from the force of the current on its downstream side. She at once walked to the protected side and downward to the water. First, wrapping her wings about her abdomen, she made several attempts to immerse her head and thorax. This appears to be the critical stage in the performance, and many mayflies are washed away while attempting it. Once under the water she started on a tour of inspection. This lasted for several minutes during which she continually walked to and fro, pausing, feeling the stone with the tip of her abdomen, and passing on unsatisfied. When she finally found a suitable place she braced her legs firmly, bending the end of her abdomen downward and her tail filaments upward. She then began swinging her whole abdomen from side to side with a slow pendulum-like motion, at each stroke leaving an irregular row of minute white eggs adhering to the surface, the first ones circular and somewhat longer than those which came later. As the egg mass grew larger she moved forward a little to allow the eggs to lie in succeeding rows. When her supply was exhausted she jerked her abdomen upward and abruptly clambered out of the water.

Habitat and season.—Mayfly nymphs live in clean fresh waters, flowing rivulets or rivers, tumbling waterfalls or quiet pools; they have become adapted to every aquatic situation except foul water. In many ponds they far outnumber all other animals anywhere near their equal in size.

Spring is the mayfly season and the fullgrown nymphs with their black wing-pads are abundant from March to late June and adults are emerging and swarming at this time. Young nymphs can be found in shallow brooks the year around.

Food.—These nymphs are confirmed vegetarians; their staple food is the great crop of diatoms and desmids which makes the golden-green color upon stones of the brook bottom and covers almost every object in the water. Besides this they eat the soft tissues of larger plants either living or dead.

Fresh-Water Sponges in Winter

There were nearly twenty animals on one stone—caddis worms, mayflies, water pennies, planarians, Bryozoans and sponges; they were creeping and sprawling, clinging or stuck fast, each according to its kind. Yet it was in the middle of January and the stone had been pulled through a hole in ice which was two inches thick. Even in a shallow brook like that things were far from frozen, and although one animal population had dug down into the bottom, another had stayed up in the water swimming and clambering after food, making nets and waiting for their catch. Most of these were young animals whose rapid growth would begin in February when the early spring food supply became abundant in the brooks. This community in winter resembled a similar one in spring, the bronze copper pennies looked like themselves, only smaller, and the Mayflies were unmistakably like those of April and May. But the winter sponges hinted nothing of their animal relations. They were like so many fig-seeds held to the stone in a bed of bristles. The bristles were the spicules, the skeleton remains of its summer colony, and the seed-like spheres were the gemmules or winter buds of the sponge. Gemmules are little balls of sponge cells, literally samples of sponge, which can grow into a complete colony when there is a proper stimulus from the warm water of spring.

Gemmules may look nothing like sponges, but they will do so speedily if they are given a chance. [Sponges Morgan collected] were taken from a shallow brook completely frozen over, in January. They were crowded among the spicules holding them to the stones, and no better picture of clustered fig-seeds could have been wanted. But a lens revealed their spicule-covered shells with the one small hole in each quite invisible to the naked eye. Some of them were scraped from the rock, taken into the house and put into a dish of water which was set near the window, but outside the path of direct sunlight. Pieces of clean glass were put into the dish, and as the gemmules were dropped down upon them they fell a little distance apart. . . . For the first few hours they would roll about at the slightest jar of the dish, but within a day or two they had stuck fast. The water was kept fresh and moderately cool, and in three days white plugs were just visible at the holes in the shells which by now had begun to swell and crack open. In another day sponge cells had come through all the crevices and creamy white streams of them had grown down onto the surface of the glass and surrounded the emptying husk of the gemmule.

Five days after the gemmules had been dropped on the glass each hollow shell lay in the midst of a small but flourishing sponge colony with thousands of cells, with true sponge osteoles and gastral cavities. Within a couple of days the transparent borders of the colonies had spread over the surface of the glass and run together so that the gemmule shells were the only signs left of the separate colonies. Several chimney-like pipes had grown upward and had osteoles at their tops, while shorter sacs were stretched thin at their swollen knob-like ends but did not yet have any openings there. Canals and chambers forming beneath the surface began to show as transparent streaks and spots and finally the glass-like spicules began to appear in clusters, visible through a hand lens along the transparent border of the colony. When carmine, a very fine red powder, was scattered lightly over the colony it rested on the surface only a very short time before a few particles of it, probably the very finest, came out on the gentle currents of water which were issuing from every osteole. This too could be seen with a hand lens and was enough to show that the little patch of cells was already carrying on the activities of a sponge. Although it was still smaller than the head of a carpet tack and had been growing outside the gemmule shell for only six days it now both looked and behaved like a sponge colony.

In order to understand either the anatomy or the activities of sponges it would be necessary to study young and full-grown colonies very carefully. Mature fresh-water sponges, such as the common Spongillas, are low cushions of cells whose surfaces are pierced with thousands of minute pores, and with hundreds of larger holes, the osteoles, mounted upon little peaks above the surface level. The pores lead into cavities, the already mentioned chambers first showing as transparent streaks in the sponge. Water is drawn into the so-called dermal chambers and on through minute incurrent canals which carry it into still another series of very small and numerous chambers out of which it passes by other small channels, the excurrent canals. These converge into the gastral chamber from which it is finally passed by way of the osteole to the outside. It was these currents of water from the osteoles that brought the particles of carmine carried through all of these passages after it had been scattered upon the surface of the young colony. Thus water carrying the food and oxygen supply passes in a steady current, as long as the sponge lives, through the pores to the dermal chambers, on through the incurrent canals and the adjoining small chambers through the excurrent canals and into the gastral chamber to its final exit by way of the osteole.

In summer sponges are much more conspicuous than in winter, but they do nothing which is so spectacular as this burst of growth in the new colony. Fresh-water sponges grow in many lakes and brooks, beneath lily pads, on the undersides of floating sticks and over the stones of brook beds. If the water is muddy or carries a load of dropping particles, their pores become clogged and they are starved and smothered, but clear water bears oxygen to them and a sufficient food supply, either dissolved or of microscopic plants and animals. Sponges flourish under these conditions and are abundant in many waters.

Colonies of Spongilla and other common fresh-water sponges

often measure several inches in extent, while still others form clumps as large as a quart measure. The Spongillas which grow in direct sunshine are soft green or even brilliant green with chlorophyll, but individuals of the same species hidden beneath rocks or even shaded by brook banks are straw colored or creamy white. The pale ones are more easily recognized as sponges; they are the color of the dried or bleached ones which we are used to seeing; their surfaces are full of holes like bath sponges; they will squeeze dry in the same way and will give off the sulphury smell suggestive of a salt-water sulphur-sponge.

The Spongillas harbor some constant but very inconspicuous visitors, larvae of Spongilla flies which later emerge into the air as four-winged flies. These immature Spongilla flies have long antennae and six legs which readily identify them as insects. They are small, never more than a quarter of an inch long. They are yellowish green with faint dapplings of brown on their backs and with little bristles sticking out from their bodies. Bits of debris and broken sponge catch upon these bristles and hide the shape of their bodies. Being hidden in all these ways they also eat the sponge tissue; they fill their food canals full of it and so become literally sponge colored inside as well as outside. No one could want a more convincing camouflage than a young Spongilla fly which has eaten its way down into a sponge. It may be resting there with its whole length in full view, but be quite invisible even to careful scrutiny through a lens. It is only when it clambers over the sponge that it may be caught, and even then it is much more like a piece of sponge on legs than like an insect.

In early fall the Spongilla colonies, like the rest of the fresh-water sponges, begin to shrink and shrivel away. By October and November many of the cells have died and the spicules are left bare. But other cells have been drawn together in closely packed balls and have secreted a protecting crust about themselves. They have become the gemmules or the winter buds. These gemmules are the winter representatives of fresh-water sponges, and are seed-like in their looks and behavior; like seeds they can endure hard weather, but are so sensitive to changes that they will start to grow with any encouragement from warmth and fresh water.

FURTHER READING

Alexander, Charles P. "Ann Haven Morgan 1882-1966." *Eatonia* 8 (February 15, 1967): 1–3.
Morgan, Ann Haven. *Field Book of Animals in Winter.* New York: G. P.

Putnam Sons, 1939.

———. *Field Book of Ponds and Streams.* New York: G. P. Putnam Sons, 1930.

———. "Fresh-Water Sponges in Winter." *Scientific Monthly* 28 (February, 1929): 152–55.

———. "Mayflies of Fall Creek." *Annals of the Entomological Society of America* 4 (June, 1911): 93–117.

———. Papers. Williston Memorial Library Archives. Mount Holyoke College, South Hadley, Mass.

19

Margaret Morse Nice

1883–1974

No one knew the "language and customs" of song sparrows better than Margaret Morse Nice. Affectionately referred to as the "Song Sparrow Lady" by those who admired her pioneering life history study of those common birds, Nice employed the same meticulous, painstaking methods of research while observing many other bird species. Appropriately enough, she called her one popularly written book published about her work *The Watcher at the Nest*. Although a large portion of it is devoted to her eight-year song sparrow study, several chapters, such as "Loti: the Tale of a Bobwhite," recount her observations and relationships with other bird species.

The study of Loti and what he ate had earned her a master's degree at Clark University in Worcester, Massachusetts. While she was there, she also acquired a husband, fellow student Leonard Blaine Nice. While he finished his Ph.D. and then accepted a faculty position at the University of Oklahoma, she was sidetracked for years from her natural history study by family obligations, most notably the raising of five daughters, one of whom died in childhood.

Then came her "awakening," as she called it in her posthumously published autobiography, *Research Is a Passion with Me*. Recalling her early love of nature, especially birds, during her childhood in Amherst, Massachusetts, she resolved in her adulthood to once again make the study and protection of nature her life's work. At the age of thirty-six, enthusiastically supported by her husband and daughters, she set out to prove that mourning doves were not finished nesting by August, an assertion made by Oklahoma hunting advocates in their effort to open the hunting season early. With the help of her tree-climbing daughters, Nice quickly discovered that mourning doves nested through September and even into October, information she used to torpedo the proposal for August mourning dove hunting.

Encouraged by her success, she and her husband, accompanied by their daughters, drove and camped all over Oklahoma the next couple of summers in an effort to compile a bird list of the state. As a result, they co-authored *The Birds of Oklahoma,* which was published in 1924 as a University of Oklahoma bulletin. It was, according to one ornithologist of the time, "the first important step that has been taken in putting Oklahoma in the ornithological world." Years later, in 1967, when ornithologist George Miksch Sutton published his definitive *Oklahoma Birds,* he gave full credit to their work, declaring in his introduction that the Nices' book had been of "inestimable value" for the information it contained.

In 1928 Leonard Blaine Nice accepted a professorship at Ohio State University Medical School, and the family moved to the outskirts of Columbus in a home, surrounded by "perfect song sparrow habitat." There Nice launched her song sparrow study, primarily to bolster the research by European ornithologists of bird territoriality. She not only proved that song sparrow males defended defined territories, but she also learned more about the life history of one single species than any previous researcher. Her work, ethologist Konrad Lorenz later wrote, was "a major break-through in the methods of studying animal behavior . . . the first long-term field investigation of the individual life of any free-living wild animal."

With the publication of her *Population Study of the Song Sparrow,* Nice became an ornithological celebrity. In 1937 the American Ornithologists' Union made her a fellow, only the second woman to have been so honored at that time. That same year she also assumed the presidency of the Wilson Ornithological Club. In 1942 she received the coveted Brewster Medal from the A.O.U., again for her song sparrow work.

Although she continued her bird study, she became increasingly involved in conservation efforts, triggered perhaps by her dismay over the "sanitizing" of her song sparrow habitat by city officials. In 1955 she received an honorary Ph.D. from her alma mater, Mount Holyoke, and another in 1962 from Elmira College. In addition she had a Mexican song sparrow subspecies named for her—*Melospiza melodia niceae.*

Nice wanted to be a success as a popular writer too, but *The Watcher at the Nest* sold only 1,006 books. Before her death at the age of ninety in 1974, she could not find a publisher for her autobiography. Nevertheless, both books are filled with insights about her life and

190

Margaret Morse Nice with husband Dr. Blaine Nice (*left*) and daughter
Constance Nice (*right*) at Delta, Manitoba, Canada, summer, 1953. *Courtesy
American Ornithologists' Union Collection, Record Unit 7150, Smithsonian Institution
Archives.*

work. The excerpt from "The Awakening" in *Research Is a Passion
with Me* succinctly sums up her goals. "On Watching an Ovenbird's
Nest" from *The Watcher at the Nest* illustrates her approach to bird
study and also includes descriptions of both the pleasures and dis-
comforts of such work.

"The Grandchildren of Uno and 4M," another excerpt from *The
Watcher at the Nest*, discusses the offspring of her two most prominent
male song sparrows: Uno was the first one she studied, and 4M was
the longest lived (eight years) and greatest singer (2,305 songs in
one day). That excerpt, in addition to giving the reader an appreciation for her hard work and dedication, describes her awakening as
a conservationist. The selection ends with her praise for the virtues
of weeds, a warning that still needs to be heeded today by most humans who believe that all weeds should be eliminated. "What good is
it?" is often the rallying cry of the ignorant. No answer could be

clearer and more to the point than Nice's reply—"where such things [weeds] are, there will birds be also."

August 20 chanced to be cool, and I escaped by myself to the river along one of our favourite paths with its tangled vines and bushes, its mistletoe-laden elms, its Cardinals, orioles, and gnatcatchers, its display of wayside flowers. Many of these flowers were armed with spines—the exquisite great white prickly poppy, the rosin weeds, golden prionopsis, weedy horse nettle, and fierce tread-softly with its coarse spotted leaves. A large hawk flew to shelter in some cotton-woods pursued by six kingbirds and a dashing Scissor-tailed Flycatcher. One of the kingbirds was so excited that he attacked an inoffensive Turkey Vulture.

At Low Brook, just east of the river bed, myriads of little moths rose around me, while a great black and white beetle with antennae two inches long buzzed as it flew by. It seemed like fairyland with new flowers at every step. Many of these belonged to the pulse fam-ily—partridge pea, wild creeping pea with long narrow pods poking out under the bright pink bonnet of the flower, tick trefoil, pink and yellow bird's foot trefoil. There was a little pink fog fruit and, loveli-est of all, a wonderful deep blue gentian, *Estoma Russellianum*, far larger than the fringed gentian of the East, and as stately as a wood lily. And for the last touch of enchantment, the hauntingly sweet refrain of the Field Sparrow.

Under the great elms and cottonwoods on the river bank I watched the turbulent Canadian River and dreamed. The glory of nature possessed me. I saw that for many years I had lost my way. I had been led astray on false trails and had been trying to do things contrary to my nature. I resolved to return to my childhood vision of studying nature and trying to protect the wild things of the earth.

I thought of my friends who never take walks in Oklahoma, "for there was nothing to see." I was amazed and grieved at their blind-ness. I longed to open their eyes to the wonders around them; to persuade people to love and cherish nature. Perhaps I might be a sort of John Burroughs [New York naturalist-writer and author of dozens of books, including *Wake Robin*] for Oklahoma.

This August walk was a turning point in my life. It was a day of vision and prophecy. But what the future really held in store for me would have seemed to me utterly fantastic.

On Watching an Ovenbird's Nest

One Monday in July as I wandered through the woods, I was suddenly stopped by loud protestations. Looking about, I saw an Ovenbird on a branch with his bill full of grubs while below on the ground beside the Dutch oven of a nest stood the mother bird, staring up at me absolutely motionless. As I walked towards her, she flew up, adding her objections to those of her mate. Inside the nest were two tiny infants, blind and naked. I retired behind a bush twenty feet away, effacing myself as much as possible, but the commotion kept on unabated. All the neighbors came to sympathize or look on—another pair of Ovenbirds, a Black and White Warbler, a Chestnut-sided Warbler, a Black-throated Green Warbler, a Phoebe, and a Chewink [rufous-sided towhee].

After a while father with a moth in his bill descended to the ground, flew up again, scolded and scolded, raising his orange crown and jerking his tail; then flew down again and ran towards the nest still objecting. His mate became frantic with alarm, on seeing such rash conduct; he reconsidered, flew up above the nest, ate his insect, and devoted himself to reproaches.

Seeing that the situation was hopeless, I moved forty feet away across the brook, seating myself beside a rock and behind a small hop hornbeam tree; with my glasses I could see the happenings at the nest. At once there was peace, and in two minutes mother went to the young to brood them. Soon Father came with a big spider and caterpillar; his mate slipped out and waited while he fed the babies, returning to them when he left.

Mother brooded and brooded, then slipped quietly off and walked away. For a long time she stayed away, finally reappearing as stealthily as she had left, bringing with her a large meal. The most striking thing about the routine of an Ovenbird's household is its deliberateness—broodings three-quarters of an hour long, meals sometimes an hour and a half apart—all in marked contrast to the ways of most warblers, whose broodings are short, and who bring food every five to ten minutes.

It seemed as if life stood still for me while I devoted myself to this nest, as if I had endless leisure to look, to enjoy, to think, alone in this pleasant place in the woods. The stately clusters of evergreen wood fern, the sun-dappled water beeches and hemlocks, the tiny waterfall—to these I could give but fleeting glances, for always I had to concentrate on the rocks and brown leaves about the center of activities of mother Ovenbird. A baby tree bowed; I seized my glasses, for any movement in that region was fraught with possible meaning. But the alarm was false. It is curious how one small branch will bend with a breeze that nothing else feels. In these vigils I learned much of the ways of the wind.

Often there was no sound but that of the tumbling brook. Sometimes there were discordant notes. A soft pattering across the leaves, and suddenly a red squirrel vented his wrath at my presence by the strangest of squeaks and squeals, more like those we expect from a toy than those from a real animal. A grey squirrel flirted his handsome tail in quirks and curlicues and then exploded into a snarling, jarring string of vituperations, extraordinary noises to proceed from such a soft and furry little beast.

The birds were pure delight. The Scarlet Tanager threw a wild, proud challenge to the woods in keeping with his gorgeous plumage. The solemn, continuous strain of the Red-eyed Vireo embodied the very spirit of serenity and content. Most beautiful of all was the song of the Hermit Thrush; when heard near by it has a note of courage, of triumph over the difficulties of life; at a distance it expresses ineffable sweetness and peace.

Mother Ovenbird had her notions; she did not mind me looking at her when she was by the nest, but if ever I caught sight of her on her way there, she froze at once, and would not be reassured until I had put down the offending glasses. It was curious that on Tuesday morning, of the five intervals between the meals she brought, four lasted exactly forty-eight minutes each.

That afternoon I noted:

"How pretty mother looks inside her rustic bower! She steps out and views the weather, which is threatening; then withdraws again to shelter."

Father was an almost negligible factor in the home life during the first half of the week, for he seldom came with food, sometimes absenting himself for an afternoon at a time, and he did not even proclaim his territory with the loud, insistent *teacher teacher teacher teacher,* as is the custom of his kind earlier in the season. On Wednesday I was shocked to see a Hermit Thrush chase him three times, when he had had one of his rare impulses to bring food to the young.

Although most of the authorities state that male and female Ovenbirds are identical in appearance, I was glad to find that I could distinguish my birds, not only by the brighter orange crown of the male, but particularly by the color of their backs, father's being more golden brown, and mother's having more of an olive cast.

Mr. [Henry] Mousley [of Hatley, Stanstead County, Quebec, author of several studies on birds, especially warblers and ovenbirds, published in the *Auk*] "never once approached the nest" of the

Ovenbirds he was studying; but by choosing my time I could steal across the brook each day and admire the progress of the babies without the parents being any the wiser. Although little Ovenbirds are fed so seldom in comparison with most other baby birds, their meals make up in size what they lack in number. I was repeatedly astonished at the enormous mouthfuls of spiders, caterpillars and moths that were brought to the young.

Thursday afternoon there came a change in the schedule. Mother gave up brooding and guarded instead, mounting a near-by bush and sitting quietly for fifteen minutes or so, her handsome black-streaked breast puffed out—a picture of motherly satisfaction. Father suddenly woke up to his responsibilities, and for the rest of the week outdid his mate in bringing food. Instead of meals appearing once every forty-two minutes, they now came at the rate of once in twenty minutes, the difference being largely due to father's zeal, since mother kept on the even tenor of her way, hardly hastening her return at all.

On Saturday morning the young had been fed at 10:35 and I was beginning to feel that it was full time they received further attention:

"11:35. A bird flies down two yards from the nest. She feeds; then the male comes walking over the leaves. She steps aside for him while he feeds. Strangely enough a gaping, reproachful mouth waves at them as they leave, like a comic picture of a ferocious snake. Did both large portions go into one maw?"

On Sunday morning as I neared the familiar spot, I heard mother scolding very hard and fast. It was plain that something had happened; I went directly to the nest and found it empty. I had never dreamt that the precocious little creatures would leave so soon. How could they have deserted their warm, dry, cozy home for the wild wet woods?

Sadly I returned to my accustomed post; soon it was evident that one baby was near the nest in mother's charge, while the other was in a bed of ferns tended by father. So I watched the family for some time, not realizing how far a little Ovenbird may travel at such a tender age; when I went to investigate, mother's babe was far away and well hidden. The fern bed was a baffling place to search, but all at once I heard a shrill *peep peep peep;* following the sound I discovered baby looking like a little light brown leaf, the fuzz of down outside his feathers giving him a very odd appearance. His tail had barely sprouted, and his flight feathers were not unsheathed; he could not possibly have flown, but his legs were strong and well developed.

I gently picked him up and he was not a bit afraid; in a few minutes he went to sleep in my hand. Father appeared with a caterpillar, but instead of going through the extravagant demonstration of alarm I expected, merely gave a loud *tchip* and vanished. Baby began to preen himself, then said *peep* and again *peep*. A mosquito started to bite my hand, and I brought it in front of the little bird as a small tidbit; but he did not peck at it till it flew. Another alighted on his wing and sucked itself full, while I perceived a new bond of sympathy between birds and people.

Presently baby grew hungry and called more and more frequently, so I returned him to his twig and went back to my hornbeam. Louder and more persistent came his far-reaching cries, until I could not help thinking how easily an enemy might find him. It was time for me to go home; as I passed the fern bed I stepped on a dead twig that snapped—instantly there was silence. I do not suppose the little fellow had ever heard this sound before, but something in his inherited make-up told him it spelled danger. I was not able to visit this family again, but I hope they escaped the perils of youth, and journeyed South in safety.

By good fortune the next summer I again discovered an Ovenbird's nest in the Grey Rocks [the Nices' Massachusetts summer home] woods in mid-July. The mother flew quietly away from her three eggs, but the following day she behaved differently. While her mate scolded at my approach, she hurried off, then turned back, and ran about in a peculiar attitude with her back hunched, wings dragging, tail spread fanwise and body feathers puffed out. There was no simulation of injury, but she certainly did look strange and conspicuous and well suited to draw the attention of an unsophisticated enemy to herself.

The next morning (which happened to be Monday) two babies had hatched. I settled myself twenty feet away behind a little hemlock, thankful that neither parent had seen me look at their progeny. Before long there was a rustle in the great hemlock to the south and I became motionless while mosquitoes settled over my face. I felt like St. Macarius who, inadvertently crushing a gnat and thereby missing an opportunity of enduring mortification patiently, stationed himself for six months in the marshes of Scete. Fortunately for me, little mother took only three minutes to decide that I was not too alarming a neighbor. She flew to the ground and walked to the nest where she fed the babies and stepped in to brood. Then I began once more on my occupation of reducing the pests of the world.

Mother hovered her children for fifty-four minutes, then walked away, but to my surprise returned in ten minutes with another large meal—the other mother had never spent less than seventeen minutes away. This time she waited in the hemlock two minutes and the next time only one, and after that bothered no more about me. How my heart warmed to her for her good sense and devotion!

Her mate, unfortunately, felt differently about me. He came once that morning to bestow a morsel on his offspring, but upon spying me, he started to scold and for one half-hour he protested; then he departed, not to be seen again that day nor the next. In an attempt to calm his nerves, I moved farther away; but even that concession did not reassure him. Sometimes I heard his loud announcement of ownership and very occasionally the ecstatic flight song; but he refused to risk his precious skin by coming near me.

For three days the routine varied very little; long broodings; sometimes long, sometimes short, absences from the nest; ten large meals brought during eight hours the first day, eleven the next, and fourteen the next—and every bit of the work done by mother. Oddly enough there were two intervals of forty-eight minutes on this Tuesday, one of forty-six, and one of forty-four.

Wednesday father appeared with a contribution; but instead of feeding his babies all he did was to reprove me, raise his crest, flutter his wings, and give a curious, soft, three-syllabled note to his mate. She, as if in a spirit of bravado to show him the unreasonableness of his fears, did a thing without precedent, for she dropped directly down to the nest from a branch above it. (Every other time she walked from quite a distance to the nest.) Still he remained stubbornly distrustful.

One day I had a philosophic thought; namely, that pleasure was given to three sets of beings by the occasional visits from the biting flies: First, it must seem like a banquet to the flies to discover me still and tasty in the woods. Next, there was a distinct feeling of achievement within me when I dispatched the creatures. And finally the carcass was a boon to the ant that carried it off for a dinner with her sisters. My philosophizings vanished, however, the next day when I was attacked by an army of deer flies. I used to think the etymology of Beelzebub—"king of the flies"—was a prophetic reference to the noxious germs given us by our satellite the housefly, but now I knew better; it was these little demons that were meant.

This year as last, Thursday afternoon showed a change in the home life; but this time the male had no part in it. First, mother gave up brooding; then, instead of walking directly away when leaving the nest as heretofore, she browsed around for a few minutes in front of the nest, finding small insects for herself; twice she flew away instead of leaving on foot; and finally she fed her three children twice as often as before. The first three and one-half days she had brought meals once in forty minutes on an average; this afternoon she presented them once every nineteen minutes. I looked forward eagerly to what the next day would bring forth, in further variations in her behavior and a possible reform on the part of her mate.

As I watched little mother, I longed to know more of her life. I wished I could have seen the courtship, could have viewed the construction of the quaint little home, and then could have followed the fortunes of the young family after their first venture into the world, and somehow could have known how they found their way on the incredible journeys to South America and back to these Massachusetts woods. A great admiration for this quiet little bird arose in me, for her self-sufficiency, the simplicity of her life unencumbered by the possessions that overwhelm us human beings. Here she was her own architect, her own provider, bringing up her babies independently of doctors, nurses, books, and even her husband, facing unaided the elements and prowling enemies.

Each evening I left a blessing with the brave little bird, and each morning was happy to find all well. But Friday as I walked through the woods, I noticed that big mushrooms that had been standing for several days were now lying low, gnawed by some animal. A sense of foreboding caused me to go straight to the nest as soon as I reached my hemlock; the home was empty and beside it lay five feathers from little mother's wing. I trust the gallant little bird had escaped with her life.

THE GRANDCHILDREN OF UNO AND 4M

Each season I had banded as many Song Sparrow babies in the nest as I could, the number one year passing the hundred mark. The babies, once grown, did not come back to their exact birthplace and enter the trap in our garden, as did some amiable members of their species in New England. I had to go forth to find them. The first discovery was that of UNO's and UNA's daughter, nesting with 13M [coding system for thirteenth banded male] some two hundred yards from home. The next year there were no fewer than seven young resident males, banded on the right leg, sprinkled all over Interpont [Nice's enlarged study area in Columbus, meaning "between the bridges"] and even beyond its borders.

Tracking my banded young took me farther and farther afield, and trapping them to discover their identity often resulted in the capture of their mates and neighbors; so gradually I extended my interests over a larger and larger area. After I had learned the language and customs of Song Sparrows and had come to know intimately a few individuals, I became fired with ambition to discover what took place among the inhabitants on the whole of Interpont. I had begun this enterprise in the spring of 1930; for four more years I worked on it, mapping and trapping, exploring the territories for the nests, and recording the vital statistics of the population.

Up and down Interpont I tramped in sunshine, rain, and snow, grieving over the untimely death of many a bird, exulting in the return of another or the discovery of some particularly well hidden nest. Though difficulties and disappointments were great, the rewards were greater. Interpont brought me deep satisfaction and keen adventure.

To my great delight, a grandson of Uno, 50M, turned up in our garden in September, 1930; he and his grandfather must have often seen and heard each other that fall, but I fear that it was only I who knew the relationship. 50M proved to be an all-year resident. In the winter he associated in our garden with 4M and other Song Sparrows, and in his first February quarreled with his ancestral rival over territory matters. He established his territory just south of our house, including part of his grandfather's estate. Twice he nested in the very woodbine where Uno's last nest had been built. In 1931 and again two years later I had the proud privilege of banding great-grandchildren of my beloved Uno; but to my disappointment I never found any of them in later years.

Una had another grandson, 95M, son of 55M, son of 5M. Una and 5M were both summer residents, but their son and grandson were permanent residents. 55M nested on North Interpont; although twelve days younger than 50M he was the latter's uncle. 95M did not have a successful life; one leg hung broken and useless, and his handsome wife deserted him.

4M lived for so many years that one would expect his descendants to have made up a fair share of the population of Interpont. This, however, was not the case, so far as I am aware. Unfortunately in 1929 his brood of four left the nest without bands, and only the single baby in the last nest was marked. Neither this bird nor any of Rosemary's[1] four children raised the next year were found after they left the nest.

During the next five years 4M raised but four young while I was on Interpont, although in all probability more little birds were fledged later in three of the seasons. One child from each of the two successful nests survived to adulthood. Blueberry's son nested a third of a mile from home for two years; he was a resident, and his songs were all different from those of his father. On May 24, 1932, I had the pleasure of banding 4M's two grandchildren; but, to my regret, I never saw them after they left the nest.

In the early spring of 1935 I was very happy to welcome 4M's daughter to 50M's former territory, not sixty feet from her birthplace. Like her father and half-brother she was a resident, although her mother was migratory. Her husband, 223M, was also a resident. She built her nest in a lattice and astonished me by laying some of the largest Song Sparrow eggs I ever measured, although she herself was a small bird. Once again disaster befell a particularly cherished bird; 4M's and Goldenrod's daughter was killed by a neighbor's cat.

In two other family lines besides Uno's and Una's I knew of grandchildren that returned and nested; but never did I find a great-grandchild of any of my Song Sparrows as a breeding bird. The reasons were two. Since I shouldered this great undertaking alone, I could not possibly find all the nests of all the birds in whom I was interested; nor could I usually carry observations throughout the whole nesting season. The other reason was the fate of Interpont.

This pleasant place of some forty acres reached its height of prosperity in March, 1932, with the population at its peak—sixty-nine pairs of Song Sparrows (all, by heroic efforts, banded)—while Interpont itself was a lovely tangle of luxuriant weeds and elder bushes. This happy state of affairs was not to last. Three misfortunes befell the Song Sparrows that season: a cold April that delayed the start of nesting, a drought in May that reduced the insect supply, and a veritable plague of Cowbirds. The next spring an unseasonable flood covered most of the nests.

These setbacks could have been endured, and when conditions were favorable again, the Song Sparrows could have multiplied once more. But in the spring of 1933 Interpont was taken over for gardens for the unemployed. Much as I regretted this, I felt it had to be; but the inexcusable destruction of trees, shrubs, and weeds along the dikes and river banks was an example of stupidity that has been only too common of late years. The Song Sparrows with few places to nest and little cover to protect them from their enemies, dwindled to a pitiful remnant.

In the days when cover was adequate and the birds were relatively undisturbed, over sixty per cent of my nesting males had survived from one year to the next and a breeding Song Sparrow lived on the average for two and a half years. In later years, however, the average life of those birds that reached maturity was only one and three-tenths years! It is no wonder that family lines became extinct.

The Song Sparrow is well able to stand rigors of climate and to keep up its numbers despite natural enemies, provided it has sufficient cover for shelter for itself and its young. But when cats and rats are added to the list of predators, and its brushy, weedy haunts are demolished in the interest of "neatness," the odds are too great.

Let us look at the humble beauty of waste places not with prejudice but enlightenment. "How rich," wrote Thoreau of his Massachusetts haunts, "like what we love to read of South American forests, is the scenery of this river! What luxuriance of weeds, what depths of mud along its sides!"

Indeed, weeds were one of the glories of Interpont—the giant ragweeds that towered above one's head, the thistles that offered snug homes to Goldfinches, the incredible cow parsnips in May, the asters and goldenrods that wove bright patterns along the ditches. Despised by many, weeds are in reality an important element in our landscape, holding the precious soil, providing nesting places for many birds, extending hospitality to migrating hosts of native sparrows that feed upon their seeds and to warblers that find upon them a harvest of insects, and finally affording food and shelter to those hardy birds that brave the northern winter. Let us therefore leave weeds and shrubs and tangled vines wherever we can along roadsides and fence rows, for where such things are, there will birds be also.

NOTE

1. Nice gave the banded female birds more personal names that often reflected her interpretation of their personalities. For example, Xantippe was named for her shrew-like characteristics.

FURTHER READING

Bonta, Marcia. "An Extraordinary Bird Watcher." *Bird Watcher's Digest* 3 (January–February, 1981): 66–67.

———. "Song Sparrow Lady." *Birder's World* 7 (August, 1993): 24–28.

Laskey, Amelia. Papers. Cumberland Museum and Science Center, Nashville, Tenn.

Nice, Margaret Morse. *Research Is a Passion with Me.* Toronto: Consolidated Amethyst Communications, 1979.

———. "A Study of the Nesting of Mourning Doves." *Auk* 39 (1922): 457–74.

———. *The Watcher at the Nest.* New York: Macmillan, 1939.

———. Papers. Dept. of Manuscripts and University Archives. Cornell University Library, Ithaca, N.Y.

Parkes, Kenneth C. "Margaret Morse Nice." *Wilson Bulletin* 86

(September, 1974): 301–302.

Trautman, Milton B. "In Memoriam: Margaret Morse Nice." *Auk* 94 (July, 1977): 430–41.

20

Nellie Harris Rau

188?–1972

LIKE THE PECKHAMS, ANOTHER HUSBAND AND WIFE entomological team—
Phil and Nellie Rau—co-authored a book on wasps. Published in
1918, *Wasp Studies Afield* often quotes the Peckhams' observations as
justification for their own observations of insect behavior. Although
the Raus co-authored several scientific papers, Phil Rau, unlike George
Peckham, wrote a book—*Jungle Bees and Wasps of Barro Colorado Island*—
and many scientific papers by himself. So except for a brief mention
in Edwin P. Meiners's obituary of Phil Rau, in which he said that "his
devoted wife shared his interests and was co-author, with him, of many
published papers," Nellie Rau's contributions to entomology were
overlooked.

In fact, Nellie Rau herself never mentioned her own role in entomology research when she sent in her Forty-Fifth Reunion Report to
her alma mater, the University of Kansas, in 1954. "Life has been
hard and good," she wrote. She had had three children. But after
the death of her beloved Phil, she began raising a second family, the
three children of her deceased daughter-in-law. During an interview
with author Mary Chomeau in 1965, "this generous and modest soul
never mentioned that she collaborated with her husband," Chomeau
reported.

Yet Nellie Harris Rau had more formal education than Phil Rau.
Born near Athens, Ohio, she had moved with her parents and her
brother to western Kansas when she was three years old. Eventually,
the family relocated to Lawrence, Kansas, where Nellie Harris
attended high school and intermittently worked her way through
the University of Kansas to obtain a degree in library science.

Her scientist brother, J. Arthur Harris, was a major influence on her life by providing an initial path for her to follow. He received a Ph.D. in biology in 1903 from Washington University in St. Louis, and from 1901 until 1903 he served as a botanical assistant at the Missouri Botanical Gardens. In 1904, when he was made Librarian of the Garden, Nellie Harris was hired as a cataloger. Three years later her brother moved to Cold Spring Harbor, Long Island, and Harris returned to the University of Kansas to finish her studies, graduating with the class of 1909.

Sometime between 1908 and 1909, she accompanied her brother on a scientific research trip to England, gaining a deeper understanding of scientific publishing. Apparently, she then returned to work at the Missouri Botanical Garden, where she met her husband-to-be. Phil, the son of a German immigrant, had had to quit school in the fourth grade to help his family run a dry goods store. He was an avid reader with a special interest in nature study. When he was twenty years old, he spent two years as a special student at Washington University. By 1910 he had published his first paper in insect behavior, and in 1911 he and Nellie Harris were married.

Years later, after Nellie Rau's death, their daughter Martha wrote: "Phil and Nellie Rau . . . did all the writing together, and also most of the scientific observations together. Both are highly respected in the field of natural science, and they became noted as a rare husband-wife team in the production of scientific information. They both were pioneers in the study of Nature in its natural setting, . . . they went out into the field to study it as it lived." Both Martha and her brother David recalled a lively childhood. As children, they and their brother Justin had kept dogs, rabbits, and white-footed mice as pets, engaged in a mind-boggling array of hobbies, and still managed to accompany their parents on their field trips in the vicinity of St. Louis. The Raus' *Wasp Studies Afield* was the result of four years of outdoor study, probably completed after the birth of their twin sons in 1912 and before the birth of their daughter in 1917. Most of their observations were made in St. Louis or within a thirty-mile radius of the city, which included Creve Coeur Lake; Eureka; Moselle; Merramec Highlands; Fox Creek, Missouri; and Clifton Terrace, Illinois. At Fox Creek, the Raus reported that they were allowed to "prowl about people's premises [but] . . . our erratic behavior was . . . regarded with grave suspicion by the population of this rustic community."

Like the Peckhams, they dug up nest burrows to observe how different wasp species laid their eggs and to determine the eggs' shape and length. They also witnessed tool-using by *Ammophila* by observing *A. pictipennis*. Once Nellie Rau had an unusually close encounter with *Ammophila:*

> On another sunny September morning the feminine partner in these observations was sitting on the ground, busily writing up the notes of the morning's observations, when an *Ammophila* came and began industriously digging up a burrow right beside her knee, while another, homeward bound with its prey, climbed up on her dress and trundled its caterpillar down the full length of her bare forearm, pausing once and laying the cut-worm down on her hand while it washed its face and looked about inquiringly, then moving calmly on to the burrow beyond.

Altogether they described the behavior of sixty wasp species and concluded that wasps had "very definite and iron-clad instincts, [yet] there is much variation in the behavior of the individuals, [and] that, in many instances, there is much aptitude for learning, display of memory, profiting by experience and what seems to us rational conduct."

The following excerpt from *Wasp Studies Afield* illustrates the Raus' patient watching techniques and their occasional impatience when they are forced to interfere in the female Pompilid wasp's nest-building. The Raus attempt to hurry along the process in an effort to discover the shape and depth of the burrow and the condition of the spider prey and the wasp's eggs. What is especially clear from this excerpt and from the rest of the book, however, is that Nellie Rau was definitely an active and participating partner with her entomological husband.

BEHAVIOR OF POMPILID WASPS

On another morning, as we were walking across the field past a spot from which all the grass had been trodden, we suddenly scared up from the edge of the grass a *P. tropicus*. She had been engaged in carrying a spider, *Lycosa frondicola* Em. female (N. Banks), not quite mature, but larger than herself. After a quarter of an hour she appeared searching vaguely in the general region, but most of the time six to twelve feet distant from her spider. She searched by walking a few inches, then hopping and flying a foot or two, occasionally taking a circle on the wing just above the grass-tops. She seemed to gain no headway in her search, so presently she went over to a small patch of cockleburs, which was six feet from the spider, and hopped and circled over the plants with an air of getting her bearings. Her behavior made us wonder if she had originally found the spider near these plants and had gone back to retrace her steps. Then she started out in the direction of the grass-plot, but missed her prey, so she went back to the cockleburs again, repeated the performance, and this time went almost directly to her spider. She pounced upon it viciously, as if she thought it necessary that it be attacked vigorously, and got a good grip, grasping it by its ventral side back of the third pair of legs.

She dragged it thus a foot or so, walking backward and pulling like a dray-horse; then poised it in some grasses and went back to hunt a place for a hole. She found a depression in the earth, a place where we had dug with a trowel the day before. The ground was dry and hard, with much dust on top. She tried spots here and there in the side-walls of this hole, scratching and biting furiously in eight different places, but she found the ground too hard and the surface dust fell in on her. After trying thus a long while, she went straight back to her spider two feet away and brought it nearer, then returned to dig, as if satisfied that this place was as good as she could expect to find. Then she seemed suddenly to decide upon her spot, and, after just a few strokes of digging, for the first time she swept the dirt back from the space immediately in front of the hole. It was hard digging, so while she was gone to visit her spider again we pierced the firm surface crust to help start her nest. After this she dug rapidly, coming out and visiting her spider six times while it lay in this position. We do not know if she examined the spider frequently in order to see if it was behaving properly, or to gain an accurate idea of the required size of her hole. Next she lugged it one foot nearer to the opening, dug out more earth and again moved the spider nearer, to a spot only nine inches from the hole. She always grasped the spider by the middle of its ventral surface and carried it vertically, the spider's hind legs dragging behind while the front ones hung limp; she did not at any time drag it sidewise by the legs as other Pompilids do. Furthermore, she always walked backward when she had the burden and could not see her way very well, so she constantly struggled over obstacles that she might as easily have avoided if she could have seen where she was going. At one time in moving her spider she struggled through grass and over a tangle of weeds for fifteen inches, when a perfectly smooth clear path lay beside her, all the way, less than two inches from her at all points.

She seemed now to feel the enthusiasm of seeing her work nearing completion, and dug furiously for a few minutes more; then she brought the spider very near and hung it carefully on the tiny weed nearest to the hole, only four inches distant, removed a few more mouthfuls and kicked back the dirt, then dragged the arachnid to the mouth of the burrow and attempted to take it in; but it was too large, so she left it at the opening of the burrow and proceeded to deepen the hole, vigorously kicking the dirt out all over the spider. She dug on and on in this way for an hour, only occasionally kicking or sweeping a little dirt off the spider. We suspected that she did this, not for the sake of keeping her spider cleared, but merely to follow her habit of occasionally clearing away the débris around her door-way. Some tiny ants hung around a bit inquisitively; the wasp came out of the hole and bit at them, kicked at them and curled up her sting at them menacingly until they withdrew.

Once when the wasp had swept the dirt off the spider it stirred, scrambled to its feet and walked away three inches, whereupon she promptly pounced upon it and the pair rolled over in a tumble—she probably stung it—then as it lay quiet she calmly mounted its back and precisely curled her abdomen around its body and planted a deliberate sting in the ventral part of the thorax, just in front of the last pair of legs; then she took it back and laid it up-side-down with care, at the mouth of the hole and resumed her digging and kicking dust all over it. So, to try her, when she was deep in the hole we drew the spider back two inches and turned it right-side-up. When the wasp emerged she saw it but paid no attention to the fact that its position had been altered. On her second appearance it began to wiggle its legs; she pounced upon it ferociously and tumbled over, probably stinging it, as the spider did not resist further; then she casually stung it again, as if for good measure, between the third and fourth pairs of legs; then as it lay on its back she most deliberately placed her sting between the second and third right legs, near the center of the body, and left it there for several seconds, while the spider convulsively drew up its quivering legs and stirred no more. Tiny drops of juice oozed out of the wounds; she paused and seemed to drink this. Then she marched away with a most triumphant and self-satisfied air.

By this time she had apparently learned that she could not profit by keeping her prey lying at the mouth of the hole, so she carried it to a spot five inches away and proceeded with her digging, visiting it often, as if to see that it was behaving properly. She worked by dig-ging up the loose dirt in the hole and then backing out, pushing it up in a mound behind her. But, we asked ourselves, why did she dig so deep and not make the hole wide enough to admit the spider?

Time dragged by—perhaps she spent another hour in enlarging the hole. At last! for the first time she came pushing her way, head first, up through her mound of loose dirt. Once more she visited the spider and shook it enquiringly by the left leg, went in and pushed out the last bit of loose dirt, emerged head first again, grasped the spider by the left coxa and, with much labor, dragged and tugged it in. Thus we see that she made her exit head first only when the next was ready to receive the provisions. The spider fitted in the hole so tightly that its legs were all doubled straight back. At the last her economy was better than we had judged, for the hole was wide enough after all, with no wasted space, and the spider fitted in the hole so snugly that it could not possibly use its legs to kick or work itself free. After the prey was in the hole she continued pushing up loose, fresh dirt, evidently clearing the way as she moved it back in the gallery. The passage must have been of greater diameter below the surface, however, in order to allow both her and the dirt to pass beside the spider. After ten minutes she had thrown up enough fresh dirt to completely close the mouth of the burrow, so we could see no more of her doings. She did not come out on the surface any more, since her property was no longer outside.

The quarter-hours passed, yet she did not reappear. Thrilling indeed! Two rational human beings squatting in the burning sun, watching a motionless spot of earth!—But how consoling that the poet who best knew patience has said:

"He also serves who only stands and waits."

At length we were preparing to dig her up, when suddenly a speck of the loose dirt in the middle of her mound quivered and a tiny hole appeared; she was hollowing it out from underneath and slowly packing it firmly back into the channel as she came up, until now the door was falling in. She emerged gradually, slowly, packing the loose dirt back into the hole with all her legs and punching it down with the tip of her ventrally curved abdomen. She filled it in tight to the top, swept the dust back over it loosely and departed so promptly that we had trouble in intercepting her.

When we dug out the burrow the spider kicked so vigorously that it seemed it would dislodge the egg. The long, white egg was slightly curved and fitted nicely to the side of the abdomen where the larva would be in position for the juicy, tender part of its food first.

The hole, one-fourth inch in diameter, went downward at an angle of 40 degrees with the surface level, for about two inches, and terminated in an oval, horizontal chamber an inch long and a half-inch wide.

From these observations we may be sure that the egg was deposited and the spider entombed at about 11:45 A.M. At 10 o'clock that evening the spider was active and would make the characteristic

threatening spring back when touched. The legs could move actively but not coordinately, and were unfit for progression; the mandibles attempted to close, but could do no more than quiver, when
tickled with a straw. After this activity we were surprised the next
morning to find it dead. By the following day we were quite certain
that the egg too was dead.

FURTHER READING

Chomeau, Mary. "The Rau Family." *Kirkwood Historical Review* 11 (June,
1972): 297–303.
Davenport, C. B. "James Arthur Harris." *Science* 71 (May 9, 1930):
474–75.
Mallis, Arnold. *American Entomologists.* New Brunswick, N.J.: Rutgers
University Press, 1971.
Meiner, Edwin P. "Phil Rau (1885–1948)." *Lepidopterists' News* 2 (June,
1948): 62.
Mercer, Martha Rau. "A Letter from Martha Rau Mercer." *Kirkwood
Historical Review* 11 (June, 1972): 304–07.
"Nellie Harris Rau." *Kirkwood Historical Review* 11 (December 1972): 352.
Rau, Phil, and Nellie Rau. *Wasp Studies Afield.* Princeton: Princeton
University Press, 1918.

21

Amelia Laskey

1885–1973

AMELIA LASKEY MAY HAVE BEEN THE QUINTESSENTIAL LATE BLOOMER. Once she discovered ornithology at a Bird Club meeting in Nashville, Tennessee, when she was forty-three years old, she immediately joined the Tennessee Ornithological Society. A year later, she started her thirty-year study of mockingbirds. And one year after beginning that project, she applied for a bird-banding permit from the U.S. Fish and Wildlife Service in 1931—a late but auspicious beginning to an illustrious career.

During the next three years, Laskey banded 3,734 birds of 69 species. As part of 4 long-time, life history studies of individual species, she also banded 900 mockingbirds, 1,621 northern cardinals, 1,000 blue jays, and 327 tufted titmice.

But those numbers pale in comparison to the 24,006 chimney swifts that she and five high school students banded over a five-year period as part of a national effort to discover where chimney swifts spent the winter. As a result, Laskey's schedule consisted of "evening after evening, hunting roosting flocks, . . . seeking permission to work at various places, then preparation for the actual work which often kept me busy until midnight, only to rise at 3 A.M. to get the volunteer workers to the roost by daylight . . . band[ing] on roofs of buildings, in alleys, on fire escapes, and other unconventional places, often spending the entire day working with one flock." She received notice in 1944 that one of her swifts, "Chimney Swift No. 140-44267 banded Oct. 13, 1940 at Nashville, Tennessee. Killed December 1943, River Yanayaco, Peru," had finally solved the migration mystery.

To Laskey, bird-banding was "one of the most fascinating and engrossing hobbies . . . being not only a healthful, outdoor diversion but affording opportunity for discoveries of scientific and economic value." Such discoveries included the first records for Tennessee of two subspecies—Gambel's sparrow and Bicknell's thrush—and one species—Harris's sparrow.

At first she conducted all of her bird studies on her own four acres of land surrounding her home, which she called Blossom-dell. But when she launched her extensive study of eastern bluebirds, she expanded her field work into the two-thousand-acre, publicly owned Warner Park, where she erected large numbers of bluebird nesting boxes, beginning in 1936 with twenty-six boxes and gradually expanding to nearly one hundred. For each box and bird family, she kept meticulous records. According to her younger friend and colleague Katharine A. Goodpasture, "box after box, week after week, year after year. Her carefully kept notes on the number of eggs laid, the number hatched, the number of birds fledged, repeat and return records, the movements and matings of individual birds, and predation statistics are amazing."

Such attention to detail and unremitting hard work were Laskey's most notable strengths as a self-taught ornithologist. Trained as a stenographer before her marriage, the childless woman spent her earlier years gardening, keeping an immaculate house, and playing bridge. But once she discovered birds, she began reading all she could about them, subscribing to the bird journals and buying the most important old and current bird books. She also contacted Margaret Morse Nice for advice, and, although she was only two years younger than Nice, Nice mentored her and encouraged the shy woman to write up her findings for the bird journals.

It was also Nice who called her the "patron saint of the birds" because of Laskey's rehabilitation work. In 1940, in an article she entitled "Avian Orphanage and Hospital," Laskey described her banding station as "an avian infirmary and home for feathered foundlings." Sick and stunned birds, others with broken bones, baby birds that had fallen from nests, orphaned nestlings, and lost chicks were all brought to her. She raised many of the youngsters by hand or, in some cases, persuaded other nesting birds to raise the foundlings. Those with permanent injuries she kept until they died and was especially partial to birds of prey and corvids. Those two species, she observed, "responded best to human companionship," yet they were "among the species most persecuted by man."

Laskey's greatest contribution to ornithology was, like her friend Nice, her life history studies, particularly her work with mockingbirds, eastern bluebirds, and brown-headed cowbirds. She was finally rewarded for her work when she was elected a fellow of the A.O.U.

in 1966. Most of her 153 published articles appeared in national bird journals, such as the *Auk, Wilson Bulletin,* and *Bird-Banding* as well as in state publications, such as the *Journal of the Tennessee Academy of Science,* and *Migrant,* the journal of the Tennessee Ornithological Society.

Nice persuaded Laskey to try her hand at popular writing. The following excerpt, "Watching a Carolina Wren's Nest," published in the *Chicago Naturalist,* was the result. In it she illustrates the joy and tediousness of concentrated bird study. She also shows her knowledge and interest in other aspects of nature, namely wildflowers and butterflies.

Watching a Carolina Wren's Nest

Today, July 10, I shall watch the Carolina wrens that have built in a nest box at the edge of the woods just off Highway 100 in Percy Warner Park. On June 25, the nest was complete except for lining. It is built mainly of green moss, leaves, and leaf skeletons and is the typical kind of this species, with a roof and side entrance. The first of the five eggs was laid on June 30; the female was incubating when the nest was last visited July 7.

It is a little after nine-thirty of a hot, humid morning after a heavy shower last night. I find an inconspicuous spot some twenty feet from the box, where I set my little three-step ladder as a seat under the drooping boughs of an Osage orange (hedge apple) and a peach, the latter laden with green fruit. I wonder if a squirrel or some picnicker inadvertently planted the peach seed. At my feet, is a jewel weed with its first blossom, a clear yellow. Behind me are more jewel weed with blossoms farther advanced, and tall spikes of lavender-pink blossoms with the square stems of the mint family which I believe are scutellaria or skull-cap. Raspberry canes that have given up their crop border the woods, and blackberries, with other growth, are behind them. These are fruiting now. Before me, scattered in the weedy open space between the woods and a clump of trees between me and the highway, are many plants that have sprung up in the blue grass. Nearest and most conspicuous, are the tall teazle [*sic*], now displaying beautiful soft bands of tiny orchid-colored flowers on the green seed heads. These are meccas for butterflies; I see a swallowtail, a frittilary [*sic*], a sulphur and a swarm of silver-spotted skippers (according to my butterfly guide). Each teazle plant harbors from one to seven of the latter. It seems to be a great day for them for I find numbers elsewhere.

This watch period promises to be far more interesting than the monotonous time I spent at home last month watching our mail box when the Bewick's wrens had their nest there. Here is privacy with only the woodland creatures about me, and no passing neighbors and strangers to wonder audibly or inaudibly what in the world I was doing, or stopping to chat, thus causing me to miss the little wren as she slipped quietly in or out, and losing much of the time I had spent, necessitating a fresh start on the incubation rhythm observations. Life is buzzing all about me. Birds are singing and calling. A yellow-breasted chat resents my presence and directs all its attention to me, gradually encircling the area several times as it flies from tree to tree or bush, keeping its bright eyes upon me and uttering its various warning or alarm notes—a strident *zee ou,* with the accent on the last syllable, and a sharp *zick, tch,* or *tuck,* which I can imitate fairly well by a sharp smack of the tongue against the roof of mouth, or perhaps by hitting two pebbles together. Whatever activity the chat had been engaged in at my arrival was neglected for nearly two hours as it deliberately moved to view me from all angles. The warning notes gradually decreased until they were scarcely audible and the wing beats sounded louder than the vocal notes.

Closer to me came insects of many varieties. One could not venture to watch all this teeming life, interesting as it was, for eyes must not be diverted even for a minute from the box which was the big question mark at this point. Whether the little Carolina was on her eggs or not, or whether there were still eggs, I did not know. If the bird is incubating, I must not disturb her, or if she is out foraging, that will soon be evident. Yet, had I known how long this initial vigil would prove to be, investigation would have been made immediately. But I must wait, so, while the various insects flew or crawled about, I practiced side glances to see what I could, and still concentrate on the wrens. A June bug zoomed past on its way to the peaches, a fly persistently landed on my hand to crawl about. It acted like one of the parasitic flies and remained to be killed by a slap of the other hand. Wasps had to be brushed off. Once something landed on my collar to crawl to my neck. Without thinking, up went my hand to brush it off, but *wow!* a painful sting on a finger cushion sent pains into my hand and arm. I have been pulling *Polistes* out of the Warner Park bird boxes these ten years without a sting because I moved faster than they, but this one had the advantage of me.

All this time, there was a chorus of birds singing in the trees and woods about me. I did not dare look for them but at times could hear three white-eyed vireos singing at once, two yellow-billed cuckoos, and several indigo buntings. During the morning, I counted almost twenty species that I could identify from their calls and songs, besides a few others that I could not place. There were at least three chats, two chickadees, summer tanager, Kentucky warbler, wood thrush, red-eyed towhee [now rufous-sided], goldfinch, cardinal, red-eyed vireo, hooded warbler, blue-gray gnatcatcher, chimney swifts, blue jay, hummingbird, catbird. These are not in A.O.U. Checklist order, but that is the way they reached my ears and their names scribbled on my note book. The hummingbird whizzed past the nest box as I dutifully looked at it, but I could not quite trust my eyes in that one-second view of it among the insects and butterflies all about me. But before I left, it came to me. First I heard the hum in the peach tree above, then it came down to pause at the blossoms of the jewel weed, hesitating within a yard of me. I held my breath, thinking it was coming to the jewel flower beside me, but no—he moved on—his lovely ruby gorget shining in the sun. He has me ahead of my story, for his final visit was something of a climax just before I left.

Nearly three and a half hours I sat with my eyes almost glued to that box, trying to relax a bit by using one eye at a time, and other devices to relieve the tension. At times, I was wet with perspiration, then a small breeze came out of nowhere to stir the leaves gently and refresh the watcher. For the first 85 minutes, I knew nothing of what was happening in that box. Then the little gad-about came home. She apparently caught a glimpse of me among the greenery, although I was garbed in inconspicuous clothing and wore a dark, brimmed hat to shade my face. She rasped for over five minutes before going into her nest. The hot sun had been shining on the box all morning so the eggs must have been warm. She remained on them only fifteen minutes when a song from the male was heard in the woods to the east. A rasping call sounded from inside the box and out came her head, then she flew east, apparently to join her spouse in another round of visits in the woods. This time, she returned in 41 minutes by my pocket Ben. She had apparently forgotten all about me for she dashed into the box without a sound. It was now noon for me, according to the "daylight-saving-time" we are living by at this season, so I was beginning to think about the little lunch that was in my car down by the side of the road. But, judging by her other period on the nest, I decided that I must wait until the end of this one, for, surely in the heat of this mid-summer day, she would stay on only 15 or 20 minutes. Just then one of the towhees began to sing. There are many varieties of towhee songs but this was one of those *"drink your tea"* fellows. What a time to remind me of lunch! I listened closely for the song of a Carolina wren. Maybe he would call the woman off again for a tidbit, but no luck. She sat and sat. I watched

214

and watched. Towhee gave up at 12:30 and probably went for his own lunch. I began to wonder if one of the many diversions had not tempted my eyes away long enough to let the little wren slip off to the woods unseen. Finally, I promised myself that I would wait until 1:00 P.M. and then must investigate to see if she had fooled me. At two minutes to one, watch in hand, I began to ease over to the box and, at exactly 1:00 P.M., raised the box top. Mrs. Wren shot out like a flash into the woods. There she must have met her mate, waiting more patiently than I for her to leave. A musical note was sounded, then a rasping note, then a song. And I went to lunch—melted cheese sandwiches, melted by Old Sol who had made the locked car as hot as an oven. But what a lovely morning and what a perverse human-like little wren that would gad all morning and then sit so patiently all through my lunch hour. Tomorrow I hope to see how she spends her afternoons.

FURTHER READING

Goodpasture, Katharine A. "In Memoriam: Amelia Rudolph Laskey." *Auk* 92 (April, 1975): 252–59.

———. Interview with the author. March 13, 1987.

Laskey, Amelia. "Breeding Biology of Mockingbirds." *Auk* 79 (October, 1962): 596–606.

———. "Cowbird Behavior." *Wilson Bulletin* 62 (December, 1950): 157–74.

———. Papers. Cumberland Museum and Science Center. Nashville, Tenn.

———. "Some Nesting Data on the Carolina Wren at Nashville, Tennessee." *Bird-Banding* 19 (July, 1948): 101–21.

———. "Some Tufted Titmouse Life History." *Bird-Banding* 28 (July, 1957): 135–45.

———. "Watching a Carolina Wren's Nest." *Chicago Naturalist* 9 (1946): 59–62.

22

Caroline Dormon

1888–1971

"ALL I ASK OF LIFE," CAROLINE DORMON ONCE WROTE, "is to be able to stay in the woods, fooling with plants and birds." And throughout most of her life, that is what she did. Born during her family's annual vacation at their summer home called Briarwood—a 135-acre estate in the sand hills of northwestern Louisiana—Dormon moved there permanently in 1918. By then she had graduated from Judson College and had taught school for several years.

Dormon wanted an outdoor job, specifically as a forester. But forestry, she was told, was not a career for women. After pleading eloquently for the conservation of longleaf pine virgin forests at the Southern Forestry Congress, she was appointed state chairman of conservation for the Louisiana Federation of Women's Clubs. Thus, she had moved closer to her goal of working in forestry.

To make a living, she returned to teaching, this time in the remote forested sand hills of Kisatchie in Natchitoches Parish— with "mile after mile of majestic longleaf pine forests. . . . The great pines came right to the water's edge on those lovely clear creeks." There her dreams were crystallized—to save a virgin tract for future generations and to persuade the federal government to buy cutover areas for a national forest.

After years of lecturing, writing, cajoling, and leading tours of important scientists and bureaucrats into the area, she succeeded in persuading the U.S. Forest Service to purchase 75,589 acres of cutover land, but the agent offered too little for the virgin tract, and it was clear-cut by the timber company that owned it.

Still undefeated, she continued her campaign for a national forest throughout the 1920s, eventually attracting the attention of the

Caroline Dormon setting out to collect in the Kisatchie Wold. *Courtesy Archives, Eugene P. Watson Memorial Library, Northwestern State University of Louisiana, Natchitoches, Louisiana.*

Louisiana Department of Conservation. She finally realized her career in forestry when they hired her to publicize their work. Her activities included preparing posters and bulletins about the value of trees to Louisiana and teaching schoolchildren the importance of trees. She was also one of the first three women in the country to be elected an associate member of the Society of American Foresters in 1930.

Dormon also loved wildflowers, especially the unique wild irises of Louisiana. For decades she collected wild plants from all over the South and brought many back to her Briarwood property to propagate, study, and paint. She became one of the South's foremost authorities on native plants and their horticultural uses. In 1934 she published her first book, *Wild Flowers of Louisiana*. She followed that with *Forest Trees of Louisiana* (1941), *Flowers Native to the Deep South* (1958), and *Natives Preferred* (1965). Each book emphasized the importance of

217

preserving native plants both in the wild and in gardens.

As part of her conservation campaign, she fought for a state park system and a state arboretum, and eventually both were established. She also served as a highway beautification consultant to the Louisiana Department of Highways. Her goal was to persuade the agency to preserve the native trees and shrubs already growing beside state highways, but she lost that campaign to nurserymen who favored exotics.

Birds were another consuming natural interest, especially as she grew older and unable to travel. She was content, instead, to watch birds from the windows of her cabin at Briarwood and write about what she observed for *Sunday Magazine* in the *Shreveport Times*. Out of those articles came her last book, *Bird Talk,* published when she was eighty-one years old. Incensed by diminishing numbers and species of birds, she blamed the scarcity on pesticidal poisons and habitat destruction. She denounced the clearing of hardwood trees, which, she claimed, provided food for the birds, and the replacing of those trees with sterile pine plantations. "Pesky lumbermen" even tried to persuade her to cut her own trees, particularly a three-hundred-year-old longleaf pine tree she called "grandpappy."

But she was determined to save her property as a sanctuary for the flora of the South, and with the help of friends, Briarwood was preserved for future generations through the founding of the Caroline Dormon Nature Preserve. The preserve, where "grandpappy" still stands, is a living memorial to one of Louisiana's foremost ecologists.

The following article, from the July 26, 1929, issue of the Louisiana *Natchitoches Times,* was one of many Dormon wrote during her campaign to save the Kisatchie Wold for future generations. The "we" in the article refers to Dormon and her older sister Virginia, who, in their "trusty Ford," explored the Wold in every direction, taking interested and influential people at the Dormons' own expense to see the remaining virgin forests. She had hoped to retain the virgin tract between Sandy and Odom Creeks, which she describes in "Camping in the Kisatchie Wold." Only a couple of months after the article was published, the area was clear-cut, "this beautiful forest lost to posterity," she mourned.

CAMPING IN THE KISATCHIE WOLD

This had to be a tour of exploration. We had penetrated the Hills from several directions—from Natchitoches, Leesville, Alexandria—

but this, to be a proper adventure, must take on a new slant.

There is plenty of room for exploration in those parts. It is always amusing to be asked, "Please tell me how to go to the waterfall at Kisatchie"—when there are so many! Or to hear someone exclaim, "Oh, we saw Kisatchie; we spent the whole day out there!" I have spent days and days—in a car, on a horse, in a wagon, on foot—exploring, and have never yet covered half of it. The Wold extends from Cane River, entirely across Natchitoches and Sabine parishes, and over a little way into East Texas. It also laps over into the northern part of Vernon parish.

Of course we must be able to go anywhere, so we took a stout Ford touring car. In it—and around it, and on it—we put food, skillet and coffee pot; blankets; mosquito bars (a safe precaution, no matter where one goes camping); and those little roll-up canvas cots. Ready to go!

There were left to us to "take off" from Chopin and Derry. This time we chose Derry. It was afternoon before we started and we had vowed not to strike camp until we came to a typical Kisatchie creek, clear and clean, with banks of snowy sand. Just a few miles from Cane River the forest received us, and almost immediately the winding road began to ascend—we were in the hills. Up and up—soon there were rocky ledges, over which the Ford struggled and panted. Ever upward, with only dips in the road, each rise higher than the last, we followed a ridge—surely the backbone of Louisiana! In a short while we reached really high ground, and could look away in every direction to the undulating skyline, with wave on wave of blue hills in between. Much of the virgin longleaf pine timber has been cut away, but here is enough second growth to fill in so that from a distance it has the look of a primeval world.

We began to descend a long hill and as we dropped down, the shadows lengthened—and our vow weakened as we went down. But soon we began seeing the tops of the magnolia trees, and as we reached the bottom of the hill, there at last was the gleam of Kisatchie sand; just in time to save us, a little creek.

Did we immediately pitch camp? Quite the contrary. Now we had with us on this expedition one lone man—a very young man—whom we had lured on by promising never to camp except where he could fish. So—on a finny foundation rested our hopes of sojourning in this attractive spot. There must be fish for supper. All must help. With a good deal of skepticism, we strung up our lines, while the boy dug out his precious can of good old-fashioned angle worms. To our astonishment, fish were there, and bit—even that time of day—perch and mud-cat.

How sad the fate of those who have never eaten perch, caught from a clear, cold stream, and fried immediately! Eaten with hot corn hoecakes, with a ravenous appetite and the smell of wood smoke for sauce—oh, well! Only those who have tried it will understand.

No bed of a fairy princess could have been more delightful than a little canvas cot that night. Even the screams and demonical laughter of a cat-owl only lulled us to deeper slumber. I have never heard of anyone sleeping under the open sky being troubled with insomnia.

It was difficult to start moving the next day as our man-of-the-camp was so entranced with the fishing. Though we had a good map, we could not find ourselves on it, so when a man passed we asked him the name of the creek. "They call this here Bayou Seep," he replied. The name being connected with water, I could only think of s-e-e-p (I offer this reason!). Finally, however, while looking at a fine cypress tree, light broke through to a feeble brain—Bayou Cypre, of course—Cypress Bayou!

We could not get away until the morning's catch of fish was cooked and eaten. So it was afternoon when we started—and we didn't know where we were going. We were nevertheless, on our way—and such a way! Over softly rounded sand hills, and rugged, jagged rocky hills. I shall never forget one spot where I got out to take a look-around. As I walked to the highest point of the hill, a dove fluttered up from my feet. I looked down, and there between three rocks, beneath a tuft of sedge grass were two lovely snow white eggs. It was the first dove's nest I had ever seen placed right on the ground.

The pine woods were literally carpeted with the rose and pale-yellow of goat's rue, the lovely flower with the unfair name. Bergamot and Brown-Eyed Susans mingled their purple and gold. Spiderwort added an occasional touch of blue and butterfly weed flamed here and there. Wine-red poppy mallows were beginning to open, and completed the gay range of colors.

We crossed innumerable lovely little streams—in fact, there was one at the foot of almost every long hill. Our requirements for a camp site were an attractive spot, and also somewhere to fish. Just before sundown we found it, right in the longleaf pine woods. Again we had a swift, clear creek, with sandy banks and this time, big grey rocks for lagniappe. As we got really up to it I exclaimed, "Why, Little Kisatchie!" And so it was, an old friend; we had merely come on it from a new direction. Another night of campfire and stars, with the subdued roar of longleaf pines for good measure. This sound is indescribable, more like distant surf than anything else.

Not such good fishing here; the water was too clear, and the creek spread out too shallow over the sand. Now and then, in some little rocky pool we caught glimpses of brilliant red perch, but they saw us first. So we had bacon for breakfast, and then we feasted on high-bush huckleberries to round out the meal. But fish we must have for dinner, so on to the falls on Kisatchie proper, the big creek.

Can any place in the state exceed in natural charm this site of an ancient watermill? The water rushes over a bed of smooth rock; and in the rock, still plain to be seen, are the holes which held the up-right timbers of the old mill, built before the Civil War. At one side, the waters fall into a lovely foaming pool. Oh, yes! It is really in Louisiana; but only in the Kisatchie Wold need one look for such streams.

And the trees! I turned on my heel and counted 20 species in sight from where I stood. Shaggy river birches, the largest I ever saw, lean over the stream; just up the bank is a giant ash; while immense elms, gums and maples are everywhere! Pines and feathery cypress add variety.

Here we found more of these delicious little perch. How could they fail to be good, coming right from that sparkling, foaming pool?

After dinner we began our last exploring trip, again leaving the public road and following what was little more than a trail through a virgin longleaf pine forest. Who can fail to come under the spell of such a forest? Those pines! Some of the same trees, no doubt, which once looked down on painted Indian braves that slipped like shadows from trunk to trunk.

With no intimation of its nearness, we suddenly came on a gash in the pine-clad hill, and there was a gem of a little creek. We found it on the map, with the commonplace name of Odom's Creek, instead of some singing Indian words. Up the stream was a perfect natural swimming pool, with tall guardian pines reflected in the water. When we came out after our plunge, there were clean flat rocks on which to sit and bask. Below were little snowy cascades, and father down still, more pools and sandy banks, shaded by spreading beeches and magnolias.

That night we camped on a pine clad knoll. Had I not been afraid of creeping things, I would have slept right on the sweet pine straw. The voices of the pines and the stream mingled in a sound so soothing we even forgot that was our last night out. Softly they blended, became indistinguishable—"Hush, hush—sleep."

FURTHER READING

Bonta, Marcia. "One Woman's Legacy." *American Horticulturist* 67 (October, 1988): 32–35.

Crittenden, Bob. "Miss Caroline's Dream Became Louisiana's National Forest." *Forests and People* 30 (1980): 24–29.

Dormon, Caroline. "Botanical Ramblings." *Louisiana Society for Horticultural Research* 3 (1967): 80–84.

———. *Bird Talk.* Baton Rouge: Claitor's Publishing Division, 1969.

———. *Flowers Native to the Deep South.* Harrisburg, Pa.: Mount Pleasant Press, 1958.

———. *Natives Preferred: Native Trees and Flowers for Every Location.* Baton Rouge: Claitor's Book Store, 1965.

———. Papers. Watson Library. Northwestern State University of Louisiana, Natchitoches.

———. Papers and Paintings. Briarwood. Saline, La.

———. *Wild Flowers of Louisiana.* Garden City, N.Y.: Doran and Company, 1934.

Johnson, Fran Holman. *The Gift of the Wild Things: The Life of Caroline Dormon.* Lafayette: University of Southwestern Louisiana, 1990.

Moore, Diane M. *The Adventurous Will: Profiles of Memorable Louisiana Women.* Lafayette, La.: Arcadiana Press, 1984.

Rawson, Donald M. "Caroline Dormon: A Renaissance Spirit of Twentieth-Century Louisiana." *Louisiana History* 24 (1983): 121–39.

Snell, David. "The Green World of Carrie Dormon." *Smithsonian* 2 (February, 1972): 28.

23

E. Lucy Braun

1889–1971

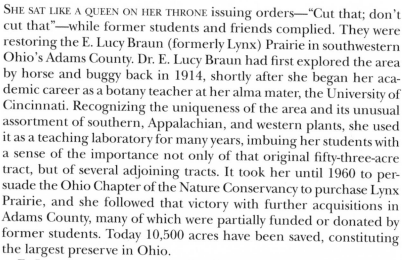

SHE SAT LIKE A QUEEN ON HER THRONE issuing orders—"Cut that; don't cut that"—while former students and friends complied. They were restoring the E. Lucy Braun (formerly Lynx) Prairie in southwestern Ohio's Adams County. Dr. E. Lucy Braun had first explored the area by horse and buggy back in 1914, shortly after she began her academic career as a botany teacher at her alma mater, the University of Cincinnati. Recognizing the uniqueness of the area and its unusual assortment of southern, Appalachian, and western plants, she used it as a teaching laboratory for many years, imbuing her students with a sense of the importance not only of that original fifty-three-acre tract, but of several adjoining tracts. It took her until 1960 to persuade the Ohio Chapter of the Nature Conservancy to purchase Lynx Prairie, and she followed that victory with further acquisitions in Adams County, many of which were partially funded or donated by former students. Today 10,500 acres have been saved, constituting the largest preserve in Ohio.

E. Lucy Braun—imperious, hard-working, fearless, and highly opinionated—was a pioneering plant ecologist and a fiercely dedicated conservationist. She fought not only to save those unique areas in her native state but to establish parks, nature preserves, and wilderness areas throughout the United States. As a charter member of the Wilderness Society, she believed that wilderness was "the environment of solitude."

To reach such areas, she and her older sister, entomologist Annette Braun, walked as many as twenty-four miles a day over rough terrain. Their favorite place in the decades between 1920 and 1950 was the deciduous forests of eastern North America, especially the still-virgin timber in remote southeastern Kentucky and Tennessee. "Nowhere in the whole world is there the equal in beauty and magnificence of our eastern deciduous forest. It is unexcelled. And in Kentucky and Tennessee this deciduous forest reached its superlative development," she said in a talk called "Save the Big Trees," which she gave in 1935 to the Garden Club of Kentucky.

With the help of a car which the sisters purchased in 1930 and Lucy drove, they reached the outlying mountain villages. At first the mountain people were suspicious of them, but soon they were calling them the "plant ladies" and telling them of special places to visit in their search for new plant species for Lucy and moths for Annette. In a letter to fellow plant ecologist Frederic E. Clements [husband of Edith Clements], Lucy described the difficulties they encountered in their attempts to penetrate remote virgin forest tracts:

> One . . . can be reached in three days round trip (on foot) from the Cumberland Valley . . . the other . . . will be harder to get into. It also must be reached by foot. . . . There is no road entering it. . . . The slopes in many places are unbelievably steep for slopes without a sign of rock, sometimes as much as 45 degrees! . . . If one steps off the trail, the ground is invisible; innumerable logs, branches, and the tangle of lower herb stuff make progress so slow that I found trails much more satisfactory, for at least it was possible to look around and up, and to move forward, without coming to 4 foot logs to scale. . . . I think there is no doubt but that the finest hardwood forests still in existence are in Ky. [Kentucky]; because these parts of Ky. have always been (and still are) so inaccessible.

For twenty-five years the sisters explored and collected in the eastern deciduous forests, not only of Kentucky and Tennessee but of Ohio, Virginia, West Virginia, and Pennsylvania, "involving in the last 12 or 15 years over 65,000 miles of travel," Braun wrote in the introduction to her definitive *Deciduous Forests of Eastern North America*, published in 1950 to general acclaim. In it she developed her concept of the "mixed mesophytic forest" with its geographical center in southeastern Kentucky. Such a forest consists of diverse species of mostly deciduous trees adapted to cool moist environments, with a rich floral and shrub understory beneath its canopy of over one-hundred-foot-tall trees.

Her book remains the best record of what those forests were like before many were subsequently destroyed. Even today ecologists, biologists, and foresters, in their search to understand the dynamics of the eastern deciduous forest, use Braun's book as a guide. And it was that book that brought her lasting fame. In the same year it was published, she became the first and only female president of the

E. Lucy Braun, at age thirty-seven in 1926, with Conrad Roth (*left*) and
Dorothy Parker (*right*), standing among two white cedar trees at Cedar Falls,
Adams County, Ohio. *Courtesy RLS Creations and Ronald L. Stuckey,
Columbus, Ohio.*

Ecological Society of America. Two years later, she received the Mary Soper Pope Medal from the Cranbrook Institute of Science in Bloomfield Hills, Michigan. The citation claimed that "her studies of the natural vegetation of eastern North America over the past twenty years and more have led to the formulation of an original principle in vegetation dynamics. . . . Her recently published synthesis . . . *Deciduous Forests of Eastern North America* . . . is no doubt one of the important books published in this field."

Her many years of conservation work through both the Cincinnati and national chapters of the Wild Flower Preservation Society was acknowledged in 1953 with an Honorary Life Membership in the Cincinnati chapter. Her decades of service to the Ohio Academy of Science, including the presidency from 1933 to 1934, were similarly acknowledged with an Honorary Life Membership in 1963. In addition she received a Certificate of Merit from the Botanical Society of America, one of fifty awarded at its fiftieth anniversary in 1956 (along with agrostologist Agnes Chase), an honorary Doctor of Science degree from the University of Cincinnati in 1964, and the Eloise Payne Luquer Medal for special achievement in the field of botany from the Garden Clubs of America in 1966.

The following article, "The Forest of Lynn Fork of Leatherwood," which she wrote for *Nature Magazine* in 1936, includes a description of Lucy's and Annette's efforts to reach a remote virgin forest in Kentucky and an account of what they found there. To read it is to wish that Braun's repeated pleas to save such areas had been heeded. Unfortunately, Lynn Fork was logged in the late 1930s or early 1940s and logged again in 1992, according to William H. Martin, Commissioner of Kentucky's Natural Resources and Environmental Protection Cabinet. Its lower slopes are now abandoned fields dominated by twelve- to sixteen-inch-diameter tulip trees, a far cry from Braun's description of the magnificent forest, which was crowned by the largest tulip tree in North America.

The Forest of Lynn Fork of Leatherwood

Little does the outsider know of the beauty hidden in the mountain section of Kentucky; little does he realize that remnants of the eastern wilderness of the eighteenth century remain in our midst, surrounded by the din, the progress, the civilization of the twentieth century. Yet there are whole counties almost without what today is termed a good road. There are forests that until recently have been too remote to tempt the lumberman; forests where even the walnut remains; forests where even tulip trees, or yellow poplar, tower above their more than average size companions.

The forest of Lynn Fork of Leatherwood is one of these. For several years we had heard of "the big poplar of Perry County," but it was not until the summer of 1933 that we learned the approximate location. We were near enough to attempt the trip, which had to be made on foot down Line Fork to Jakes Creek, up Jakes Creek to its first branch, along a trail up that branch and over the ridge into Stony Fork, down Stony Fork to Leatherwood Creek. There we were to inquire and find a guide if possible. Our course lay down Leatherwood Creek to Lynn Fork; up Lynn Fork, choosing, about one half mile up, the Left Fork; then a sharp climb up through a cornfield, and the narrow trail enters the forest. Somewhere beyond is the "big poplar." But all about is forest, forest of superlative beauty, forest of towering trunks, of luxuriant undergrowth, of exquisite ground cover. Destroying man had never entered here, nor had his animals—hogs or cattle.

Onward and upward the trail leads. Every change of slope is reflected in changing composition of the forest. Here white oak prevails, massive and tall, columns four feet in diameter. There, on a protected slope where ledges of sandstone outcrop, the whole aspect changes; hemlock mingles with the deciduous trees; the dense summer-green understory opens up; few of the delicate herbs of the deciduous forest thrive in the deep duff. The forest of the deeper valleys is in places unbelievably dense, scarcely a ray of sunlight penetrating the dense canopy; rhododendrons clothe the lower slopes, obscuring the little stream from view. Or, in "bottoms," it opens up and the lighter crown of red maple seems to permit the entrance of more light. Mountain magnolia and oil-nut, with here and there a mass of mountain laurel, are grouped with such perfection of design as only the Master Hand could plan. And all between are beds of ferns.

To the right is a tributary valley and up this we turn, for the "big poplar" grows at the foot of the last rise, well up at the head of the valley. Soon the forest changes again. We are entering a veritable cathedral, its roof upheld by huge towering columns—the tall and stately tulip trees. Where before they had been scattered, rising here and there between the other trees, now they outnumber all others, sheltering in their shade large beech and sugar maple. The herbaceous growth is even more luxuriant than before; masses of narrow-leaved spleenwort and silvery spleenwort, waist-high, are all about. Hidden more or less by this luxuriance, and inconspicuous because past blooming, are yellow lady's slippers and showy orchids.

227

The leaves of trillium, bellwort, phlox, spotted mandarin, butter-cups, foam-flower and a host of other spring-flowing plants stirred our imagination and painted the hillsides in spring bloom. But dom-inating all is the primeval grandeur of a forest. Each changing vista brings to view additional large tulip trees, each larger, it seems, than those before. And then, ahead, rises the majestic column of the "big poplar"—straight, sound and perfect, towering eighty feet to the first branch, lifting its crown far aloft. In reverence and awe we stood and gazed upon this tree, the *largest living individual* of its kind in North America. Such monarchs of the forest are not grown in decades, nor yet in centuries. Few but the mountain folk had ever seen it, even knew of its existence. If the people of this nation loved and revered this splendid tree as do those mountain people—they once held church service in this cathedral of Nature—its safety would be assured. It would not, as now, be threatened with destruction as is all this splendid forest. Only through purchase by the gifts of public-spirited, Nature-loving citizens can it be saved.

Realization of the irretrievable loss that will result if our last remaining stands of virgin deciduous forest are cut prompted the formation of the Save-Kentucky's-Primeval-Forest League, with its first objective the saving of the forest of Lynn Fork of Leatherwood for posterity as a monument of the primeval. We need the help of every lover of the primeval forest. In the words of Theodore Roosevelt:

"There is nothing more practical in the end than the preserva-tion of beauty, than the preservation of anything that appeals to the higher emotions of mankind."

Here we have, in the words of one who was in the foremost ranks of those who battled for the preservation of beauty and who was also a veteran in the advocacy of practical ends, an assurance that there is no conflict between these two objectives. We need a more general realization of this principle in our multiple activities.

If this reasoning can be invoked in the campaign to save this particular forest, it will turn the tide. The Forest of Lynn Fork of Leatherwood is a thing of beauty; it appeals to the higher emotions of mankind.

FURTHER READING

Braun, E. Lucy. "The Forest of Lynn Fork of Leatherwood." *Nature Magazine* 37 (April, 1936): 237–38.
———. Papers. Frederick and Amey Geier Collections and Research Center. Cincinnati Museum of Natural History, Cincinnati, Ohio.

Martin, William H. "Characteristics of Old-Growth Mixed Mesophytic Forests." *Natural Areas Journal* 12 (1992): 127–35.

Peskin, Perry K. "A Walk through Lucy Braun's Prairie." *Explorer* 20 (Winter, 1978): 15–21.

Stuckey, Ronald L. "E. Lucy Braun (1889–1971), Outstanding Botanist and Conservationist: A Biographical Sketch, with Bibliography." *Michigan Botanist* 12 (March, 1973): 83–106.

———. "E. Lucy Braun: Ohio's Foremost Woman Botanist." A Collection of Biographical Accounts, Maps, and Photos Compiled for the E. Lucy Braun Symposium, May 5, 1990. Cincinnati Museum of Natural History.

———. *Women Botanists of Ohio Born before 1900.* Columbus, Ohio: RLS Creations, 1992.

24

Ruth Harris Thomas

1900–1973

LIKE HER MENTOR MARGARET MORSE NICE, Ruth Thomas was a nest watcher, meticulously recording the life history of several species, most notably eastern bluebirds and brown thrashers. Beginning in 1937, two years after she joined the American Ornithologists' Union, Thomas also started banding birds. After four years she had banded 1,253 birds of twenty-eight species on her property near North Little Rock, Arkansas. She characterized the fifteen-acre area as "rocky upland with thin woodland" and later named it "Crip's Hill" after the male brown thrasher whose life she chronicled over the eleven and a half years he lived in her dooryard.

A native of Kentucky, Thomas spent her childhood in Georgia, Alabama, Mississippi, and Louisiana. After graduating from Louisiana State University at Baton Rouge in 1923, where she had edited the weekly student newspaper, she became a newspaper reporter for the *Arkansas Gazette* in Little Rock. Two years later she married Rowland Thomas, whom she called Stan. He was several decades older than she and had abandoned a successful career as a reporter for the *New York World* to work as an associate editor of the *Gazette*. Together they moved to the country, north of Little Rock, where they raised two dogs (Nora and Dinah) and goats and gardened.

While her husband commuted daily to work, she enjoyed her bucolic setting. "I loved everything in country life," she later wrote, "from weather to the crawly creatures of my garden. . . . But more than anything else, wild birds."

In 1933 she began writing a monthly nature column—"The Country Diarist"—which became a weekly two years later and continued until her death in 1973. As the column evolved, birds increasingly took center stage. With the help of Margaret Morse Nice, who taught Thomas how to temper her love for the birds with an honest analytical mind, she contributed sound ornithological observations to such journals as the *Auk, Bird-Banding,* and the *Wilson Bulletin.* Her research led, in 1946, to her detailed, forty-page "Study of Eastern Bluebirds in Arkansas," which was widely regarded at the time as one of the most definitive monographs on the species. Because of that work, she was made Fellow of the A.O.U. in 1950.

Thomas was also active in conservation issues, which was reflected in her newspaper columns. Because of her influence, Arkansas passed a state law protecting raptors. A founder of the Arkansas Audubon Society, she was honored for her work when the Society established Ruth Thomas Scholarships to provide training for teachers and youth leaders at National Audubon Society study camps.

Both Nice and Amelia Laskey befriended and corresponded with Thomas, and the Nice-Laskey correspondence frequently mentioned Thomas's struggles to publish *Crip, Come Home,* her popularly written, book-length study of her male brown thrasher. In 1950 *Audubon* reprinted portions of that book, and Harper and Brothers published it. It received excellent reviews because of its ornithological accuracy and readability. Interspersing journal entries with narrative, Thomas closely followed the life of the banded brown thrasher she named "Crip" after he broke his right wing. The wing healed crookedly, but Crip doggedly persevered and relearned to fly, although awkwardly and for short distances. Before he migrated again, Crip stayed in Thomas's vicinity for two years, eating the grains and nutmeats she personally fed him beneath her lilac bush. Thomas and Stan worried that he would not make it back the following spring:

> Crip could fly less than a hundred yards; I had seen him force his wings till his strength was spent and he fluttered to the ground. There would be open spaces to cross in the woodland and, night or day, there would be enemies quick to pounce on a weary, crippled old thrasher. . . .[then,] on the morning of March twenty-sixth, Crip came home. . . . That was a wonderful morning, and I think I was happier than the old thrasher that had come to the end of his migratory journey. Only half believing what my own eyes saw, I hurried to tell my husband, "Crip's home!"

At the same time Thomas watched Crip cope successfully with his infirmities, she also watched Stan lose his battle with cancer. "All the months of Stan's illness, the old thrasher was a joy and a care beyond ourselves," she wrote. After Stan's death, her interest in Crip's domestic affairs was all that kept Thomas going.

A year and a half after Stan died, on October 12, 1946, Crip disappeared forever. Altogether Thomas had observed his life for four years before his injury and seven and a half years after it. "Stan's love and the old cripple thrasher, somehow they seemed one, and when I faltered, gave me strength. 'Do not walk and weep and brood by the fire. Somewhere is another need, another pattern. Have courage to seek,'" she concluded. She left the country home she had shared with Stan and Crip and moved into a small, ridgetop house near Morrilton, Arkansas. There she wrote *Crip, Come Home* and continued her bird observations and column writing for the remaining twenty-seven years of her life.

The following excerpts from *Crip, Come Home* illustrate Thomas's ability to tell a poignant story in lyrical prose while slipping in her accurate observations of brown thrasher domestic life.

From Crip, Come Home

On April 9th, the Crips' idleness was explained. That was the day Mrs. Crip laid her first egg. . . .

Then mid-April. Summer birds were coming home, winter birds leaving. The white-throated sparrows, growing more beautiful every day, would linger through May's first week. Their tremulous songs were like a farewell. "A good journey, little sparrows, a good summer, and may we meet again in next October's golden days."

In my heart I knew there would be no more golden days. Stan was weaker. I could not think even of tomorrow, and all the past had slipped away. Today's moments were a narrow, trembling bridge, there was no backward way and I was in terror of the darkness ahead.

Crip's roses bloomed, Van Fleet with pink buds, Silver Moon spreading snowy petals. On April 24th, the thrashers' eggs hatched; Mrs. Crip brooded the tiny babies, and old Crip searched for small caterpillars to feed them.

That season was kind to birds, all the nests near our house were successful. Bewick's and Carolina wrens, titmice and chickadees, cardinals and mockingbirds went to and fro with food for nestlings. Bluebirds led their speckle-breasted children to the table and stuffed them with peanuts. Downy woodpecker father liked to fill his youngsters with suet. When the downy pecked at the fat, many bits fell to the ground and Crip picked them up for his family.

The roses came to the end of their flowering, the petals drifted down through the canes. In a curious way, the Silver Moon's shattering made work for the thrashers. Like most passerine birds, they kept their nest meticulously clean. After each feeding, they waited a moment, watching, and when one of the babies wriggled and hoisted his small stern skyward, a parent seized the white cloacal sac and flew off with it. Instinct told them to remove any white object, and now the foolish birds snatched up the petals that fell in the nest. Crip would carry a scrap of rose up to a tree, carefully drop it and then wipe his beak back and forth on a branch.

On the morning of May 6th, the four baby thrashers left the nest. For an hour before the leaving they were restless, standing tall and stretching, now gaping their wide yellow mouths, now picking at their new feathers, then one would tower above his brothers and flap his little wings. Through all this they were silent. At last the moment came. One baby climbed upon the rim of the nest, and with a flutter and a scramble was out. In the same moment he made his first utterance of small grunty notes. Not planning or thinking, not knowing what he said, he told his parents, "Here I am, here, here, come find me, come feed me." Within twenty minutes two more were out and at once chirping like the first. Fifteen minutes longer the last little thrasher stayed in the nest, and three times Mrs. Crip came and fed him. When he was all the way out, his feet no longer feeling the familiar floor of the nest but closing around a thorny cane, he cried with his brothers, "Here I am, here, here, come find me, come feed me."

May 6th, the day Crip's babies left the nest, the last day Stan was up for a while. It was clear and bright, the sun like a flood from the sky, and he lay in his long chair on the porch, watching the old thrasher lead the little ones across the lawn.

For the next four days Stan was very weak, but on the morning of the fifth day seemed wonderfully improved. I know that day by heart. Many weeks I was to live it over in my mind, every minute, every word. Breakfast, gay, with Nora and Dinah by his bed, waiting crusts of toast. The morning letters and the newspaper, talk before lunch. And while he was having lunch, a Baltimore oriole blundered into one of my traps. A male, his head and throat of deepest satiny black, his breast like flame, and I took him in for Stan to see. He put out his hand, so white and smooth, and touched the bird's bright breast, murmuring, "How pretty." Even then, the pain had returned, and that afternoon we went to the hospital. He died early on the morning of May 14th. . . .

Greta! Next to Crip I loved her best of all the birds. Two summers she had been our thrasher's wife. The next year it was because the poor wing made him late coming home that she joined Red. And the next year there had been the conflict; she was moved by Crip's songs but held to Red by his persistence. Greta, in spring, was not free, deep instinct and circumstances ordered her life. In autumn's idle days she returned to the thrasher who was her first mate and to the roses that sheltered her first nest.

On the evening of October 2nd, at a quarter of six o'clock, Crip made his way to the cedar. Greta had stayed in the roses, and in the full darkness of six-twenty cried three sharp "smacks." Did a cat prowl or a screech owl brush against the trees? There was no alarm in the voice—what moved Greta to cry in the dark? And then I knew—she was about to leave! Next morning, only Crip came for peanuts, only Crip turned the leaves on the ground and then rested in the roses. All that day I thought of the thrasher flying off in the night.

Then a fear grew in my heart that Crip would leave. All the dear meaning of my home was gone, my garden and my love of the garden were lost, other birds were as shadows. Only the old crippled thrasher needed me. Watching over him, thinking of him first in the morning and seeing each evening that he was safe in the cedar, were the ties that held me to the lonely walls of my home. If he left I would close the doors, and with Dinah and Nora go away forever.

Rain dripped steadily, promising the gloom of winter. Crip, alone in the roses, shook out his wings and hunched his shoulders. Perhaps he felt dim impulses, now to stay now to leave, a vague distress like the sickness of irresolution.

OCTOBER 10, 1945

Sun, clear light and cloudless sky. In every wild place, the asters of autumn, in the garden a gold and scarlet flowering.

Crip lives placid days. Evenings he peers down at me from his place in the cedar, gives an uneasy twitch of the stiff right wing, and then is quiet for sleep.

I know Crip in the spring, sleek and tall, hurrying in the intensity of his need for a mate. I know him in new mated happiness, whispering songs. I know him as he drives a jay away, his yellow eyes blazing. I know him in the gentle work of feeding babies, as the frantic father in time of danger. I know him in late summer's contentment, in the lazy days of molting, his eyes sleepy, his feathers ragged and pale with dust. I know him as new fall energies come and he grows cross and peevish, bustling and old-womanish, and drives his mate away. With the turning of the season, the time for thrashers to go south, I know him perched in the roses, humped and brooding. I know him in these halcyon days of sun and plenty. I have known him in winter, forlorn and miserable.

Crip, my dear brown bird, stay with me till I grow stronger in the way of loneliness.

FURTHER READING

Halberg, Henry N. "Ruth Harris Thomas." *Auk* 92 (1975): 646.
Laskey, Amelia. Papers. Cumberland Science Museum, Nashville, Tenn.
"Ruth Thomas." *Audubon* 52 (May–June, 1950): 202–203.
Thomas, Ruth Harris. "A Study of Eastern Bluebirds in Arkansas." *Wilson Bulletin* 58 (September, 1946): 143–83.
Thomas, Ruth Rowland. "The Constant Carolinas." *Audubon Book of True Nature Stories*, Edited by John K. Terres. New York: Thomas Y. Crowell Co., 1958.
———. *Crip, Come Home.* New York: Harper & Brothers, 1950.
———. "Ticks Affecting Birds' Eyesight." *Auk* 58 (October, 1941): 590–91.

25

Rachel Carson

1907–64

Like a religious convert, Rachel Carson felt called upon to write about pesticides, so she put aside her passionate interest in the sea and natural history to write one of the most pivotal environmental books of the twentieth century. Eight years after the publication of *Silent Spring*, a newspaper editorial summarized its impact: "A few thousand words from her and the world took a new direction."

But changes did not happen soon enough. Every year since then more pesticides have been manufactured and distributed than during Carson's lifetime. Because of Carson's warnings, however, today's public is at least better informed and less willing to accept the rain of poisons. Instead, they now question the effects of progress on humans and the natural world. Essentially, *Silent Spring* marked the end of humanity's naive love affair with technology.

While Carson was enrolled in rigorous graduate courses at Johns Hopkins University, she took many laboratory courses. But abstract science never really interested her. She wanted to be out in the field instead, observing and trying to understand the intricacies of the natural world.

By writing about what she saw, she hoped to engender in her readers an appreciation for nature, which would compel them toward its conservation instead of its exploitation. That was what she had done in her previous best-sellers on the sea—*Under the Sea Wind* (1941), *The Sea around Us* (1951), and *The Edge of the Sea* (1956). "Nature's Advocate," Vera Norwood called her, in Norwood's excellent book *Made from This Earth: American Women and Nature*. Carson "taught the world to wonder," the National Council of Women declared when they announced their selection of *The Edge of the Sea* as the outstanding book of the year in 1956.

Ironically, Carson was not a child of the sea but of the rolling green hills of western Pennsylvania. Born and raised in Springdale, north of Pittsburgh, Carson won a four-year tuition scholarship to the Pennsylvania College for Women (now Chatham College), where she majored first in English and then in zoology, planning, even then, to write about the wild creatures she was studying.

When she won a summer-study fellowship from her college to the Marine Biological Laboratory at Woods Hole, Massachusetts, she finally saw the sea she had dreamed about all her young life. After summers of field work combined with graduate work in marine biology at Johns Hopkins, which resulted in a master's degree, Carson landed part-time teaching positions both at Hopkins and at the University of Maryland.

In 1935 she was hired as a junior aquatic biologist by the U.S. Bureau of Fisheries, which merged in 1940 with the Biological Survey and was renamed the U.S. Fish and Wildlife Service. From then until 1952, when she resigned to become a full-time writer, Carson advanced steadily through a series of bureaucratic promotions—from assistant to associate to aquatic biologist, then to information specialist, biologist, and, finally, chief editor, writing pamphlets and booklets on marine issues and national wildlife refuges.

With the fabulous success of *The Sea Around Us* (eighty-six weeks on the *New York Times* best-seller list), she was able not only to leave her government job but also to buy a summer home in Maine. There she spent happy hours exploring "the edge of the sea" for the book she most enjoyed writing. Before too long she was plunged, almost against her will, into writing *Silent Spring* when a friend told her how the birds had started dying in her Massachusetts backyard after DDT aerial spraying.

Once alerted, Carson took four years to research and write her literate account of pesticide abuse. By the time she finished, she was a very sick woman, but she still withstood vitriolic attacks by chemical and agricultural interests and defended her findings. Before she died of cancer two years after the publication of *Silent Spring*, she received vindication by President John F. Kennedy's Science Advisory Committee report. Honors were heaped upon her, including the Audubon Medal (the first ever bestowed on a woman), the Cullum Medal of the American Geographical Society, the Albert Schweitzer Medal of the Animal Welfare Institute, Conservationist of the Year designation from the National Wildlife Federation, and the first Woman of Conscience Award from the National Council of Women.

Best of all, though, was her election into the prestigious American

Rachel Carson looking in a tide pool near her home in Maine, circa mid-1950s. Photograph by Shirley A. Briggs. *Courtesy Rachel Carson History Project, Bethesda, Maryland.*

Academy of Arts and Letters which cited her as "a scientist in the grand literary style of Galileo and Buffon, [who] used her scientific knowledge and moral feeling to deepen our consciousness of living nature and to alert us to the calamitous possibility that our shortsighted technological conquests might destroy the very sources of our being."

The excerpts that I have called "Sea Pansies" and "Basket Starfish" from *The Edge of the Sea* illustrate both the extent of Carson's field work and her use of library research not only to educate her readers but to nourish their sense of wonder toward the sea.

Portions of "The Other Road," her concluding chapter in *Silent Spring*, offer readers a choice between "disaster" and "alternatives to chemical controls." In poetic terms of Robert Frost's "The Road Not Taken," she pleads that the world choose the "road less traveled by"—that of cooperation with and respect for natural forces instead of the usual approach of confrontation and arrogant domination—an approach, she prophesies, that will lead to worldwide disaster.

Today, more than ever, *Silent Spring* should be read and pondered anew, especially its dedication, which reads: "To Albert Schweitzer who said, 'Man has lost the capacity to foresee and to forestall. He will end by destroying the earth.'"

SEA PANSIES

On one of the sea islands of Georgia is a great beach that is visited only by the most gentle surf, although it looks straight across to Africa. Storms usually pass it by, for it lies well inside the long, in-curving arc of coast that swings between the Capes of Fear and Canaveral, and the prevailing winds are such that no heavy swells roll in upon it. The texture of the beach itself is unusually firm because of a mixture of mud and clay with the sand; permanent holes and burrows can be dug in it, and the streaming tidal currents carve little ripple marks that remain after the tide goes out, looking like a miniature model of the sea's waves. These sand ripples hold small food particles dropped by the currents, providing a store to be drawn on by detritus feeders. The slope of the beach is so gentle that, when the tide falls to its lowest ebb, a quarter of a mile of sand is exposed between the high-tide line and the low. But this broad sand flat is not a perfectly even plain, for winding gullies wander across it, like creeks across the land, holding a remnant of water from the last high tide and providing a living place for animals that cannot endure even a temporary withdrawal of the water.

It was in this place that I once found a large "bed" of sea pansies at the very edge of the tide. The day was heavily overcast, a fact that accounted for their being exposed. On sunny days I never saw them there, although undoubtedly they were just under the sand, protecting themselves from the drying rays of the sun.

But the day I saw them the pink and lavender flower faces were lifted so that they were exposed at the surface of the sand, though so slightly that one could easily pass them by unnoticed. Seeing them— even recognizing them for what they were—there was a sense of incongruity in finding what looked so definitely flowerlike here at the edge of the sea.

These flattened, heart-shaped sea pansies, raised on short stems above the sand, are not plants but animals. They belong to the same general group of simple beings as the jellyfish, sea anemones, and corals, but to find their nearest relatives one would have to desert the shore and go down to some deep-lying offshore bottom where, as fernlike growths in a strange animal forest, the sea pens thrust long stalks into the soft ooze.

Each sea pansy growing here at the edge of the tide is the product of minute larva that once dropped from the currents to this shore. But through the extraordinary course of its development it has ceased to be that single being of its origin and has become instead a group or colony of many individuals, bound together into a whole of flowerlike form. The various individuals or polyps all have the shape of little tubes embedded in the fleshy substance of the colony. But some of the tubes bear tentacles and look like very small sea anemones; these capture food for the colony, and in the proper season form reproductive cells. Other tubes lack tentacles; these are the engineers of the colony, attending to the functions of water-intake and control. A hydraulic system of changing water pressure controls the movements of the colony; as the stem is made turgid it may be thrust down into the sand, drawing the main body after it.

As the rising tide streams over the flattened shapes of the sea pansies, all the tentacles of the feeding polyps are thrust up, reaching for the living motes that dance in the water—the copepods, the diatoms, the fish larvae small and tenuous as threads.

And at night the shallow water, rippling gently over these flats, must glow softly with hundreds of little lights marking out the zone where the sea pansies live, in a serpentine line of gleaming points, just as lights seen from an airplane at night wander across the dark landscape and show the path of settlement along a highway. For the sea pansies, like their deep-sea relatives, are beautifully luminescent.

In season, the tide sweeping over these flats carries many small, pear-shaped, swimming larvae from which new colonies of pansies will develop. In past ages, the currents that traversed the open water then separating North and South America carried such larvae, which established themselves on the Pacific coast, north to Mexico and south to Chile. Then a bridge of land rose between the American continents, closing the water highway. Today the presence of sea pansies on both Atlantic and Pacific coasts is one of the living reminders of that past geologic time when North and South America were separated, and sea creatures passed freely from one ocean to the other. . . .

Basket Starfish

My first meeting with a live West Indian basket star was something I shall never forget. I was wading off Ohio Key in water little more than knee deep when I found it among some seaweeds, gently drifting on the tide. Its upper surface was the color of a young fawn, with lighter shades beneath. The searching, exploring, testing branchlets at the tips of the arms reminded me of the delicate tendrils by which a growing vine seeks out places to which it may attach itself. For many minutes I stood beside it, lost to all but its extraordinary and some-how fragile beauty. I had no wish to "collect" it; to disturb such a being would have seemed a desecration. Finally the rising tide and the need to visit other parts of the flat before they became too deep-ly flooded drove me on, and when I returned the basket star had disappeared.

The basket starfish or basket fish is related to the brittle stars and serpent stars but displays remarkable differences of structure: each of the five arms diverges into branching V's, which branch again, and then again and again until a maze of curling tendrils forms the periphery of the animal. Indulging their taste for the dramatic, early naturalists named the basket stars for those monsters of Greek mythology, the Gorgons, who wore snakes in place of hair and whose hideous aspect was supposed to turn men to stone; so the family comprising these bizarre echinoderms is known as the Gorgonoceph-alidae. To some imaginations their appearance may be "snaky-locked," but the effect is one of beauty, grace, and elegance.

All the way from the Arctic to the West Indies basket stars of one species or another live in coastal waters, and many go down to light-less sea bottoms nearly a mile beneath the surface. They may walk about over the ocean floor, moving delicately on the tips of their arms. As Alexander Agassiz long ago described it, the animal stands "as it were on tiptoe, so that the ramifications of the arms form a kind of trellis-work all around it, reaching to the ground, while the disk forms a roof." Or again they may cling to gorgonians or other fixed sea growths and reach out into the water. The branching arms serve as a fine-meshed net to ensnare small sea creatures. On some grounds the basket stars are not only abundant but associate in herds of many individuals as though for a common purpose. Then the arms of neighboring animals become entwined in a continuous living net to capture all the small fry of the sea who venture, or are helplessly carried, within reach of the millions of grasping tendrils.

To see a basket starfish close inshore is one of those rare happen-ings that lives always in memory. . . .

THE OTHER ROAD

We stand now where two roads diverge. But unlike the roads in Robert Frost's familiar poem, they are not equally fair. The road we have long been traveling is deceptively easy, a smooth superhighway on which we progress with great speed, but at its end lies disaster. The other fork of the road—the one "less traveled by"—offers our last, our only chance to reach a destination that assures the preservation of our earth.

The choice, after all, is ours to make. If, having endured much, we have at last asserted our "right to know," and if, knowing, we have concluded that we are being asked to take senseless and frightening risks, then we should no longer accept the counsel of those who tell us that we must fill our world with poisonous chemicals; we should look about and see what other course is open to us.

A truly extraordinary variety of alternatives to the chemical control of insects is available. Some are already in use and have achieved brilliant success. Others are in the stage of laboratory testing. Still others are little more than ideas in the minds of imaginative scientists, waiting for the opportunity to put them to the test. All have this in common: they are *biological* solutions, based on understanding of the living organisms they seek to control, and of the whole fabric of life to which these organisms belong. Specialists representing various areas of the vast field of biology are contributing—entomologists, pathologists, geneticists, physiologists, biochemists, ecologists—all pouring their knowledge and their creative inspirations into the formation of a new science of biotic controls. . . .

Through all these new, imaginative, and creative approaches to the problem of sharing our earth with other creatures there runs a constant theme, the awareness that we are dealing with life—with living populations and all their pressures and counterpressures, their surges and recessions. Only by taking account of such life forces and by cautiously seeking to guide them into channels favorable to ourselves can we hope to achieve a reasonable accommodation between the insect hordes and ourselves.

The current vogue for poisons has failed utterly to take into account these most fundamental considerations. As crude a weapon as the cave man's club, the chemical barrage has been hurled against the fabric of life—a fabric on the one hand delicate and destructible, on the other miraculously tough and resilient, and capable of striking back in unexpected ways. These extraordinary capacities of life have been ignored by the practitioners of chemical control who have brought to their task no "high-minded orientation," no humility before the vast forces with which they tamper.

The "control of nature" is a phrase conceived in arrogance, born of the Neanderthal age of biology and philosophy, when it was supposed that nature exists for the convenience of man. The concepts and practices of applied entomology for the most part date from that Stone Age of science. It is our alarming misfortune that so primitive a science has armed itself with the most modern and terrible weapons, and that in turning them against the insects it has also turned them against the earth.

FURTHER READING

Anticaglia, Elizabeth. *Twelve American Women*. Chicago: Nelson-Hall Co., 1975.

Briggs, Shirley. "A Decade after Silent Spring." *Friends Journal* 1 (March, 1972): 148–49.

Brooks, Paul. *The House of Life: Rachel Carson at Work*. Boston: Houghton Mifflin Co., 1972.

Carson, Rachel. *The Edge of the Sea*. Boston: Houghton Mifflin Co., 1955.

———. Miscellaneous Papers. Rachel Carson Council Library. Chevy Chase, Md.

———. *The Sea Around Us*. New York: Oxford University Press, 1950.

———. *The Sense of Wonder*. New York: Harper & Row, 1956.

———. *Silent Spring*. Boston: Houghton Mifflin Co., 1962.

———. *Under the Sea Wind*. New York: Oxford University Press, 1941.

Christopher, Barbara. "Rachel Carson: American Author-Biologist." *National Business Woman* 53 (May, 1963): 4–5.

Gartner, Carol. *Rachel Carson*. New York: Frederick Ungar, 1983.

Graham, Frank, Jr. *Since Silent Spring*. Boston: Houghton Mifflin, 1970.

Lear, Linda. "Rachel Carson's *Silent Spring*." *Environmental History Review* 17 (Summer, 1993): 23–48.

Moore, Lillian. "Rachel Carson's *Silent Spring*: Its Truth Goes Marching On." *Smithsonian* 1 (July, 1970): 4–9.

Seif, Dorothy Thompson. "Letters from Rachel Carson: A Young Scientist Sets Her Course." Typescript.

Sterling, Philip. *Sea and Earth: The Life of Rachel Carson*. New York: Thomas Y. Crowell, 1970.

Afterword

For readers interested in visiting the homes of women naturalists, there are three such places open to the public.

The Stanwood Wildlife Sanctuary (Birdsacre) in Ellsworth, Maine, includes Stanwood's home, which is listed in the National Register of Historic Places, woodland trails over the 130-acre property, and a Wildlife Recovery Center. The Stanwood Homestead Museum, a modest Cape Cod–style house, is filled with the essence of Cordelia Stanwood's life—her bird photographs, the Indian baskets she made to augment her income, and the desk containing her field notebooks.

Funded by private donations, the Stanwood Wildlife Sanctuary was the brainchild of the late Chandler Richmond, a local insurance man and bird lover, who saved the home in 1959 when he learned it was to be replaced by a motel. With the help of Ellsworth business leaders and other interested neighbors, Richmond steadily expanded the scope of both the property and the sanctuary. He was assisted by his late wife, Marion, and his son, Stanley Richmond. Stanley is now President of the Stanwood Wildlife Sanctuary and continues to expand its mission both through its bird rehabilitation work and the newly-constructed Richmond Nature Center. For further information contact the Stanwood Wildlife Sanctuary, P.O. Box 485, Ellsworth, Maine 04605.

Before she died, Caroline Dormon, with the help of her friends, formed the Foundation for the Preservation of the Caroline Dormon Nature Preserve in late 1970. Today, at the Caroline Dormon Nature Preserve (Briarwood) near Saline, Louisiana, visitors can find not only the remains of the many native plants Dormon planted along a network of trails but also a headquarters building erected with

244

donated materials and labor from the lumber industry and local businesses. Dormon's log home has been preserved just as she left it along with an ever-expanding collection of southern native wildflowers, trees, and shrubs planted and cared for by Dormon's friend and protege Richard Johnson and his wife Jessie.

Recognized in 1966 as a "sanctuary for the flora of the South" by the American Horticultural Society, the Preserve is wholly funded by friends and members of the Foundation. For further information write the Foundation for the Preservation of the Caroline Dormon Nature Preserve, P.O. Box 226, Natchitoches, Louisiana 71457.

The Rachel Carson Homestead Association was founded by Pittsburgh friends of Carson in 1975. The partially renovated two-story, white clapboard home has memorabilia relating to Carson. Visitors can tour the home and grounds. The goals of the Association are to fully restore Carson's birthplace and early home and to develop educational programs based on her life and career. For more information contact the Rachel Carson Homestead Association, 613 Marion Avenue, Springdale, Pennsylvania 15144.

Althea Sherman's family homestead is today a cornfield with a tract house built upon the foundation of the old Sherman home. Sherman had left her land to the National Cemetery Association, with the understanding that it would remain a bird sanctuary. But her heirs contested her will, the land was sold, and only her chimney swift tower was preserved through the efforts of conservationist R. W. Daubendiek and later the Kruger family, on whose property it recently stood. However, the tower is in the process of being restored by members of the Johnson County Songbird Project in Iowa City under the leadership of Jim Walters and Barbara Boyle. They plan to fully reclaim the tower so that it might continue to educate and delight another generation of bird lovers. For further information contact the Johnson County Songbird Project, 2511 Highway 1 Southwest, Iowa City, Iowa 52240.

Selected Bibliography

Abir-am, Pnina G., and Dorinda Outram, eds. *Uneasy Careers and Intimate Lives: Women in Science, 1789–1979.* New Brunswick, N.J.: Rutgers University Press, 1987.

Ainley, Marianne Gosztonyi. "The Contribution of the Amateur to North American Ornithology: A Historical Perspective." *Living Bird* 18 (1979–80): 161–71.

———. "Family and/or Field-Work in Science: North American Women Ornithologists, 1900–1950." Simone de Beauvoir Institute, Concordia University, Canada. Photocopy.

———. "Women in North American Ornithology during the Last Century." Paper presented at the First International Congress on the Role of Women in the History of Science, Technology, and Medicine, Veszprem, Hungary, August 15–19, 1983.

Anderson, Lorraine, ed. *Sisters of the Earth: Women's Prose and Poetry about Nature.* New York: Vintage Books, 1991.

Bonta, Marcia. *Women in the Field: America's Pioneering Women Naturalists.* College Station: Texas A&M University Press, 1991.

Brooks, Paul. *Speaking for Nature.* Boston: Houghton Mifflin, 1980.

Keeney, Elizabeth Barnaby. *The Botanizers.* Chapel Hill: University of North Carolina Press, 1992.

Norwood, Vera. *Made from This Earth: American Women and Nature.* Chapel Hill: University of North Carolina Press, 1993.

Porter, Charlotte M. *The Eagle's Nest: Natural History and American Ideas 1812–1842.* University: University of Alabama Press, 1986.

Rossiter, Margaret. *Women Scientists in America.* Baltimore: Johns Hopkins University Press, 1982.

Rudolph, Emanuel D. "Women in Nineteenth Century American Botany:

A Generally Unrecognized Constituency." *American Journal of Botany* 69 (September, 1982): 1346–55.

Smallwood, William Martin, and Mabel Sarah Coon Smallwood. *Natural History and the American Mind.* New York: Columbia University Press, 1941.

Strom, Deborah, ed. *Birdwatching with American Women.* New York: W. W. Norton and Co., 1986.